Computational Grammar

An Artificial Intelligence Approach to Linguistic Description

Computational Grammar

An Artificial Intelligence Approach to Linguistic Description

GRAEME D. RITCHIE

Research Fellow, Electronics Laboratories,
University of Kent at Canterbury

THE HARVESTER PRESS · SUSSEX

BARNES & NOBLE BOOKS · NEW JERSEY

First published in Great Britain in 1980 by
THE HARVESTER PRESS LIMITED
Publishers: John Spiers and Margaret A. Boden
16 Ship Street, Brighton, Sussex

and in the USA by
BARNES & NOBLE BOOKS
81 Adams Drive, Totowa, New Jersey 07512

British Library Cataloguing in Publication Data
Ritchie, Graeme D
Computational grammar. - (Harvester
Studies in cognitive science; 15).
1. Linguistic models
I. Title
401'.84 P128.M6

ISBN 0-85527-801-3

Barnes and Noble
ISBN 0-389-20048-4

Printed in Great Britain by
St Edmundsbury Press, Bury St Edmunds, Suffolk

To my friends

CONTENTS

Introduction

1. Methodology and Metatheory 1

 1.1. Theories, Paradigms and Frameworks 1
 1.2. Some Assumptions 3
 1.3. Terminology and Grammaticality 9
 1.4. Computer Modelling 11
 1.5. Detailed Analyses 16
 1.6. Psychology, Linguistics and Artificial Intelligence 16

2. Other Frameworks 20

 2.1. Preamble 20
 2.2. The Aspects Model 21
 2.3. Deep Interpretive Semantics 23
 2.4. Surface Interpretive Semantics 26
 2.5. Generative Semantics 27
 2.6. Montague Grammar 29
 2.7. Preference Semantics 30
 2.8. Conceptual Dependency 32
 2.9. Transition Network Grammars 36
 2.10. The SHRDLU System 39
 2.11. Wait-and-See Strategies 43
 2.12. Semantic Networks 45

3. Structural Combining Rules 48

 3.1. Tree Structure 48
 3.2. Semantic Rules as a Form of Surface Structure 51
 3.3. Representing Syntactic Information 53
 3.4. Immediate Semantic Processing 59
 3.5. Separating Syntagmatic and Paradigmatic Information 62
 3.6. Adjectives and Classifiers 69
 3.7. The Syntax of Verb Phrases 74

4. Processing Levels 77

4.1. PUSH and POP 77
4.2. Predictive Aspects of the PUSH command 79
4.3. Complexity in Embedded Structures 83
4.4. Left-Embedding 84
4.5. Right-Embedding 86
4.6. Centre-Embedding 89

5. Temporary Storage 94

5.1. Registers 94
5.2. Different Types of Register 94

6. Semantic Representation 98

6.1. Sense and Reference 98
6.2. The Semantics of Noun Phrases 102
6.3. Semantic Representation 108
6.4. Verbs and Cases 112
6.5. Definers 116
6.6. Semantic Categories 122

7. Levels of Description 124

7.1. Syntagmatic and Paradigmatic Information 124
7.2. Different Types of Feature 125
7.3. Some Grammatical Classes 126

8. Decisions, Mistakes and Predictions 128

8.1. The Methodology of Mistakes 128
8.2. Exhaustive Strategies 128
8.3. Weighting and Preference 132
8.4. Top-Down and Bottom-up 134
8.5. Bottom-up Devices for ATN analysers 135
8.6. Decisions within an ATN analyser 141
8.7. Specifying Structural Locations in Advance 143

9. Conversational Structure 145

9.1. The Need for Dialogue Procedures 145
9.2. Conversation Games 147
9.3. Some Typical Games 149

10. Summary of the Framework 151

- 10.1. The Story So Far 151
- 10.2. Structural Combining Rules 153
- 10.3. Recognition Rules 154
- 10.4. Semantic Representation 155
- 10.5. Syntactic Properties and Features 157
- 10.6. Analysis Procedure 157
- 10.7. Registers 162
- 10.8. Conversation Routines 163
- 10.9. Guidelines for Analyses 164

11. English Wh-Clauses 171

- 11.1. The Surface Structure of Wh-Clauses 171
- 11.2. The Complex Noun Phrase Constraint 175
- 11.3. Semantics of Wh-Clauses 180
- 11.4. Non-Restrictive Relative Clauses 184

12. Tense and Time in English 188

- 12.1. The Previous Descriptions 188
- 12.2. Nested Tense Settings 191
- 12.3. The Function of Time-binders 194
- 12.4. Disembodied Time References 196
- 12.5. Tense Clash 198
- 12.6. A Summary of the Tense-Slot System 199
- 12.7. Time Semantic Structures and Relationships 199
- 12.8. Perfect Aspect 205
- 12.9. Some Rules and Structures 206
- 12.10. 'When' Clauses 208
- 12.11. Summary of Rules 211

13. A Computer Implementation 213

- 13.1. The MCHINE program 213
- 13.2. Overall Structure 214
- 13.3. Sample Dialogues 215
- 13.4. Comparison with Other Programs 218
- 13.5 Summary of Grammar 221

14. Conclusions, Problems and Speculations 224

- 14.1. Preamble 224

14.2. Structural Combining Rules 224
14.3. The Analysis Procedure 226
14.4. Semantic Representation 229
14.5. Syntactic Markings 231
14.6. Methodology 232
14.7. Constraints 233
14.8. Conversational Rules 234
14.9. Epilogue 235

References 237
Subject Index 247
Author Index 253

PREFACE

This book is a revised version of my PhD thesis which was originally submitted in April 1977. It has been radically re-structured in order to change a technical project report into an interdisciplinary monograph, but no new material has been added. Apart from re-organising the chapters and sections the only changes have been the omission of many technical details, some minor corrections and stylistic improvements, and the addition of explanations of certain concepts as they are introduced. I have refrained from employing hindsight to repair inadequacies in the ideas or to comment on later work (although the final chapter gives a few references to more recent research). The original thesis was a product of the state of artificial intelligence and linguistics in the period 1973–6 and this book retains that perspective, even at the risk of seeming out of date.

I should like to thank: my thesis supervisors, Christopher Longuet-Higgins and Hamish Dewar, for their assistance during the original project; Stephen Isard, for discussions which made essential contributions to the ideas outlined in this book; my thesis examiners, Rod Burstall and Michael Arbib, for their advice and encouragement regarding the publication of the thesis; Maggie Boden, for much constructive editorial advice on the presentation of the material; Chris Miller and Chris Mellish, for their extremely useful comments on the intermediate drafts; the Science Research Council, for generous and helpful support throughout the research period; the Departments of Artificial Intelligence and Computer Science, University of Edinburgh, for providing a good working environment.

Edinburgh, April 1979 G.D.R.

INTRODUCTION

Since the early 1960s many computer programs have been written which analyse, in some way or another, limited ranges of English. This line of research has given rise to various computational techniques for processing and representing the form and meaning of natural language. The theoretical investigation outlined in this text attempts to integrate these techniques with the sophisticated descriptive methodology that has simultaneously evolved within transformational linguistics, in order to lay the foundations of a computational model suitable for general linguistic description. This book is not a report of another English dialogue program; rather, it is a sketch of a linguistic theory which borrows many concepts from computing, while retaining the general linguistic goal of elucidating the structures and processes underlying human use of natural language. This embryonic theory will be referred to as 'computational grammar'.

The inspiration for computational grammar comes from many sources in artificial intelligence, linguistics and formal logic, so that it is not so much a new idea as a particular way of combining existing concepts for linguistic purposes.

The problem of language is so vast and complex that most theories start by considering only a few aspects, thus giving each framework its own idiosyncratic emphasis (see Chapter 2). Computational grammar focuses primarily on the process of 'sentence comprehension', i.e what processing is necessary to convert a string of English words (a phrase or sentence) into a representation of its 'meaning'.

Investigations of language can generally be categorised as either linguistic competence models (in the sense of Chomsky), psychological models (to explain experimental data) or computer implementations (working programs). Computational grammar does not fit clearly into any of these categories as it is a description of processing (rather than of 'competence'), but it is not an experimentally-based simulation or a working program. This is one of the metatheoretical issues which will be discussed in Chapter 1.

The detailed implementation of linguistic descriptions in program form is a central aspect of the methodology of computational grammar, as will be discussed in Chapter 1. The ideas outlined here developed in the course of a project which involved writing an English dialogue program (the 'MCHINE' system — see Chapter 13), but the performance of that program is not the main topic of interest. In fact, the performance of the program is quite pedestrian, as can be seen from the sample dialogues in Section 13.3. However, we will not be primarily concerned with the problems of producing banal conversations with a computer. Instead we shall be investigating theoretical questions such as:

(i) how can we represent the surface structure of a sentence in a way which is appropriate both syntactically and semantically?
(ii) how can we capture generalities of structure and of processing in one model?
(iii) do we need special constructs to cope with the branching structure of English?
(iv) what temporary storage is needed during the processing of an English sentence?
(v) how can a computational model handle the sense/reference distinction?
(vi) do we need separate syntactic and semantic categories?
(vii) how can a sentence-processing model handle incorrect predictions about the items that are to come in the input?
(viii) what connections are there between consecutive utterances in a conversation?
(ix) is it possible to replace transformational constraints with processing principles?
(x) how is 'tense' used in English conversation?

It may be useful to start with a brief summary of the framework. The two main components of the model are a set of recognition rules which define the steps to be taken in analysing an English sentence from left to right and a set of structural combining rules which define surface structure trees in syntactic and semantic terms. Together these rules can convert an English sentence into a representation of its 'meaning' (a semantic network) which is then available for higher-level routines (conversation rules) to operate on. Since the emphasis of the model is on the sequence of decisions during sentence analysis the processing rules are designed, as far as possible, to make decisions only as necessary, without relying on blind 'guesses'. To this end, a system of temporary storage is included for retaining information during processing. (There is a brief summary of the model at the beginning of Chapter 10 which the reader may wish to read at this stage.)

Chapter 1 sets out the assumptions and guidelines on which the framework is based and Chapter 2 summarises some of the main influences on the development of computational grammar. Chapters 3 to 9 develop the various facets of the model showing how they are natural improvements of existing constructs and illustrating their application where possible with examples from English grammar. Chapter 10 summarises the components of the framework (without defining them formally) and Chapters 11 and 12 give two fairly detailed linguistic descriptions of areas of English grammar to demonstrate how the processing rules can be used in a traditional descriptive way. Chapter 13 is a brief informal summary of the experimental program used to explore some of these ideas and Chapter 14 discusses some of the inadequacies of the model with a view to future improvements.

CHAPTER 1

METHODOLOGY AND METATHEORY

1.1. Theories, Paradigms and Frameworks

The phrases 'theory of language' or 'linguistic theory' are often used in discussing research into natural language. The aim of this section is to question whether we always have 'theories' and to suggest that something weaker is guiding current research.

One widely accepted version of how scientific investigation proceeds is characterised by Hempel (1966). In such an approach a theory is a coherent, structured body of ideas concerning some subject, which makes predictions that may be verified, and which can be used to 'explain', in some sense, observations made about the subject matter. Hempel presents a very neat picture of a highly organised objective scientist using a carefully constructed theory in an unprejudiced fashion. A somewhat different analysis is presented by Kuhn (1970) who has less faith in the objectivity of the scientist. Kuhn sees science working within a series of 'paradigms'. A paradigm is an accepted theory which not only guides research but positively straitjackets it by defining problems, and possible solutions, in such a way as to narrow the scientist's view greatly. A paradigm is not just a theory but has an attached set of ways of working and a whole terminology of its own. Hence it imposes a very definite structure on the way research proceeds. Whereas Hempel discusses the notion of choosing between competing theories by gathering evidence, Kuhn asserts that these rational choices are not possible between paradigms, since each paradigm defines differently the criteria for such choices.

A case could be made for regarding linguistic research as proceeding in Kuhnian paradigms. A paradigm in this sense contributes to research at two levels — it provides a theory which can be regarded as 'true' or 'explanatory'; it also provides guidelines for the everyday investigations of the subject matter. It is this latter aspect that is more relevant in artificial intelligence and computational linguistics, since both lack an overall 'theory' to provide a received body of 'facts' or 'explanations'. In the period before the development of a paradigm there is, according to Kuhn, an atheoretical stage in which a body of techniques and concepts are built up which serve to guide investigation and description of a topic. Let us call such a collection of devices a 'framework'. A framework is weaker than either a theory, in Hempel's sense, or a paradigm, in Kuhn's sense. It makes no really precise predictions since it is not sufficiently elaborated. It cannot, therefore, claim to provide any explanation since it does not relate all observed phenomena to some systematic generality. It has no use for 'critical experiments' or 'crucial counter-examples' since it is not an integrated edifice that can be demolished by removing one brick. It contains no 'truths' which can be taken as unquestionable by the community using the framework. However, it is of great use to what Fillmore (1972) calls the 'ordinary working grammarian'. It provides tools for investigation and describing the subject-matter. It provides a terminology which workers in the field can use to communicate with each other. It suggests problems that must be attacked and, often, ways of attacking them. It provides some means of assessment of putative solutions (usually using some general classification of 'elegant' against '*ad hoc*'). It is a cluster of related ideas rather than a tightly structured whole, so that different workers may disagree over the acceptance of certain aspects of the framework and yet still be able to share the rest of it.

Current artificial intelligence work definitely has a framework, but it is doubtful if it has a paradigm, since it lacks any real theory. To demonstrate that there exists a common cluster of ideas and techniques it is necessary only to list some of the terminology currently used in artificial intelligence: top-down, bottom-up, depth-first, breadth-first, goal-directed, procedural-embedding, distributed knowledge, flow of control, access environment, subroutine call, pattern-invocation, demons, middle-out, backtracking, plan formation, interacting goals, updating a world model, etc.

It might be thought that, without the concept of a critical experiment, there could be no notion of 'refutation' or 'incorrectness' within a framework. If we consider the form of argumentation conducted in transformational linguistics during the 1960s it can be seen that a weak form of 'refutation' was achieved even without a full theory. Although the results of Peters and Ritchie (1971, 1973) showed that the mechanism of transformational grammar was so general as to be virtually irrefutable, linguists continued to produce 'counter-examples' to each other's claims. Despite the fact that the formally defined transformational grammar could, strictly speaking, perform any operations whatsoever, there was an additional notion of 'simple' against '*ad hoc*'. This could be used to eliminate many of the technically possible manipulations — a 'counter-example' was an 'example which could not be handled *neatly*'.

This has to be borne in mind when discussing computational linguistics. In order to cope with the detailed complexity of grammatical phenomena computational descriptions normally contain mechanisms which have totally general computing power. (Technically, they are equivalent to a Turing machine, i.e. an abstract mathematical device which can perform any definable computation — see Hopcroft and Ullman (1969), Gross (1972).) However, what makes such models distinct from each other is the different structuring that is imposed on the mechanisms. The different models (or rather, the different sub-frameworks) may well make different claims when combined with a notion of 'simplicity' or 'elegance'.

1.2. Some Assumptions

In examining a framework it is important to be aware of the assumptions which are its initial basis for investigation. This section outlines the assumptions for later chapters without providing any real justifications for any of the positions adopted.

It is possible that a language-understanding system might be constructed in which all tasks (such as inference, detection of ambiguity, etc.) can be performed using the word string as the sole representation of the input sentence. That is, no independent level of 'meaning' is required to show, for example, the similarities between the pairs of sentences below, or to detect the ambiguity of (3).

(1)
(a) John bought an alligator from the zoo manager.
(b) The man who administers the zoological garden sold John an alligator.
(2)
(a) The alligator attacked John.
(b) John was attacked by the alligator.
(3) Attacking alligators can be dangerous.

Years of linguistic and philosophical research have demonstrated the unsuitability of word strings for manipulations such as inference, so we will not explore the possibility here. Instead, we shall follow recent linguistic research in associating a 'semantic structure' (i.e. a representation of the 'meaning') with each sentence.

This does not necessarily involve claiming that the surface string contains 'less information' than some other 'semantic structure' for the sentence; if the latter is computed from just the surface string this cannot be true, although the information may be in a more usable form in the computed structure. However, the computation might use information from outside the word string itself (contextual clues) which will make a contribution to the semantic structure. Not performing the conversion might entail storing these contextual clues (if they could be isolated) along with the surface form so that the information they contained could be used whenever the 'meaning' of the sentence was required.

Some balance must be struck, nevertheless, between the simplicity of semantic operations (for making inferences, etc.) and the complexity of the conversion from surface form to semantic structure (cf. comments in Section 2.3 on interpretive semantics).

The assumption used, therefore, in computational grammar is that there is some level of representation which can be called 'semantic structure' which is logically distinct from the surface form, and which is computed from the surface form together with other (contextual) information.

It might be argued that to produce a 'structure' is misguided as the best way to analyse an English utterance, in context, is to consider the effect that was intended by the speaker (on any hearers) or the effect that the utterance had on the hearer(s), or both. Thinking in terms of conversational effects is extremely valuable and may be the most general way to describe an utterance, but this does not contrast with the 'structure' approach outlined here, except in terminology. Suppose we have a linguistic model in which sentences are described in terms of their effects or intended effects. This model (unless it is to be totally unilluminating) will have to provide a precise representation, in some formal terms, of these 'effects'; if we are careful this representation may even allow some comparison of 'similar effects' so that similarities like those in (1) and (2) are shown. Such an arrangement will not differ fundamentally from the vague outline presented already — 'semantic structure' is being used in such a broad sense that it does not contrast with 'representation of conversational effect'.

In certain logical languages like the predicate calculus (Schoenfield (1967)), syntax has a clearly defined purpose and is distinct from, though systematically related to, semantics. Syntactic rules specify which strings in the language are to be classed as 'well-formed', and only well-formed strings need be considered for inference or semantic interpretation. This is similar to the notion that Chomsky adopted in his theory of natural language (1957, 1965), although it has now been widely questioned (see Section 2.2 for further discussion). It is possible that a natural language may not have a comparable concept of 'well-formedness' characterised by a set of syntactic rules, although some sentences may express an odd idea and some sentences may be more complex to process. Also, some sentences may sound odd because they are uttered in an inappropriate context.

The investigation in later chapters assumes that we need not search for rules of syntactic well-formedness, and that it is sufficient to search for rules of semantic manipulation, together with rules for converting between surface form and semantic structure. Many of the phenomena attributed to syntax (particularly Chomskyan 'grammaticality') may be more accurately describable in terms of semantic or conversion rules (see also Section 1.3 below). This may sound as if syntax is merely being banished to lurk under another heading, since syntax has traditionally been a fundamental part of the process of conversion between surface form and meaning. This is true, since any conversion rules which are postulated will almost certainly have to make extensive use of traditional syntactic notions such as 'verb', 'preposition', possibly 'transitive' and perhaps even 'subject'; the change that is being highlighted here is more a change of emphasis. In computational grammar the primary aim of writing these grammatical rules is not to specify any 'well-formedness' for sentences; the goal is to show how surface strings relate to semantic structure. In view of this the terms 'syntax' and 'syntactic' will be used in the later chapters for rules or structures whose sole task is to guide the conversion process, and which cannot reasonably be said to be describing patterns of meaning. For example, the class of verbs which appear at the front of the sentence in English questions (auxiliary verbs) is a useful syntactic class, since it aids in the detection of the question construction; it is not clear whether auxiliary verbs are a semantic class (although some more sophisticated analysis might show this to be so).

Notice that it is still possible that some notion of 'well-formedness' will result from such rules. If there are conversion rules and semantic rules, then certain items may fail to be processed by one or the other. An accurate model would be one whose rule-failures, or complexities of processing, correspond to utterances or strings which sound bad to the traditional native speaker. However, it is the model as a whole which will characterise such ill-formedness, not just one component. In fact, the existence of these native judgments of 'good/bad' provide much of the evidence for rules of any kind, and the Chomskyan style of argument can be adopted in discussing such data. (See Section 1.3 and Chapter 8 for further remarks on this topic.)

So far, the (deliberately vague) term 'conversion' has been used for the relationship between surface form and semantic structure. This concept can now be examined in greater detail.

A complete model of a language-user will have to specify, among other things, how semantic structure can be converted to strings of words (production) and how strings of words can be converted to semantic structure (recognition). One obvious way of making such specifications would be to present two (probably enormous) algorithms, one for production and one for recognition. To allow for alterations to the language (or idiolect, if modelling a specific user) it might be preferable to separate out some items called 'rules' which the algorithms use to perform their tasks; language-expansion could consist then of alteration to the rule-system, or to the algorithms, or to both. The two algorithms (i.e. for production and for recognition) are distinct, since the form of input used for one is the form of output for the other (and vice versa). It might be possible, nevertheless, to find common aspects of the two processes. Ideally, it would be neat if all such points of similarity could be separated out and built into the rules; then there might be two totally distinct interpreters (in the computational sense) working on one common set of data (the rules). This could of course be done trivially just by taking the union of the two disjoint sets of 'rules' to be the common set, but that is not what is meant. (See Kay (1975) for some comments on this topic.)

Some linguists claim to be building a model of language which is not biased towards either production or recognition (this was one of the claims of Chomsky (1965)). In a sense this is true but it is reminiscent of the joke about a blind horse seeing equally well at both ends. Chomskyan linguists usually ignore the need for effective production and recognition procedures, and so in a sense the models are equally incomplete answers to both problems. Such an approach also has to assume that *all* aspects of language can be described in such a neutral, non-directional way. Hence, if there are any phenomena which are direction-specific (i.e. are consequences of the algorithmic parts) either these phenomena will not be describable or else the neutral formulation will have to be distorted to accommodate them.

Computational approaches to language have generally treated the two processes separately. This is largely because computer models must include effective algorithms for whichever of the two processes they simulate; hence the task of investigating both problems at once is inconveniently large. Also, there is probably a greater conviction among computational linguists than there is among theoretical linguists that the two processes have substantial differences. The justification for this approach is that similarities between the two processes are a further topic for exploration. Common sub-processes are to be found empirically, and we do not start from the assumption that the whole processes differ only trivially.

Chomsky has often stated that any human language must be subject to constraints on what it is possible for the human mind to 'know', in some sense. It should not be forgotten that whatever 'know' is taken to mean here it must cover the constraint that language must be able to be produced and to be recognised. The assumption in Chomsky (1965) seems to be that constraints on production and recognition are both obvious and trivial (e.g. the limits on multiply centre-embedded structures — see Section 4.6), but this is not necessarily true. Hence some characterisation of the production and recognition processes is just as fundamental to the study of linguistic universals as the investigation of 'deep structures' (Section 2.2).

The focus of computational grammar is on the recognition process, but some attempt has been made to separate out generalisations in the form of rules so that frequently-occurring mechanisms are explicitly emphasised. However, no mechanisms has been included for bi-directional rules, although there are some parts of the various grammatical descriptions which obviously ought to be shareable with a production-oriented model.

1.3. Terminology and Grammaticality

In later chapters expressions such as 'noun phrase' and 'subject' will be used frequently in discussing examples of English grammar, but this does not mean that these terms are constructs in computational grammar. 'Noun phrase' is a term which is extremely useful for describing English informally but which is very difficult to define rigorously. Some traditional concepts (e.g. 'verb') are used directly in computational grammar; others (e.g. 'subject') could be defined if necessary, although they are not used at present; some (e.g. 'person' and 'number' markings) are not used in the standard way. Nevertheless, these traditional expressions are so well known that they provide the best expository vocabulary for describing English informally and they are employed for that reason.

Chomsky (1957) used the word 'grammatical' to refer to a string of words which a native speaker accepts as belonging to his language; strings which are not in the language were 'ungrammatical'. In 1965 he introduced a further classification — a sentence could also be classed as 'acceptable/unacceptable', depending on whether or not it was easily processed (under 'performance conditions'); also, a sentence could be classified as 'semantically normal/semantically anomalous', depending on the well-formedness of the meaning expressed. Chomsky made the assumption that these three dimensions of classification were relatively independent (although grammaticality was a prerequisite for the other classifications to be made). He also assumed that it was easy enough for the linguist to say which native-speaker judgments pertained to which dimension.

Later papers in semantically-based grammar (see Fillmore and Langendoen (1971)) use the asterisk (the traditional Chomskyan sign for an ungrammatical string) to condemn sentences (or strings) for a wide variety of reasons. McCawley (1971b) uses [*] to mark 'presuppositional oddity', and the device of inserting one or more question marks to mark degrees of 'oddity' is very common in linguistic literature.

What emerges from these post-1957 developments is that the 'oddity' of a putative sentence (as judged by a native speaker) is graded not just along one dimension but along several. Also, despite Chomsky's original assumption, neither the native speaker nor the linguist may have clear intuitions about which dimension(s) he is using to classify a string as 'odd'. It is the task of the linguist to construct a theory in which 'odd' strings are classed as ill-formed in some respect (if the theory is to model human behaviour), but the native speaker does not provide judgments which are rigidly pre-sorted into boxes labelled 'perceptually difficult', 'semantically anomalous', etc.

This is a suitable point to introduce some informal terminology. The term *grammatical* will be used not in the Chomskyan sense but in the sense of 'pertaining to grammar'; its contrary will therefore be *non-grammatical*, rather than 'ungrammatical'. An utterance which sounds, in some way, strange to a native speaker, will be classed as *odd*; the contrary to this is *acceptable*. Both 'odd' and 'acceptable' are classifications of the data, with no assumptions about the type of strangeness involved; both may be context dependent, since the judgment may be of the form 'sentence S would sound strange in context C'. An utterance which would sound strange in virtually any context may be referred to as *ill-formed* (this is the nearest equivalent to Chomsky's 'ungrammatical' that will be used). An utterance whose strangeness results entirely from contextual effects (rather than from its internal properties alone) will be termed *inappropriate*. A string which is deemed, for some theoretical or linguistic reason, to be abnormal in some way will be called *anomalous*. That is, 'inappropriate' and 'anomalous' refer to the way that the linguistic theory or grammar classes the item, not to the judgments about the original data.

These do not constitute precise definitions of the way that these words will be used, but they should clarify the informal usage in later chapters.

Within computational grammar a full linguistic description

(including both semantic rules and recognition rules) should specify how a sentence or phrase can be converted to semantic representation. Since there may be several possible ways of performing the conversion we must introduce more detailed evidence concerning the way that it is done. The assumption will be made here (following Chomskyan linguistics) that 'odd' sentences result from rule-failures of some kind or from abnormal structuring. That is, there should be a direct correspondence between anomaly (something going wrong in processing or in the final structure) and oddity (sentences sounding bad). Adding this criterion to the grammar-writing methodology enriches the information available concerning the details of English grammar (see Section 1.6) and has consequences for the way that linguistic analyses are produced (see also Chapter 8).

1.4. Computer Modelling

If we regard a grammar as a procedure for converting surface form into semantic structure it is useful to have a way of experimenting with the way that different grammatical rules act. One possible way of carrying out such tests is to implement the rules in a computer program. It is worth giving an explicit outline of the relevance of computer programming to computational grammar as the advantages may not be obvious.

One advantage of expressing ideas in program form is that one can build on an existing descriptive language. In trying to describe some complex subject matter where there is not an established theory problems of notation quickly arise. It is difficult to make statements which are detailed and yet comprehensible to the reader if the descriptive system is completely new and special purpose. To some extent the widely-used transition network notation (see Section 2.9) has helped matters in computational linguistics but there are still uncharted areas. If the model-builder uses a programming language he can at least express his constructs in primitive terms which will be understood by those who know that language. If, for example, the way that some 'mapping' operates is slightly obscure, the corresponding piece of program can be examined to provide an alternative description.

A computer also acts as a stern (although undiscriminating) critic. To have a machine take all of one's half-formulated ideas to their logical (if absurd) conclusion is an edifying (and humbling) experience; to see the intermediate stages of this development (by tracing the steps of the program's execution) is positively enlightening. In this way, testing a computationally-expressed grammar at a computer terminal develops a strong intuition for the details of a language. It also forces the grammar-writer to be rigorous and precise in the expression of his rules — a device has yet to be designed that takes hand-waving as its input.

However, perhaps the biggest advantage of using a computer to test one's ideas is the complexity of model which can be handled. It is very difficult to keep track, on paper or in one's head, of how various rules and different sub-components interact, so that non-computational models must remain either fairly simple or wholly unchecked.

One of the biggest contributions that computer modelling has made to the development of computational grammar is in the range of concepts it has provided. As noted in 1.2 one obvious way to express language comprehension is in the form of steps that must be performed on an input sentence. Computer programming is based on algorithmic description and hence provides a natural way of expressing a series of instructions which must be performed. There are also certain computational concepts (subroutines, registers, assignment, etc.) associated with this form of description which are useful notions to use in describing a process. For example, the augmented transition network notation (Section 2.9) is really just a form of programming language with primitives which are particularly useful for describing the task of processing English, and many of its aspects are just re-formulations of ordinary programming devices. See Winograd (1972, pp. 44–6), and Ritchie (1978a).)

It is also worth mentioning some possible justifications that are not relevant to computational grammar, although they might apply to other computational approaches to

English. A possible aim of using computers in linguistics might be to allow the use of English as a high-level programming language. (That is, a programming language in which the commands are designed to suit a human user rather than being based on the idiosyncracies of a particular computer.) This is not only not the aim of computational grammar, it is a somewhat misguided aim. The reason English works so well as a vehicle of communication is that people are extremely clever at using it. Partial utterances, oblique allusions, etc., are frequently used in everyday speech in a way which would be hopelessly inefficient if one was not talking to a very sophisticated understanding device. In situations where efficient human communication is required (for example, between aircraft crews) stylised forms are often used. If we had a machine which was as intelligent and subtle as the human hearer English might be a feasible means of communication — but it would still not be the best. (See Longuet-Higgins and Isard (1970) for discussion of some of the difficulties.)

Also, there is not a significantly useful similarity between the structure of English and that of a programming language, although inspection of certain program texts in high-level languages like COBOL, POP-2, etc., (full of 'IF . . . THEN . . . ELSE', 'MOVE', etc.) might suggest to a naïve reader that there is no essential difference between the two. This is not very helpful, as the differences between English and a programming language are greater than the similarities. Many of the similarities are superficial and often result from the attempts of the language designer to make the text understandable to humans. 'IF . . . THEN . . . ELSE' is more transparent than (say) 'TEST . . . OPTION . . . DEFAULT', but it should not delude the reader into thinking he is reading English. Ambiguity, use of pronouns, lack of a clear notion of syntactic well-formedness, the ability to be self-referential, are all features of English which are generally absent from (and even undesirable in) programming languages. This is not to say that it is impossible to build a language which has some, or all, of these features — but this would be narrowing the gap by constructing an unusual 'programming language' rather than showing the gap to be small already.

For some time artificial intelligence was a field in which the main research activity was writing programs. Sometimes no separate statement of theories or suggestions was forthcoming along with the program. If challenged, a writer might reply that his program *was* his theory — that the actual lines of the program embodied clear hypotheses about intelligent behaviour which could be assessed by running the program. Such a claim cannot be taken literally, unless the LISP programmer intended to assert that intelligence is formulated in CARs, CDRs and CONSs, or the FORTRAN programmer meant that non-recursive subroutines were fundamental parts of his model. Clearly there are some parts or aspects of a programmed model that can be taken to constitute the substantive proposals and some which are merely implementation details. Fortunately this deficiency is being gradually remedied, with artificial intelligence workers being more explicit about what they are suggesting rather than dumping a mass of code and output in the lap of the reader. Although the implemented version of a model is the only one that can actually be regarded as 'tested' in the fullest sense it is still necessary to be clear about which aspects of it are to be taken seriously. (See the exchange between Simmons and Giuliano, in Simmons (1965).)

Allied to the approach just mentioned is the attitude that any program which actually works and produces impressive output must be of value and that any ideas which cannot be directly expressed in a working program are meaningless hand-waving. Almost no one holds this view in such an extreme form, but it is a detectable thread in some discussions in artificial intelligence. Although the first part of this attitude is slightly absurd, it cannot be denied that much of the impact of the Winograd (1972) thesis came from the sample dialogue. It is important to bear in mind here the performance of the ELIZA program (Weizenbaum (1966)). ELIZA could carry on a superficially plausible typewritten conversation with a human user without using any analysis of the 'meaning' of the sentences. The program's responses were formed either by shuffling the previous utterance (or parts of it) into a stereotyped pattern (e.g. 'Why do you think

. . . ?') or by producing one of several standard questions (e.g. 'In what way?'). This program cast very little light on how a human can understand a sentence (although it may have modelled a polite party conversation) but it illustrated how careful we must be not to be misled by a program's output.

Even people who hold very strongly that ideas must be programmable tend nevertheless to criticise or praise ideas on grounds (e.g. generality, elegance, intuitive appeal, etc.) other than whether they have been (or can be) programmed. Ultimately, ideas can be assessed in various terms and the existence of an implemented program is just one (important) criterion among several.

An even stronger version of the 'working program' attitude just described further stipulates what kind of performance the working program should have. Since one of the essential uses of language is to carry out conversations it is a very rigorous test of a linguistic model if it can describe precisely the process of human dialogue. In fact, Schank (at the NATO Advanced Study Institute, Santa Cruz, 1975) commented that modelling conversation was perhaps the hardest task facing researchers in language processing. It is somewhat unreasonable, in the current state of the field, to demand of any computational linguistic hypothesis that it be demonstrated within a fully conversational system. Many interesting theories and programs have been produced which would not meet this criterion. (Again, ELIZA would score disproportionately well on this count.)

In addition one practical disadvantage of writing a full program in a project like this should be mentioned. Program-writing and debugging is time-consuming and usually introduces many implementation problems which have no theoretical content. This means that there is a 'law of diminishing returns' concerning what should and should not be programmed, in that a section of program is worthwhile only if it will demonstrate some useful point, or will in some way enlighten the programmer himself. Unfortunately often this can be determined only after the programming has been done.

1.5. Detailed Analyses

Another justification for writing computer implementations of grammars (e.g. the program described in Chapter 13) is a general argument which applies to linguistic description whether done with pencil and paper or implemented on a computer. It is important not to lose touch with the real details of grammatical phenomena, since any hypothesis should derive from natural language observations and must fit future observations. It is easy to become intoxicated with strong hypotheses and seduced by loose conclusions and not devote enough time to seeing if the claims are even half true. This is not to say that strong, false hypotheses are worthless — the Popperian idea of learning by refutation is relevant — but we must first find that they are false, not assume them to be true.

This is not to suggest that linguistic investigation proceeds in the fashion outlined by a textbook on scientific method — hypothesis construction, experiment design, experiment execution, confirmation or refutation. The whole process is much less tidy than this, with partially-formed ideas being tried out on small collections of data only to be modified in the light of what is found, and then applied again to more items. There is a constant repetition of hypothesis-formation and testing, with concepts growing gradually (and often quite patchily) as a result. Neatness can often be achieved by working apart from the data for a while but one always has to return to the examples eventually, whether at the computer terminal or the desk.

The framework described in Chapter 10 developed gradually and various grammar fragments were written and tested at early stages. In the course of this the details of the model altered as certain initial ideas were found to be empirically inadequate (see Ritchie (1977)). This illustrates the gain in knowledge which can result from attempting to follow up the detailed implications of a theoretical proposal.

1.6. Psychology, Linguistics and Artificial Intelligence

Linguistic theories frequently occupy an ambiguous position

with respect to psychology. On one hand, language is an essentially human activity, and the only evidence for the linguist is the way humans use language, (where 'use' is taken in a very broad sense, to include, for example, the intuitions and judgments employed as data by transformational grammarians). On the other hand, linguists do not generally claim to be carrying out psychological experiments, and their notion of 'empirical' differs radically from that of an experimentalist. This dual position was highlighted by Chomsky's controversial attempt to distinguish between 'competence' and 'performance' (Chomsky (1964, 1965)). Generally, linguistic descriptions have been what Chomsky would regard as 'competence' theories, since linguists have usually aimed at describing patterns in linguistic structure without specifying processes for producing or interpreting sentences. Hence the methodological stance of linguists has been fairly consistent — they merely attempt to describe, in a theoretical fashion, the nature of linguistic structure; how this would actually be used by a human speaker or hearer in a real situation is another matter, to be investigated by psychologists. Unfortunately, anyone attempting to design a 'performance' model is in a more difficult position, and it is desirable to clarify at this point some of the aims of the framework described here.

The partial model presented in later chapters is primarily a linguistic model of performance, with an obvious but wholly speculative relationship to a psychological model. This approach was adopted largely because it seemed on intuitive grounds to be more productive, but it can be justified in greater detail (see Section 1.2). The main point is that it is observable that people do interpret and produce sentences (subject to philosophical provisos which are too complex to discuss here); hence it is reasonable to investigate language in terms of two analogous processes. There is no guarantee that any regularities or constructs will be formed in language outside these processes (e.g. Chomskyan 'competence'), so to search for such non-processing patterns may well be fruitless.

The evidence used in constructing the model has been

wholly linguistic in nature, since it consists of considering intuitive judgments about the use of language (oddity of utterances, difficulty in understanding of sentences, notions of similarity or difference in meaning, etc.). The main advantage of using such 'evidence' is its potential richness. If we allow judgments of synonymy, oddity, etc., as data for our model-building we will be able to fill in many details which are not easily amenable to treatment by experimental technique. The linguistic style of argument (largely developed within transformational grammar) yields a mass of 'information' of debatable reliability, whereas the experimental method gives strongly-supported results in minute areas.

This raises another point — the need for a fairly full model. Psycholinguistic evidence does not yet constrain the set of possible theories far enough to tell us much about it; stipulating that the theory should be detailed, coherent and fairly consistent does, however, provide a fairly stringent set of constraints. In fact they are probably enough to rule out all current linguistic theories or frameworks, including the one outlined here, but these properties can be regarded as criteria that the ideal theory should try to meet. They have the advantage that they can be applied at every stage in theory construction without recourse to experiment.

If we ever get near to having a full model, its usefulness as a psychological theory becomes relevant. This does not imply that even a detailed model is easily tested within the experimental paradigm, since it is not a trivial matter to state how aspects of the model should reveal themselves in measurable psychological parameters. For example, certain experiments (see Carey *et al*. (1970), Garrett (1970)) suggest that when people are faced with a potential structural ambiguity while listening to a sentence they consider all possibilities. This seems, at first glance, to support a 'breadth-first' model rather than a 'depth-first' one (see Chapter 8). However, further consideration shows that this is an over-interpretation of the results. The results really show that when a hearer is faced with a multiple choice he requires more processing time — it shows nothing about how he uses this extra time and so does not distinguish between two models in which all options are attempted in some way; it is also compatible with a strategy in which a careful selection of one option is made after some estimating process.

What, then, are we attempting to model in a computational grammar? A grammar is not a model of some abstract 'competence', but it cannot be claimed to be a psychological model of a human. This dilemma is not unique to linguistic performance models but is a common aspect of much of artificial intelligence. The main justification that can be offered for artificial intelligence models, from a psychologist's viewpoint, is that, while not directly psychological, they may furnish suggestions and concepts for an eventual psychological description. (This is also true of linguistic models which, like Chomsky's, aim to form part of an eventual performance model). The disciplines of cognitive psychology and artificial intelligence now overlap, as some psychologists recognise the need to work out full models of a fairly speculative nature before attempting to seek experimental support.

The framework in later chapters forms a partial linguistic model of the English language. It is phrased in terms of 'processing' primarily because this seems to be an obvious way to look for patterns in language. It includes the concept of a 'model hearer', which is a device capable of performing certain operations on linguistic structures. The model hearer includes certain subparts (e.g. an 'analyser') which deal with specialised tasks in these operations. Occasionally the notion of a 'program' will be referred to. A computer program is intended to be an implementation of the model hearer, which may serve to clarify certain points of detail, but it is not the central descriptive device (see Section 1.4). The data to be used in sketching the model hearer include various intuitive judgments about English sentences and English dialogues. This follows the principle that all we know about the workings of language is what the language-users can tell us about it; this principle is as old as field-work in linguistics, if not older. A fairly agnostic approach will be taken towards judgments of 'oddity' (see Sections 1.2, 1.3), in that as few assumptions as possible will be made about the cause of the oddity.

CHAPTER 2

OTHER FRAMEWORKS

2.1. Preamble

Work in artificial intelligence tends to impinge on the fields of linguistics, psychology and philosophy, so there are relationships (of varying strength) between computational grammar and a wide variety of other investigations of the English language. No attempt will be made here to give a complete guide to these other frameworks, but the aspects most pertinent to later investigations will be discussed. The more detailed arguments of Chapters 3 to 9 will also incorporate comments on the other frameworks, particularly those most relevant to computational grammar.

It is noticeable that most of the schools of thought that will be examined here are 'frameworks' in the sense of Section 1.1, rather than theories. Generally, language research operates with a cluster of ideas and guidelines (which often are not related by any necessity), rather than with some monolithic theory with clear boundaries. For example, it is hard to say what are the defining principles of the 'conceptual dependency' of Schank (1972a). It is fundamental to conceptual dependency that meaning can be described by a small set of primitive elements which are not language-specific. However, Schank's work has associated ideas and methods which are not logical conclusions from this assumption, e.g. the use of a particular set of primitives, the avoidance of traditional syntax, etc. Someone could therefore adhere to the central tenet (description of meaning in non-linguistic elements) but still not be working on conceptual dependency as it is normally recognised. Some frameworks are even harder to define precisely, although all are clearly recognisable to their users. Katz explicitly states (1972, Chapter 8) the defining principle of deep interpretive semantics, and discards as peripheral certain notions often attributed to him. His minimal definitive statement might surprise some linguists, since it contains so little of the framework that has come to be associated with interpretive semantics.

The discussions in this chapter will therefore deal with the loosely linked packages of ideas that are normally taken to characterise the various viewpoints, rather than attempting to isolate and examine defining properties. A framework exists in the minds of the users, rather than in explicit definitions, unfortunate though this often is.

Sections 2.2 to 2.6 describe the frameworks that provided the background in linguistics and logic for computational grammar, Sections 2.7 to 2.10 outline the artificial intelligence influences on the framework, and Sections 2.11 and 2.12 summarise work which was carried out independently but which has certain similarities to the overall model.

2.2. The Aspects Model

One of the most influential linguistic theories of recent years has been transformational grammar as developed by Chomsky (Chomsky (1955, 1956, 1957, 1958, 1959, 1961, 1964, 1965, 1966)). The remarks here will be addressed to the more complex 1965 version, rather than the 1957 prototype.

Chomsky proposed a model of grammar in which there were separate (but closely related) syntactic, semantic and phonological components. (The phonological component as outlined in Chomsky and Halle (1968) is not of interest here.) Although some work was done on the semantic component by others (see Section 2.3), Chomsky's own suggestions were primarily concerned with the syntactic component.

There were to be two main kinds of syntactic rules — phrase structure and transformational. The former characterised a set of labelled trees and the latter defined a set of tree-manipulating operations. Each sentence was analysed as having a surface structure (a labelled tree whose terminal nodes represented the words of the sentence), a deep structure (a labelled tree describable by the phrase structure rules) and a derivation (an ordered subset of the transformational rules, which defined the relation between the deep structure and the surface structure). The deep structure was supposed to be the level at which certain linguistic generalisations (e.g. categorisation of verbs) were represented, and formed the interface with the semantic component (in that the semantic rules were defined on phrase-structure-generated deep structures). Ambiguous sentences, therefore, might have more than one associated deep structure, thus providing more than one possible input to the semantic component.

One major asset of this model is that it was a fairly detailed and complex system which attempted to systematise a wide range of phenomena. Certain problems and linguistic patterns were simultaneously drawn to the attention of linguists and described in an elegant fashion. This stimulated a great amount of work which uncovered a vast number of regularities in natural language (especially English). The resulting literature provides a vast store of linguistic patterning which subsequent theories can take as partially-digested data. Over recent years many criticisms have been aimed at Chomsky's work, but only the three which emphasise the contrast between transformational and computational grammar will be mentioned here.

The model was not one of language-processing (despite a tentative suggestion at the end of Katz and Postal (1964)), but was a static description of patterns. (See Section 1.2 for a discussion of this issue.) Chomsky (1965, pp. 30-31) seems to imply that the mode of employing transformational rules to comprehend language would be some kind of general rule-interpreter, but no details are given of how such a mechanism might work.

Secondly, the model was dominated by syntactic generalisations. Although deep structures were supposed to provide the interface with the semantic component, the criteria for postulating particular deep structures and transformational derivations were almost always based on syntactic patterns. The assumption seemed to be that if the syntactic generalisations were captured the semantic rules would work correctly (see Section 2.3 for further remarks).

Also, (as a consequence of the two preceding points), the model was disproportionately dependent on the separation between ill-formed and well-formed sentences. Instead of this providing just one criterion to apply in the construction of analyses, it formed the central task of the grammar, with the latter being wholly syntactic. (See Sections 1.2, 1.3 for more discussion.)

2.3. Deep Interpretive Semantics

Katz and Fodor (1963) sketched a semantic theory which was intended to provide a semantic component suitable for the linguistic model being developed by Chomsky (see Section 2.2, above). They provided some simple examples of how their model was to operate, but not all the details were explicitly stated. Katz and Postal (1964) elaborated on this theory and suggested how the semantic component might interface with a syntactic component in the style of the 'Aspects' model. This semantic theory was gradually developed in a series of articles (Katz (1967, 1970, 1971)) and the fullest description so far is contained in Katz (1972). It is this latest version which will be discussed here.

Katz maintains the position that the relationship between syntax and semantics is as follows. For each sentence, there is an associated deep structure, in the form of a labelled tree, related to the surface structure by a sequence of syntactic transformational rules (see Section 2.2). There are semantic interpretive rules which relate each deep structure to a *semantic representation*. The semantic representation for an item consists of a set of *semantic markers*. Other forms of information in Katz's model are held in *redundancy rules*, which impose a hierarchical organisation on the markers, and *antonym sets*, which cluster mutually exclusive markers. These latter two devices seem to capture generalisations and are a useful contribution to the problem of defining and describing 'semantic anomaly'.

A semantic marker is not (as it appeared from the original Katz and Fodor formulation) an unanalysable unit (like a syntactic feature), but can have internal structuring. That is, 'semantic marker' is roughly equivalent to 'piece of semantic structure', with no atomic connotations. Hence the 1972 version allows a wider range of operations to be defined on markers, whereas the 1963 theory permitted little other than ordinary set operations (union, intersection, etc.) on the sets of markers. This can be regarded as an improvement or a retrograde step, depending on the metatheoretical standpoint, but from the point of view of building working models it is a useful enrichment for exploring the complexities of natural language semantics. Unfortunately, Katz does not use a fully formal notation for his markers, so it is hard to determine all the details. For example, it is not clear exactly how the internal structuring of a marker like

(EVAL: seat for one)

can be operated upon, or what elements are atomic in his system. Also, it may be that Katz has not taken full advantage of the potential enrichment of having non-atomic markers, for the following reasons. In the 1963 and 1964 versions of the theory, there were *projection rules* which showed how the meanings of the immediate constituents of a syntactic item were combined to form the meaning of the whole. There were different projection rules for different syntactic constructions, and so different rules could combine meanings in different ways (subject to the proviso that the items they were acting on were unordered sets of atomic elements). Katz suggests that such rules can be removed from his theory and their function performed by syntactic annotations on each semantic lexical item, showing how other items may be attached to or combined with it. He illustrates this by describing how the lexical meaning of a verb can have annotated 'slots' showing which syntactic constituents will provide the meanings to be inserted in the meaning of the main verb. It is not clear how this approach will work in general; presumably the lexical meaning for a noun will require annotations showing where all possible modifiers (e.g. adjectives) can be attached. Possibly only nouns and verbs will need these markings and other items can be dependent on them (cf. dependency grammar, Robinson (1970)). This seems a little cumbersome — having semantic items carrying details of all possible combinations that they can undergo, including syntactic details of the way that their associated items will be expressed (cf. comments in Section 10.9 on where to represent information). Also, it restricts the modes of combination, unless the marking system is to be expanded in some way to allow the markings to be lists of different ways of combining. In Katz's verb example there is one mode of combination (roughly equivalent to filling in a case-frame, in the model of Fillmore (1968)), so no more needs to be specified. This seems to be inherent in the mechanism, whereas the 1963 version allowed the projection rules to describe different semantic patterns in terms of different inter-constituent relationships. Abolishing projection rules seems to tie the linguist's hands and eliminate one of the more useful parts of the theory (cf. Montague's rules (Section 2.6)).

The annotations on semantic items can specify only one syntactic form that related items may have, so this innovation is, like most of Katz's theory, heavily dependent on having a canonical syntactic form (deep structure) for the semantic rules to operate on. This dependence means that any simplicity or elegance that Katz's rules achieve is conditional upon the syntactic component being able to define the requisite deep structure. Whereas Chomsky made the assumption that a grammar which captured syntactic generalisations would define the appropriate deep structures for the semantic component, Katz makes the assumption that the syntactic component will provide whatever structures are needed for the semantic rules. Such assumptions are unavoidable in a modular model (this is how some complex computer systems are written, for example) but great care needs to be taken to ensure that the interfaces are compatible, and that simplification on one side of the line does not cause complication on the other.

Katz' earlier model and computational grammar both employ hierarchically-organised semantic rules (see Chapter 3, below), but there is not much else in common between the frameworks. Interpretive semantics uses a different kind of semantic representation, and the level at which the semantic rules operate (i.e. 'deep structure') is 'deeper' in interpretive semantics than in computational grammar.

2.4. Surface Interpretive Semantics

One development from the 'Aspects' model was the introduction of semantic rules which operated on syntactic structures other than deep structures, as proposed by Jackendoff and others (Jackendoff (1968, 1973), Dougherty (1969), Bresnan (1970)). There are certain aspects of this approach which might seem to bring it slightly closer to computational grammar than the original Katz semantic theory. Unfortunately, there are many unexplained details in Jackendoff's proposals (as has been observed by opponents of surface interpretive rules) so it is hard to deliver an overall verdict.

Jackendoff suggests the use of a wider variety of semantic representations rather than just sets of semantic markers (e.g. 'coreference tables', a 'thematic hierarchy', etc.). This is an important step, since it frees the linguist from the restriction of having to capture every aspect of the meaning of a sentence in a set of markers. It seems plausible that coreference (i.e. whether two phrases refer to the same object) can be incorporated in a model of langugage-use more easily if it is explicitly handled as part of referential semantics rather than if it is squashed into syntactic rules. It is not quite so easy to see how benefits will accrue from Jackendoff's notation for opaque contexts, since no mechanisms are outlined (e.g. inference) which use the notation.

As observed in Section 2.3, deep interpretive semantics depends on a fairly sophisticated syntactic component to connect deep and surface structure, and so presents problems for a model of language understanding. Surface interpretive semantics replaces many previously formulated syntactic transformations with semantic interpretation rules, and so makes a start on the problem of determining semantic representation from surface form. However, it is only a partial step, since very few of Jackendoff's rules operate directly on the *surface* structure. The rules usually operate on some structure intermediate between deep and surface, and so it would be more appropriate to call them 'derived structure interpretation rules'. From the point of view of trying to model language understanding as a process, this introduces as many problems as it eliminates (if not more), since an analyser which followed a transformational derivation would have to perform semantic processing at arbitrarily interleaved parts of the syntactic processing. That would not be impossible, but it requires a more complex processing model than the term 'surface interpretive semantics' might suggest.

One issue which becomes rather confused in the course of Jackendoff's arguments is the question of 'syntactic well-formedness' (or 'grammaticality' in the Chomskyan sense). Although he adheres to the position that there is a notion of syntactic well-formedness which is independent of semantics, Jackendoff's proposals regarding undeveloped nodes lead to rather bizarre strings being classed as syntactically well-formed. Jackendoff admits that his notion of well-formedness has changed from the original Chomskyan idea in certain respects, but does not regard this as a problem. His position is quite consistent, and it emphasises the point made in Section 1.3 that well-formedness is defined by the *theory* rather than being given in the data, but it raises anew (without fresh debate) the question of what role syntactic well-formedness is to play in the theory.

Although certain of Jackendoff's innovations are similar to ideas in computational grammar (in particular, handling certain semantic phenomena outside the syntactic component and applying semantic rules at a 'shallower' level), there is little resemblance between the two frameworks.

2.5. Generative Semantics

Another development stimulated by Chomsky's work in the

mid-1960s was that of 'generative semantics' (Lakoff and Ross (1967), McCawley (1968, 1971a), Bach (1968), Postal (1972)). This framework retained certain parts of Chomsky's model (in particular, the notion of a transformational derivation of tree-structures) but discarded the idea of a separate syntactic component. A generative semantic derivation related the semantic representation (a tree of predicates, arguments and propositions) to surface form by a uniform sequence of transformational rules, with no intermediate level of syntactic deep structure. A later development (see Lakoff (1971)) was the incorporation of *global derivational constraints* which were general rules with the power to influence the operation of transformational rules in any way.

The initial tenet of generative semantics (that it is undesirable to posit separate syntactic rules and structures) is shared by computational grammar, but there are few other similarities. The main difficulty in assessing the advantages of the theory (as opposed to the attractiveness of its assumptions) is that it is very hard to assess whether a given solution falls within the predictions of generative semantics, since global derivational constraints allow any manipulation whatsoever, and the concept of 'transformation' has changed so much. As observed in Section 1.1, most theories include theoretically powerful devices, restrained only by the idea of 'ad-hoc-ness', but this theory seems to allow any 'rule' to be inserted without the linguist's conscience compaining. Also, since there is no good independent definition of 'syntax' or 'semantics' (a frequent problem), it is difficult to see whether the hypothesis of there being no wholly syntactic rules has been verified. (These issues have been covered very fully elsewhere — Partee (1970, 1971), Lakoff (1970), Chomsky (1971, 1972), Postal (1972), Katz (1970).)

The methodology adopted in computational grammar is that independent syntactic constructs should not be postulated unnecessarily, but that the linguistic description (or the notion of 'semantic') should not be distorted to protect this guideline.

2.6. *Montague Grammar*

At present, one of the few formally defined frameworks for describing language is that of Montague (1968, 1970a, 1970b, 1972), which is unparallelled in its rigour and precision.

Montague's system contains many traditional notions in a mathematically formalised form. The syntactic rules are very like phrase-structure rules (see Chomsky (1957)), in that they characterise a tree-like structure with words as terminal elements. Most of the syntactic terminology is merely a tidying-up of notions like 'lexical entry' and 'phrase'. Syntax and semantics are defined separately, but there is a well-defined interface, in that each syntactic rule has an associated semantic combining rule. This is closely related to the Tarski semantics for predicate logic, and is also very similar to the Katz-Fodor system of 'projection rules' (see Section 2.3 above). The semantic concepts are related to formal logic and provide a very comprehensive generalisation of notions like 'sense and reference' (Frege (1892)) and 'indexical expression' (Bar-Hillel (1954)).

Montague uses the notion of a 'point of reference', which can be regarded as a 'context' or a 'state of the world'. A point of reference is defined as an ordered pair, consisting of a 'possible world' (in the logician's sense) coupled with a 'situation of use'. Although Montague decomposed a point of reference into only two components, presumably these two elements could in turn be defined to be n-tuples if we wished to distinguish various factors in the state of the world. For Montague, the meaning of a 'term' (i.e. what might loosely be called a 'referring expression') is a function from points of reference to sets of objects (more precisely, to functions which define sets of objects). Thus the meaning of a term is always the same function, but it can refer to different sets of objects if evaluated at different points of reference.

The main advantages of Montague's work are its precision and generality. Also, it has started to illuminate such difficult and confused areas as the distinction between categories of meanings and categories of objects referred to, and the way that meanings can vary systematically with changes in the context of use.

The main disadvantages of Montague's work are that it is not a process model, and there is no place in the theory for any form of production or recognition rules.

There seems to be a feeling within artificial intelligence that Montague's semantic system is based too strongly on traditional, Tarski-style truth-values. For example, Wilks (public lecture at Edinburgh University, 1976) stated that one deficiency of Montague's ideas was that it assigned the same 'meaning' to 'Snow is white' and 'Two is prime', namely 'TRUE'. This misrepresents Montague's theory, which provides two distinct intensional meanings (i.e. different semantic structures) for these two sentences, with the same extensional meaning (i.e. truth-value) in some worlds. Also, it is currently fashionable to advocate describing sentences in terms of their use in a dialogue. It is important to notice that such an approach does not necessarily contrast with a truth-valued system of meaning unless a model of conversation can be developed which genuinely uses a different method of describing conversational effect. For example, the SHRDLU, LSNLIS and MCHINE programs (see Sections 2.9, 2.10 and Chapter 13) all treat a yes-no question as requiring a pattern (the 'meaning' of the sentence) to be tested against the 'hearer's' model to see if that state holds (or held at some time). This is very much a truth-value system, although improved by making 'truth' relative to each hearer or speaker.

Computational grammar uses many traditional syntactic and semantic ideas, and Montague's writings have been particularly useful in clarifying certain distinctions (particularly in semantics) which are often not considered elsewhere.

2.7. Preference Semantics

One of the most distinctive approaches to language-processing in recent years has been that of Wilks (1972, 1973, 1975). Although the implemented versions have generally been aimed at machine translation, it is worth considering whether any general principles of language-processing can be extracted from the ideas he uses. The form of 'interlingual representation' used is influenced by the translation task, so it is not very relevant to try to assess its adequacy for general purpose meaning representation. However, the processing strategies are interesting, since Wilks claims that they are predominantly *semantic*, rather than syntactic, and are capable of processing metaphors and other non-standard constructions.

A preference semantics grammar can be thought of as being in two sections — structures and procedures. There are three principle kinds of structures — primitive elements (like Katz-Fodor 'semantic markers'), formulae (corresponding to lexical entries) and bare templates (corresponding to structural rules or patterns). Each word has an associated formula, which consists of a binary tree of primitive semantic elements, with one element designated the 'head'. A bare template is a triple of primitive semantic elements representing three formulae-heads to be sought in the input words.

The procedures are many and varied. The input string is first put through a 'fragmenter' which clumps the words into small phrases ('fragments'). There is a matching routine which tries to find a bare template to match each fragment, inserting 'dummy' elements where necessary to complete the match. The bare template together with the elements that matched it are called a 'full template'. Then various routines (referred to in the 1973 paper as EXTEND and TIE) attempt to find links between the filled templates so far built; in later versions of Wilks' system further structures called 'paraplates' help to perform these connections. The notion of 'preference' is introduced because the routines which fill out connections between structures will not discard a structure simply because its internal semantic specifications are met — however, a structure where all the specifications are met will be preferred to a deficient one, thereby resolving possible ambiguities on semantic grounds.

The main advantage that this system has is that it has been implemented, and has translated passages of English and French. The main difficulty in trying to assess the details of the mechanisms is that Wilks tends to highlight certain areas at the expense of others. His papers generally concentrate on the notions of 'template', 'formula' and 'preference', and imply that most of the linguistic information is contained in the structures plus the simple notion of counting semantic connections. In fact, much of the work is done by the routines for matching templates and tying together structures, and information is encoded in a wide variety of forms. Although the central aspect of the system is supposed to be that it is based on *semantic* matching and not syntactic structure-building, much of the processing (e.g. the 'fragmenting' and 'extending') is traditionally syntactic. Since the preferential semantic accounting occurs only once the building routines have made ties, the overall demarcation is not vastly different from that in the programs of Woods, Winograd or Marcus (see Sections 2.9, 2.10, 2.11), where semantic checking is applied to the results of syntactic building. The main differences are that the template-matching is at least partly semantic and that Wilks' semantic checking does not discard possibilities but merely gives them a preference ordering.

Wilks' central claim (that semantic constraints give an ordering of alternative possibilities rather than rejecting unusual combinations outright) seems correct, but computational grammar has not incorporated a suitably subtle mechanism for carrying out the assessment of different semantic structures (see Section 8.3 for further discussion).

2.8. Conceptual Dependency

One of the more influential artificial intelligence approaches to natural language in recent years has been 'conceptual dependency' as developed by Schank and others (Schank (1969, 1970, 1972a, 1972b), Riesbeck (1974, 1975), Goldman (1973), Rieger (1974)). The main aim of conceptual dependency is to provide a system of 'conceptual representation' which can be used to describe the meaning of natural language in terms which are unanalysably primitive and which are independent of the natural language involved.

By constructing a vocabulary of primitive constructs, and rules for using them, Schank hopes to develop a single representation system which will serve for all language-processing and inferential tasks, e.g. machine translation, question-answering, etc. This seems a worthwhile aim and the desire for generality is a great improvement over earlier artificial intelligence approaches to meaning-representation. As argued in Chapter 1, some of the most interesting questions in language research concern the processing that must be done either to convert a string of words to the meaning representation, or vice versa. Although it is clear that Schank regards language comprehension as fundamental, his articles have tended to concentrate on issues regarding semantic representation rather than processing.

Nevertheless, papers by Riesbeck (1973, 1974, 1975) have given some indication of how a conceptual dependency sentence-analyser is intended to operate, and this outline will be examined here, as it is the aspect of conceptual dependency which contrasts most strongly with computational grammar. There are two slightly different proposals concerning analysis strategies; the first is described in Riesbeck (1973, 1974: part I) and the second in Riesbeck (1974: part II, 1975).

Roughly, the system is as follows. The central device is a 'request', which is a *test* coupled with an *action*, processed in the following way. Each word has an associated list of requests and the analyser maintains a list of currently active requests. As each word is taken in its requests are added to the list. The list is then scanned and if the test part of any request yields TRUE the action part of that request is carried out and the request removed from the list. Hence a 'request' is much the same as a 'demon' (Charniak (1973)). The second version of Riesbeck's system attempts to fill in more details of this process. 'Expectations' (an alternative term for requests) are now annotated with information about what they do, in terms of which variable value is relevant to the TEST (or 'FOCUS'), and which slot will be filled if the action is executed (the 'NEED'). This seems to help in indexing the expectations, since the FOCUS device will make the implementation more efficient, but it does not impose any structure on how the expectations operate.

The main problem with Riesbeck's suggestions are that they say virtually nothing about the details of language processing. All that he says about the form of the processing strategy, or the shape of grammatical rules, is that the grammar is in the form of 'demons'. This can be contrasted, for example, with the more subtle proposals of Marcus (see Section 2.11), where the notion of 'demon' is taken as a building block for making further detailed suggestions, rather than being left as the entire theory. Riesbeck asserts that his program treats syntax and semantics in a uniform manner and allows concepts of both types to communicate freely. This is true, in as much as all information is programmed into expectations, but it could equally well be said that any program written wholly in one programming language achieves the same uniformity — the whole problem is in elucidating *how* different information interacts, not merely expressing it in some common computing language. Demons (or expectations) are a wholly general computational device, and this kind of mechanism is a common implementation detail of language processing systems — what are needed are some rules about *how* these demons can or cannot be used.

Despite Riesbeck's claims to the contrary, it is not the case that syntactic information is not used in his program. He merely puts it into expectation form and re-labels it. For example, the worked example in Riesbeck (1975) starts with the expectation 'Is INPUT an NP?' — a very appropriate (but syntactic) prediction. In the same example, the word 'a' causes the action to be performed:

> 'save the current set of expectations and replace it with "6 — does INPUT end an NP?" '

This seems to recognise the surface integrity of the traditional noun phrase, and the saving of expectations seems to be analogous to the nesting devices in syntactic systems, such as the 'PUSH' in Woods' transition networks (see Section 2.9), or PROGRAMMAR's 'PARSE' (see Section 2.10).

This saving of expectations raises doubts about one of Riesbeck's other examples.

(4) John was mad at Mary. He gave her a sock.

He suggests that in (4), the word 'sock' would be disambiguated as soon as the word 'sock' was read (not when the whole NP was processed) using the expectations set up at the higher level. If 'a' has caused the higher level expectation list to be temporarily shelved it is not clear how this can happen.

Even Riesbeck's attempts to enrich his theory by annotating each expectation with a 'NEED' and a 'FOCUS' does not help much. He suggest that if expectations E2 and E3 are both active, and both would have to fill the NEED of E1, and if E2 'cannot produce a structure that will satisfy the predicate of the first expectation' (i.e. E1), then E3 is tested first. This is strange for two reasons. If E2 'cannot produce a structure' that is suitable why test it at all? It could just be discarded. Also, where does this useful information come from? Neither NEED nor FOCUS indicates what kind of structure an expectation-action will produce.

The NEED/FOCUS system can apply only to some of the manipulations performed by the analyser since, as Riesbeck admits, 'Unfortunately, there are no constraints on what sets of functions can appear as predicates and programs', and arbitrary side-effects are allowed. In an attempt to broaden the notion of a NEED to cover a particular operation that he needed, Riesbeck (1974) distorts the original idea to the extent of making it vacuous. He argues that certain constructions can be handled by the 'need' for all words in the sentence to be used up; this is hardly the name of a conceptual slot being filled.

Fundamental to the approach of Schank and Riesbeck is the idea that conceptual (not syntactic) predictions will provide the mechanism for analysing a sentence. They seem to overestimate the extent to which predictions of conceptual meaning will constrain the possible input forms, which is what the analyser ultimately has to deal with. (See Ritchie (1978a, b) for an elaboration of this point.)

Schank and Riesbeck suggest that, while it is necessary for a theory of language to specify some way of converting surface strings to meaning representation, it is not important to specify that process in any theoretically interesting way. If a program can be written which produces the desired output from particular inputs, that is all that is required at present. As can be judged from Chapter 1, this is a fundamental difference in attitude between computational grammar and conceptual dependency.

2.9. Transition Network Grammars

The LSNLIS program (Woods *et al.* (1972)) is a major implementation of various ideas which contribute to the basis of computational grammar. In particular, the recognition grammar is written using a formalism which has become widely used in language processing, and which has been the basis of the mechanisms used in computational grammar, so it is worth digressing to give the background to this formalism (see also Bobrow and Fraser (1969), Woods *et al.* (1969), Woods (1970, 1973)).

The kind of grammar Woods uses are known as *augmented transition network grammars*, or 'ATN grammars' for short. (The abbreviations 'RATN' — Recursive Augmented Transition Network — and 'AFSTN' — Augmented Finite-State Transition Network — are also used sometimes.) The grammar is a standardised description of a sequence of tests and operations that have to be

(5)

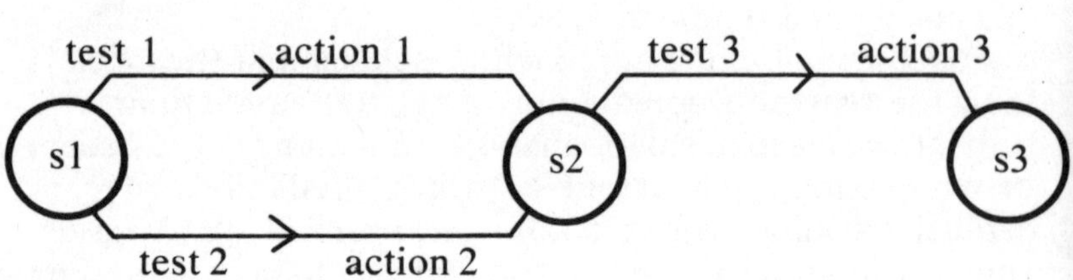

performed when a sentence is being processed. This can be represented graphically by a directed graph, where arcs represent test-action pairs and states (or nodes) indicate common points joining arcs, e.g. (5) (cf. Conway (1963)).

The tests are generally (but not necessarily) conditions on an input word and the network represents the possible ways of analysing a sentence. A complete analysis is produced by a path through the network on which all the tests are satisfied by the input words (which are scanned gradually as the path is traced through the network) and all the actions are carried out in order. The 'augmented' in the title refers to the fact that any arbitrary tests or actions can be included, making the ATN a totally general computational formalism (i.e. equivalent to a Turing machine).

One of the most important aspects of the ATN formalism is the mechanism for handling embedded constituents. Where a test on an arc simply checks the grammatical category of the next word, processing is simple, but if the network is to check for the presence of a particular kind of *phrase* things become more complicated. There is a special kind of arc (called a 'PUSH' arc by Woods) for including phrase-tests.

(6)

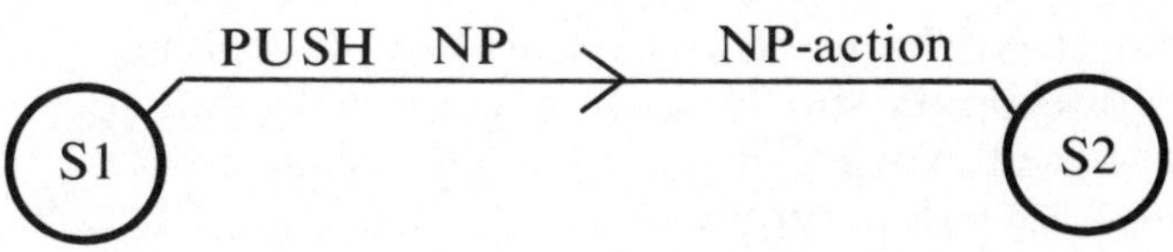

In a network like (6) the PUSH NP indicates that the category being checked (i.e. NP) may be made up of more than one word and independent processing space is needed for it. The destination state (S2 above) is saved (as in the 'NP-action' in some versions) and some other part of the network (indicated by the label 'NP') is used to process the incoming phrase. If the phrase is processed successfully another special arc (a 'POP' arc) will be encountered in the NP network. Traversing a POP arc causes processing to be resumed in the saved part of the network (S2 in example (6)), with the whole phrase that has been found acting as the input item for the action on the original PUSH arc (in (6), 'NP-action'). This jump and return mechanism is analogous to the use in a computer program of a subroutine (i.e. a self-contained section of program for some particular computation). The PUSH mechanism can be invoked again while processing a phrase so that constituents can be nested inside each other to an arbitrary depth. (In practice, the ability of any particular ATN system to process nested items will be limited by the space available for storing information about the return point.)

In any implementation of an ATN system there has to be a program which interprets grammars written in the ATN notation and carries out the appropriate processing of the input words. That is, an ATN analyser consists of an ATN *grammar*, together with an ATN *interpreter* which defines the exact significance of the various network constructs. The interpreter will, for example, keep track of what is the current state in the network and what is in each register. (Strictly speaking, a whole ATN grammar could, as an alternative, be translated (or 'compiled') into a set of program instructions, but this technical distinction is not relevant here. The ATN interpreter can be regarded as an abstract machine, whether it is implemented by 'compiling' or not.) It is therefore natural to define any given ATN construct (such as the PUSH arc) by describing what an ATN interpreter should do on encountering that construct. This form of exposition is used in later chapters.

The LSNLIS program contains a large bank of geological data (concerning moon-rock samples) and the syntactic-semantic components are designed to allow a scientist to interrogate this store of facts. Hence there is a slight bias in the type of sentence tackled, since questions and certain imperatives are the main types needed. There is a general semantic representation (related to predicate logic) which provides the necessary routines to search the stored bank of data for specific details (see also Woods (1968)). The system has a syntactic recognition grammar (written in ATN form) which converts input sentences to (approximately) a deep structure representation in the sense of Chomksy (1965). This syntactic structure is processed by a set of interpretive rules into the semantic form necessary for examining the data. All conversion of syntactic form to semantic representation is performed at the end of a sentence, with no interaction between the two components other than this. The semantic interpretive rules are hierarchically organised so that they are applied to the syntax tree as a whole and each rule can invoke other rules on the branch of the tree.

There are few significant differences between the overall organisation of the linguistic components in the LSNLIS program and the structure of computational grammar. The main difference is that LSNLIS includes a full, separate syntactic component, which the semantic interpretive rules are geared to handling, whereas the structure built by analyser in computational grammar is directly part of the setting up of the semantic rule hierarchy — the surface structure in computational grammar *is* the interpretive rule sequence (see Chapter 3).

One other main difference is in the research methodology adopted. LSNLIS is a practical working system using generalisations and patterns only to improve the efficiency of the overall service to the user. The program described in Chapter 13, on the other hand, has been written only as a testing device for linguistic ideas, and the general aim is to experiment with linguistic descriptions and devices, in order to illuminate the structure of language. Woods (at the workshop on Theoretical Issues in Natural Language Processing, Cambridge, Mass., June, 1975) claimed that working with the goal of achieving practical efficiency will achieve the goal of linguistic discovery as a by-product, but this remains to be seen.

2.10. The SHRDLU System

The SHRDLU program (Winograd (1972)) is one of the best known English dialogue programs of recent years. It is interesting here since it includes some of the devices developed and used in computational grammar. Winograd did not use the ATN notation but instead designed a programming language PROGRAMMAR which provides more or less the same facilities (he comments (pp. 44-6) on the similarities of these two mechanisms). The overall organisation of the SHRDLU syntactic and semantic components is similar to that of the LSNLIS system, and the two programs are very close in their linguistic analyses (although Woods gives credit to Chomsky for the structures, and Winograd discusses Halliday's systemic grammar).

Syntactic classification is entirely in terms of *features*, where a feature is an unanalysable marking. The written description of SHRDLU (Winograd (1972)) emphasises that these features are interdependent in ways that can be perspicuously represented by a particular form of graph (a 'systems network'). Since Halliday (1967a, b, 1968) uses this notation, this has been taken to mean that Winograd is using Hallidayan grammar. This is slightly misleading, as the program itself does not use the systems networks — they are merely a good expository device for describing the relationships between the features. The program in Chapter 13 also uses features but at no stage have these been organised into systems networks; nevertheless, a close examination of that program would allow a reader to draw up his own system network for the way that the features are distributed throughout the grammar. This would be true of any grammar that employed features. There is more to Halliday's ideas than this part of the notation.

In the SHRDLU system the lexical entry for a word consists of a list of features and a semantic entry, the latter being a data structure which will act as the 'meaning' of the word. The parser, written in PROGRAMMAR, builds a surface syntactic tree. Each node in the tree has a category label (indicating that it is a Noun Group, Clause, etc.), a list of features, and an associated semantic structure. The features are attached to the nodes directly by the parser on the basis of the words it finds in the sentence (and other tests). The semantic structure is constructed by a 'semantic specialist' which will be described below.

The PUSH/POP facility of the augmented transition network is replaced in PROGRAMMAR by the 'PARSE' command which takes a constituent label (e.g. NG) as an argument. Hence

(PARSE NG . . .)

is a command to try to parse a Noun Group (the other arguments '. . .' indicate what to do on completion or failure, using various standard options). Successful execution of this command should produce a subtree, which is then attached to the part of the syntactic tree currently being constructed. During the execution of this command the line

(PARSE DET . . .)

might be encountered. This is similarly a command to parse a particular category (this time one word) and attach it to the tree. In this way the tree-structure results from the hierarchical processing; parsing commands may be nested within each other to produce a correspondingly branching tree-structure.

One exception to this left-to-right, top-to-bottom flow of processing is the use of 'demons'. Winograd suggests that the best way to handle a conjunction (a difficult construction for any parsing system) is to define a special type of lexical entry for 'and'. Instead of 'and' having a small 'semantic structure' which is handed statically to a semantic specialist, the entry for 'and' contains a special program, which must be run on encountering the word in the input, and which causes an interruption of the ordinary flow of instructions. The 'and' program makes the PROGRAMMAR system suspend its current parsing task and start trying to parse another constituent of the same type as the one it is currently parsing.

The SHRLDU program converses about a small world of toy blocks sitting on a table ('the BLOCKS world'). It has an internal representation of these items in the form of a relational structure. That is, there is a data-base of items where each item represents a relationship between entities. Each entity is represented by an atomic one-word symbol.

Thus the data-base item

(SUPPORT B1 B2)

records the fact that there is a relation of 'SUPPORT' between the two 'blocks' B1 and B2. The whole state of the BLOCKS world can be recorded in statements like this. The 'meaning' of a sentence for SHRDLU is therefore expressed in terms of items and operations in the BLOCKS world data-base. For example, the meaning of 'a red cube' is a small program to find an equidimensional block which is marked as red. The meaning of 'pick up a red cube' is a program to find such a block and pick it up.

The conversion from input words to BLOCKS world actions is in several stages (not necessarily consecutive, but logically separate). Firstly, the syntactic tree is built. Secondly, each major constituent node (NG, CLAUSE, etc.) is converted to semantic representation by the 'semantic specialists'. Thirdly, the semantic representation is used to examine or alter the BLOCKS data-base. In fact the syntax to semantics conversion may be carried out at stages during the syntactic tree-building, since, when a major category node is completed, the semantic specialists may be used to transform the node to a BLOCKS world item. (Unfortunately, Winograd's exposition is not too clear about certain aspects of the interleaving — see Ritchie (1976).)

The SHRLDU program is related in various ways to computational grammar, but there are major differences, as in the case of the LSNLIS system, in the methodological approach. Winograd was not constructing a practical program for non-linguists to use for information retrieval (cf. Section 2.9), but the goal of implementing a working program with an impressive performance was fairly central. This may have led to some blurring of the distinction between implementation details and proposed principles, and to the use of slightly *ad hoc* measures. It is possible to look on computational grammar as an attempt to clean up some of the ideas in SHRDLU, LSNLIS and related systems in order to perform linguistic description. (More detailed discussion of Winograd's program is included in Chapters 3 to 9, as various themes are developed.)

2.11. Wait-and-See Strategies

It is worth examining in detail the suggestions made by Marcus (1974, 1975), since he adopts goals and techniques which are closely related to those of computational grammar. The emphasis in Marcus' work is on *deterministic processing*, and he wishes to design a parser which contains enough grammatical knowledge to avoid making mistakes or having to follow up several analyses simultaneously. This is a worthwhile aim, and work done with this goal should help to elucidate the sentence-understanding process. Marcus observes that many language-understanding programs in artificial intelligence rely on exhaustive, mistake-driven strategies, instead of incorporating more specialised decision-making devices (see Chapter 8 for further comments on this). He then proposes a system which, he claims, will perform more efficiently without such mistake-based control.

Marcus' grammar is organised as follows. The smallest units are *modules*, which are structure-building procedures, invoked by the presence of certain features in the input (each module has its own feature pattern), and modules are grouped into *packets*. A module can be invoked only if it is *active*, and a module is active if and only if some packet which contains it has been made active. Certain packets are active at the start of the analysis and others become active as a result of modules explicitly activating them. It is not clear from the papers cited here how a module or packet ceases to be active. Each module has a priority and those with higher priorities will be invoked in preference to those with lower priorities. Processing occurs at two levels — *group* and *clause* — with each level having an input buffer of items waiting to be tested by the modules and an output buffer of structures produced. At the group level the input buffer contains the words of the sentence and the output buffer contains the groups (small phrases) formed by clustering the words. At the clause level the input buffer is the output buffer of the group level (i.e. it contains groups) and the output buffer contains clauses. The feature-pattern on a module is compared with the first few items in the input buffer, and if the features match the module is invoked. If the feature-patterns of several active modules match the input the analyser may use a 'differential diagnostic' to narrow down the range of possible hypotheses. Differential diagnostics are a 'series of easily computed tests that decides between the competing hypotheses' (1975, p. 7). Clause structures are built by 'a case-frame interpreter that is intended to serve as an interface between it [the parser] and deep world modelling' (1975, p. 8). Also, 'the parser can ask pre-compiled fill-in-the-blank questions of the world model itself (the world model in question being the author)' (1975, p. 8).

This overall outline is similar enough to other current frameworks and programs not to be too controversial. The interesting aspects of Marcus' suggestions are the constraints within which he wants the mechanism to operate, and the performance which he claims is possible within these bounds. Marcus makes various speculative claims regarding processing time, use of world knowledge and ways of processing semi-grammatical of elliptical sentences, but these are more peripheral aspects. The main strong claims regard syntactic processing.

Marcus claims that, at any point in the analysis, the feature-patterns of active modules are to be matched against only the first few items in the input buffer — no extended look-ahead is required. This initial testing should narrow the possibilities down to what he terms two or three 'hypotheses'. If several hypotheses are possible the parser executes a 'differential diagnostic' (see above) to determine which single 'hypothesis is correct, before attempting any of them' (1975, p. 6). It is crucial to Marcus' claims that this test uses very limited look-ahead, is simple, and yields a definite result. It is unclear from the two papers cited whether recursive levels are allowed (e.g. a clause level within the group level), or whether just one clause level and one group level can exist simultaneously. If recursive levels are involved (e.g. a clause level producing items for the input buffer of a group level) then look-ahead of three *constituents* is not very restrictive, since one constituent may contain an arbitrarily large nested structure; if recursive levels are not incorporated presumably short look-ahead tests will fail in any example where some embedded structure occurs in the group that is being built (e.g. a relative clause within a noun phrase).

The simplicity of the tests is also open to question. The example he gives (1974, pp. 15–16) includes a test to see if the next item will be an adverb or a time adjunct; this does not seem to be a simple test and would probably require the item in question to be parsed. Marcus' grammar is fairly narrow in scope and it is fairly easy to construct simple rules if only a few examples are to be covered; it is another step to claim that grammars of this form will never need complex rules. It is not clear whether 'hypothesis' corresponds to 'successfully matched module' on a one-to-one basis; if they do not, it is not clear how 'hypotheses' are to be counted. It may be that the counting of hypotheses, and resorting to a differential diagnostic if the total exceeds one, occurs in the grammar-writer's mind, rather than in the execution of the program, since Marcus talks of a differential diagnostic being a particular kind of module constructed so that it is invoked only when the modules it has to choose between will also have been invoked. Maybe this describes the way that the modules are constructed rather than an algorithm which they actually obey.

There are several aspects of Marcus' work which are similar to the work described in later chapters here. For example, both frameworks accept the principles that structure, once built, must not be re-built or dismantled during an analysis, and that look-ahead should be avoided if possible. However, the more central claims of the 'wait-and-see' approach remain unproven so far. (For further coments, see Chapter 8.)

2.12. Semantic Networks

Simmons (1973, 1975) has outlined an English language

understanding system which has many similarities to the framework used here. Simmons uses a form of augmented transition network grammar to process input sentences directly into a 'semantic network' representation.

A 'semantic network' is a form of representation closely related to the standard semantics for predicate logic (cf. Shoenfield (1967)). There are a set of 'relations' which can occur between items and the items can be virtually anything. The word 'network' is used because such relational structures are often represented as graphs with labelled edges, and 'semantic' merely refers to the use of this representation for language meanings. For example, Simmons gives the representation of 'Napoleon suffered defeat at Waterloo' as:

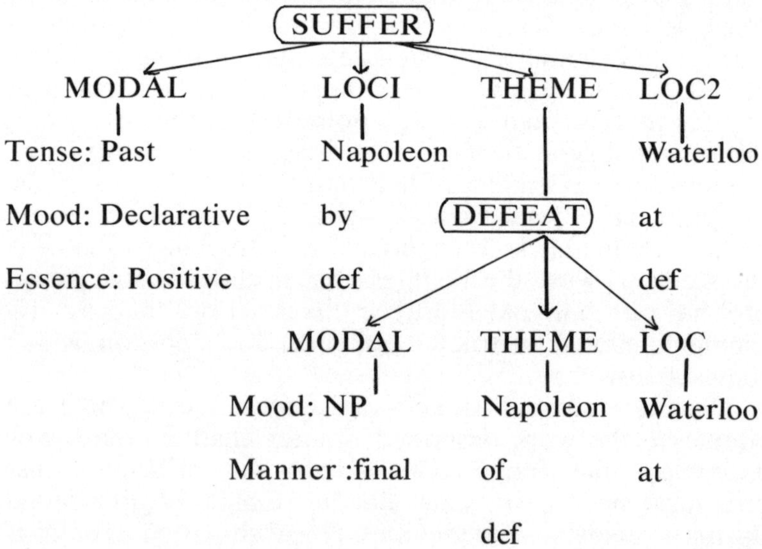

(For other semantic network systems, see Quillian (1969) and Rumelhart and Norman (1973).)

This method has been used to build a program which accepts declarative statements (e.g. 'A clown holding a pole balances on his head in a boat') and displays corresponding pictures on a graphics screen.

The grammar used does not alter the surface order or relation of the input string greatly, but each verb has an associated set of 'paradigmatic ordering rules' which express permutations of the surface subject, object and indirect object into a deep case frame for the verb. This is very similar to the computational grammar way of handling verbs, as will be seen in Chapters 3 and 6. However, this action is performed in Simmons' program by a particular operation ARGEVAL, rather than by having anything corresponding to structural combining rules (see Chapter 3). The semantic network is built directly by the actions on the ATN arcs. This approach is difficult, since the suitable constructs for a surface ATN are different from those for a semantic representation if there are no intermediate rules (see Ritchie (1978a)). Simmons can use one-stage processing largely because his semantic network is very close to a traditional surface syntactic structure, apart from the permuting of the verb arguments, and any deeper semantic patterns have to be covered by inference rules. It is not very clear how the verb-permuting operation (ARGEVAL) chooses which 'paradigmatic ordering rule' to use in arranging the verb arguments, since Simmons says that this is done using the *semantic* characteristics of the items. Since much of the case information in English is conveyed by surface syntactic aspects (order, prepositions, inflections, etc.) allotting items to verb places using solely semantic information will not in general be possible.

The main difference between computational grammar and Simmons' model is that the latter has no constructs corresponding to 'structural combining rules'. Hence Simmons' grammars have to try to capture all syntactic and semantic regularities at a *single* level of semantic representation (which may be impossible), and this semantic structure is built directly on the ATN arcs (rather than by separate rules).

CHAPTER 3

STRUCTURAL COMBINING RULES

3.1. Tree Structure

Many models of language assume that words, phrases and clauses can be seen as built up hierarchically from smaller units, thereby imposing a tree-like structure on sentences (e.g. Wells (1947), Harris (1946), Postal (1964), Chomsky (1957), Montague (1970b), Winograd (1972)). This idea is retained as one of the central parts of computational grammar, and the rules which define the combinations of linguistic structures are referred to as 'structural combining rules'. These rules are an attempt to represent grammatical relationships between constituents in the same linguistic string; that is, they deal with *syntagmatic* relationships, not *paradigmatic* classes (i.e. categories which relate items in a sentence to other items in the grammar). (See Hudson (1971) for a fuller discussion of this distinction.)

The details of this mechanism can be best presented by considering the related constructs which have been used within artificial intelligence, particularly the versions employed by Winograd (1972) in the SHRDLU program.

Syntagmatic relationships between units are decoded in two ways in Winograd's program. First, the parser builds the syntactic tree. This gives a grouping into constituents, together with a labelling (using features) of each constituent. Then, these labelled subtrees act as inputs to the semantic specialist programs which produce semantic forms. The semantic specialists are treated more or less as 'black boxes' constrained only to produce a particular output from a given input. The lack of constraints on these two stages (other than the need to interface with each other) has two slightly unfortunate consequences. The inscrutability of the semantic specialists means that they contribute little to the important question of how syntax is related to semantics.

The second consequence is directly linked to this lack of a systematic method of semantic interpretation. The syntactic component lacks criteria for what is 'good' or 'bad' grouping or labelling of a surface structure, other than the fact that it should 'work' when handed to the appropriate semantic specialist. *Ad hoc* feature markings (of the sort discussed in Chapter 7) are successful solely because they serve as the input to the equally unconstrained semantic interpreter.

If we wish to illuminate the process of extracting meaning from surface strings we must dissect the semantic specialists and try to organise the inner mechanism as systematically as possible. Consider the noun group semantic specialists. Winograd used what he called the 'slot-and-filler' approach to the structure of the noun group — there are various slots for modifers, etc. on the group node which may or may not have entries. This meant that 'null' entries had to be made on many noun groups (giving rise to features like NDET — see Chapter 7). The semantic specialist had to examine all the slots and make its decisions on the basis of the various entries. This obscured any internal semantic regularities between subunits. For example, the relationship between determiner and head noun is not separable from the relationship between adjective and head noun — both are buried somewhere in the deliberations of the semantic specialist. Winograd suggests that his 'flatter' trees are more semantically useful than the more deeply-branching trees used by transformationalists (op. cit., pp. 16–17), but this overlooks two points. First, he uses elaborate feature markings, some of which convey further structural information (which is inherently present in the transformationalists' tree already). Also, the deep branching was an attempt to reflect semantic groupings; with Winograd's method one has to deny these groupings, or hide them in the viscera of a specialist, or encode them in further 'features'. If we were to take Winograd's method to an absurd extreme, we might end up with trees like (7), a single semantic specialist (for 'Sentence') and a vast collection of features.

The whole point of further grouping, as Winograd himself states, is to find generalities that can be dealt with at a local level, and make use of all semantic regularities. If we can

(7)

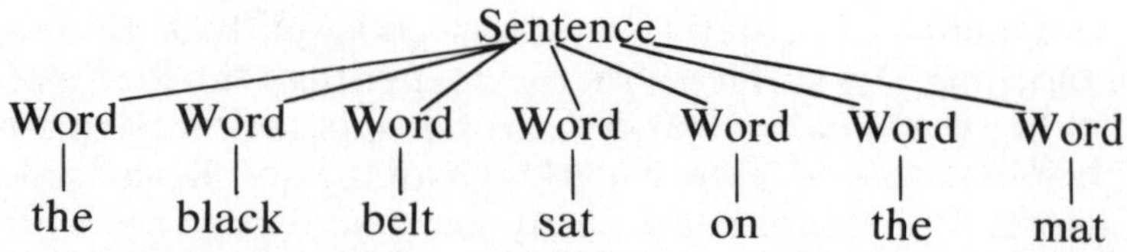

find syntagmatic regularities *within* the noun group then there is a case for separating these out into individual semantic specialists. During the analysis of a sentence the program would need to invoke only those semantic specialists for which non-null arguments existed. The tree might look like (8), where each node is marked with the semantic specialist used.

(8)

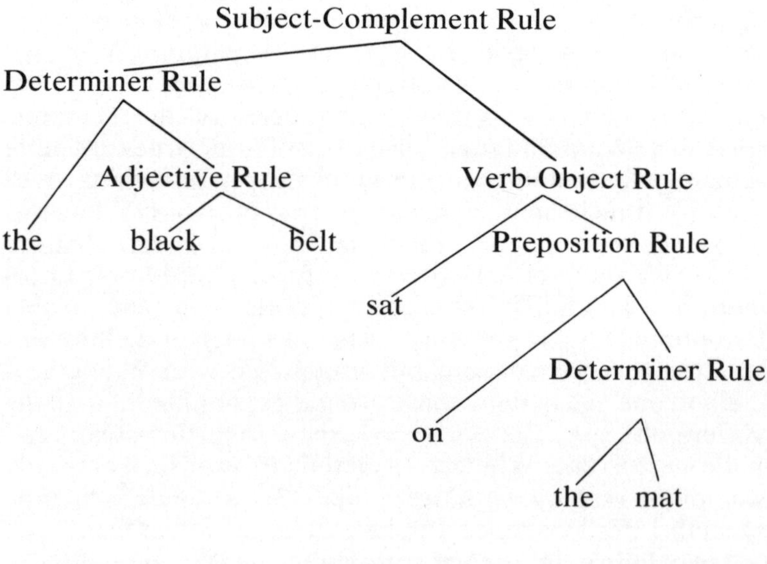

It may appear that this produces a proliferation of specialists, but that is misleading. The rules which we are referring to as semantic specialists here are much smaller than those in Winograd's program, and have been obtained by dismantling his rules. One could keep a small number of large specialists by building more and more alternatives into the body of each rule, but that would not really be simpler.

In Winograd's system the semantic specialist was selected according to the major category label on the node (e.g. NG). If we do not have specialists indexed to major categories, the question arises of how to select the rule. This question is not trivial and will be considered in the next Section.

3.2. Semantic Rules as a Form of Surface Structure

Winograd's parser acted as a pre-processor for the semantic specialists by grouping and labelling constituents. As commented in Section 1.2, the only justification for syntactic rules is that they contribute to the language-decoding (or encoding) process. It may be possible to link semantic processing more directly to the actions of the analyser, thus breaking down Winograd's two-stage conversion. There is a sense in which Winograd's parser makes all the semantic decisions, since the grouping and labelling defines how the semantic specialists will act; on the other hand, these decisions are re-encoded (in arbitrary features) instead of being used directly to build a semantic structure. The feature-laden tree is then dissected by the semantic specialists so that these earlier decisions can have semantic effect. Winograd states (op. cit., pp. 16–17) that the sole justification for his features is that they convey meaning, so presumably all the features (even bizarre ones like DPRT) perform this function of passing decisions between the syntactic and semantic components.

One obvious modification to be investigated is the abolition of the arbitrarily-labelled syntactic tree as a mail-box between the components. If we could integrate the semantic specialists and the parser more closely we could perhaps allow the parser's decisions to be more directly related to the meaning-manipulations that they cause.

Consider the original form of the semantic specialists

(ignoring, for the moment, the breaking down of the specialists into several rules, as outlined in Section 3.1). The noun group specialist constructed a semantic structure on the basis of the items in the seven 'slots' (Winograd, op. cit., p. 56) on the NG subtree, together with the feature-labelling of the subtree. In a sense the seven slot-fillers were acting as arguments for the specialist, since they provided the variable information that distinguished one noun group from another. Suppose, therefore, that we re-formulate the semantic specialist as a procedure which takes seven arguments (some of which may be dummies). Instead of establishing a syntactic NG node and attaching labelled daughters, the analyser could make a copy of a semantic NG rule (i.e. a copy of this new specialist) and fill in the appropriate arguments. Not only would this avoid some tree-building, it might also simplify the internal operation of the specialist (since it would not have to 'read' the syntactic tree). Also, features which are intended solely to provide structural information (such as NDET) would be eliminated. This does not mean that no features would be needed (number-markings would probably still be required) but it would eliminate any redundant syntax and show more clearly what information was being used where.

If we also adopt the suggestion of Section 3.1 and have separate specialists for each syntagmatic combination the need for dummy arguments should be eliminated. The parser builds a tree, each node having an associated semantic specialist, all of whose arguments have to be filled. (There may be only 2 arguments for some rules if deeply-branching trees are used.) The tree would look something like (8) above.

This proposal is not particularly radical. All that we have done is suggest that, since the parser's decisions determine (ultimately) which semantic specialists are to be invoked, and what arguments are to be passed to them, these facts should be directly represented. The operation of the semantic specialists was already hierarchically organised (as observed in Section 3.1), so using them as the cement which holds the tree together is not an extension of their use; it merely makes explicit the fact that the hierarchical syntactic organisation was ultimately aimed at guiding the semantic processing. The semantic specialists themselves (both in their original form and in the revised version) have fundamentally the same purpose as the semantic interpretive rules of Katz and Fodor (1963) and Jackendoff (1973), or the rules of Montague (1970a, b). The revised notation for the semantic/syntactic tree is similar to the analysis tree of Montague (1970b). These rules are referred to as 'structural combining rules' (SCRs) to avoid having to categorise them as 'syntactic' or 'semantic', since they fulfil a dual role.

3.3. Representing Syntactic Information

The rules as described so far do not fulfil all the functions traditionally covered by 'syntax'. There is other information to be used in the sentence-understanding process and we need further constructs to handle this information.

There are certain properties of words and phrases which help to indicate how the various items are to be grouped in building the surface tree, and which seem to have no other purpose. That is, they do not contribute directly to the final semantic structure, but they help the routines which plug the combining rules together. One good example of this is 'subject-verb agreement' which (as Katz (1972) argues convincingly) is not just a semantic property.

Subject-verb agreement is often referred to as 'number-agreement', and is described in terms of 'singular' and 'plural'. This is misleading, since it gives the impression that the agreement system is based on plurality of the set of things denoted by the subject (i.e. that it is a semantic phenomenon). The two-way classification into 'person' and 'number' for verb forms (e.g. 'third person singular') may be helpful for relating English to other languages, but it does not reflect the agreement patterns which actually occur in English.

Consider regular verbs. Most of these have two present-tense forms (e.g. 'run', 'runs') which we can refer to as PRESP (mnenonic for traditional Present Plural) and ES (mnemonic from the inflectional ending) forms. The PRESP form is compatible with subjects 'I', 'you', 'we', 'they', or any 'plural' noun phrase. That is, it covers what were traditionally known as first and second person singular, plus all plural forms. The ES form is compatible with what are traditionally called third person singular subjects — 'he', 'she', etc. Regular past tense forms (or 'remote' tense forms, to use the terminology of Chapter 12) are generally compatible with any subject at all, as are the present and past forms of modal verbs (which are 'defective' in traditional terminology).

An exception to these agreement patterns is the verb 'be'. There are four classes of subject for agreement with inflected forms of 'be', as follows:

Compatible with 'am': 'I'
Compatible with 'was': 'I', 'he', 'she', etc.
Compatible with 'were', 'are': 'you', 'we', 'they', etc.
Compatible with 'is': 'he', 'she', etc.

(Chris Miller (personal communication) has pointed out that this omits certain 'subjunctive' constructions, such as 'If I were you', 'If this be the case', etc. These appear to need special agreement patterns for particular kinds of subordinate clauses.)

Although 'be' is a solitary case, and so can be treated exceptionally, we still need agreement-classes that are capable of describing this pattern as well as the regular one. The most economical set seems to be:

Agreement Class 1: 'I'
Agreement Class 2: 'you', 'we', 'they', etc.
Agreement Class 3: 'he', 'she', etc.

Other classes can then be formed by taking the union of these minimal classes. Thus the four classes for 'be' outlined above are 1, 1+3, 2 and 3 respectively. Regular verbs will generally require 1+2 and 3 to describe the present tense, and 1+2+3 to describe the remote tense.

The difference between Class 2 and Class 3 might seem to correspond to a semantic difference in the subjects involved, as in (9), but that is not always the case.

(9)
(a) The dogs run round the garden.
(b) The dog runs round the garden.

There are phrases where the 'agreement-number' differs from the 'semantic number', (e.g. (10)), so these notions are logically distinct.

(10)
(a) These scissors are blunt, and your trousers have to be trimmed.
(b) Measles are not hard to cure, but cancer is. (Katz, p. 379).

Also 'mass' nouns (like 'snow', 'rice', 'mist') cannot be given a semantic number, since they do not denote a set of discrete objects, but have a very definite agreement class (namely, Class 3).

(11)
(a) Snow falls softly.
(b) *Snow fall softly.

To emphasise the distinction between agreement classes and semantic plurality notice that 'you' is unmarked for semantic plurality (or else has two lexical entries, one for each plurality), but has a definite agreement class, Class 2.

(12)
(a) You run very fast.
(b) *You runs very fast.

The picture is further confused when we consider that verb agreement classes can (occasionally) have semantic effects in the understanding of sentences. Some subject noun phrases are unmarked for both semantic number and agreement class. In such cases the verb form used may provide the missing semantic number information:

(13)
(a) The sheep runs very fast.
(b) The sheep run very fast.

Also, agreement classes cannot just be marked statically in the lexicon, since they are a property of whole noun phrases. The assignment of phrases to agreement classes is productive (i.e. new examples can be allocated systematically) and seems to be based on semantic number. If you learn that a 'sib' is a tool for cutting cloth, and that 'latt' is a confetti-like substance, then you will probably regard (14) (a) and (b) as acceptable, but (15) (a) and (b) as somewhat odd.

(14)
(a) Twelve sibs are lying on the shelf.
(b) Some latt is pouring out of the bag.

(15)
(a) ??? Twelve sibs is lying on the shelf.
(b) ??? Some latt are pouring out of the bag.

Brown (1958, pp. 250–53) reports that children sometimes work in the reverse direction; that is, they make systematic guesses about the meaning of a new word on the basis of its verb agreement class in examples like (14).

These phenomena can be described in the following way. Each noun phrase has a syntactic agreement class (1, 2 or 3), as outlined above, and a totally distinct semantic number (SINGULAR, PLURAL or MASS). Each inflected verb is marked with a list of the agreement classes which are compatible with it. (Listing them takes advantage of the fact that some classes are formed by taking the union of the basic three classes). Nouns like 'sheep' (which are ambiguous with respect to agreement class and number) have two separate entries with different agreement and syntactic number for each. (Hence the semantic information provided in cases like (13) is conveyed by elimination of ambiguity using syntactic agreement.)

'Agreement' between subject and verb is a rather arbitrary, language-specific device which helps to signal to the analyser how (or whether) the items are to be paired, and can be represented by some suitably neat symbolic markings (see also the examples in Section 3.7 below). Such information can be recorded by associating with each word or phrase a set of 'syntactic properties'; that is, a list of attributes which can have a range of values.

In addition, there is a need for some way of describing paradigmatic classes (i.e. categories which distinguish different grammatical items — see Hudson (1971)). In writing a recognition grammar there is often a need to include a test for some class of words whose only unifying characteristic seems to be that they can occur at certain points of a sentence. For example, English auxiliary verbs generally occur at the front of a 'yes-no' question rather than after the subject. A recognition grammar needs to be able to check the first word of the sentence to see if it is an 'auxiliary', as this suggests that the sentence may be a question. It is hard to define semantically what an 'auxiliary' is, and it seems to be a purely syntactic category — 'one of those little verbs that precede the main verb and are at the front in questions'. Other examples are the various constituents within a noun phrase — determiners, possessives, articles, adjectives, etc. These constitute options which occur at various stages throughout the processing of the phrase, and the ordering of them (and the occasional parallel options) can only be described by idiosyncratic markings on the words, since their semantic characteristics provide no clue to the order in which the options should occur. This distributional information could also be covered by 'syntactic properties' as above, but there are further generalisations about the information. Firstly, a syntactic property may have a range of values, whereas the paradigmatic information usually gives simple class membership (e.g. 'is this word an auxiliary or not?'). Secondly, syntactic properties (e.g. subject-verb agreement) may need to be marked on phrases as well as words, whereas the paradigmatic classes are to guide the analyser when it is inspecting words. In computational grammar two separate constructs have been incorporated to cover these two kinds of information:

Syntactic properties, which are attributes capable of taking a range of values, and which can be marked on phrases as well as on words.

Syntactic features, which can simply be present or absent (presence denoting membership of a particular paradigmatic class) and which are marked only on lexical items, not on larger constituents. Notice that syntactic features are not like syntactic categories, in that items may be cross-classified by giving each item several syntactic features, instead of just one. (See Chomsky (1965) and Halle (1962) for arguments in favour of this form of classification.)

One further construct is needed to integrate these concepts. As mentioned above, agreement classes cannot just be marked on all noun phrases in the lexicon, since most noun phrases are constructed out of other lexical entries. Sometimes the determiner decides the agreement class, as in (16) (a) and (b); sometimes the head noun contributes the information, as in (16) (c) and (d); and sometimes both are marked for agreement class, as in (16) (e).

(16)
(a) *A sheep* is sinking in the mud.
(b) *Many sheep* are swimming in the loch.
(c) *The dogs* will attack immediately.
(d) *Your children* are spreading marmalade on our cat.
(e) *Those apples* are very sour.
(f) *These man is selling pornography.

When both constituents provide an agreement class it must be the same one or oddity results, as in (16) (f).

If syntactic properties are to be marked on phrases, how are the markings to appear on the phrases as they are built? There are a number of logical possibilities, ranging from having a phrase inherit all the syntactic properties of the lexical entries of all the words in it, to allowing the properties of the phrase to be computed in any way whatsoever from the properties of the lexical entries of its words. Writing the grammar for the program described in Chapter 13 threw very little light on this, as only one syntactic property was included which had to appear on phrases; namely, the 'verb-agreement' class of a noun phrase. The method used in the program was to allow each structural combining rule to have, optionally, a 'property inheritance rule' which specified which properties of the argument nodes were to be attached to the result-node. (Since these properties are not deemed to be part of the meaning, but merely transient annotations to aid the surface-structure routines, they are marked on the *nodes*, not on the semantic items contained therein.)

The SCR for combining determiners and head nouns can have an associated property inheritance rule, which passes up to the noun phrase node the agreement classes of both the determiner and the noun (if present). Examples like (16) (f) will cause the analyser to attempt to make two different entries for the same property, which is not allowed. Since determiners are often combined with more than a single head noun (for example, if there are adjectives or other modifiers before the head noun), any SCRs for constructing intermediate parts of a noun phrase (e.g. the adjective-noun combining rule) will also have to have a property inheritance rule which passes up the head noun's agreement class.

It is impossible to claim empirical support for this method since only the one example of an inherited property has been tried out.

3.4. Immediate Semantic Processing

The LSNLIS system postpones all semantic processing until the end of the sentence, and SHRDLU performs semantic processing at the end of major constituents. Rieger (1974) criticises Winograd's approach for having too great an emphasis on syntax, and Riesbeck (1974) claims that his analyser can build up a non-syntactic 'conceptual structure' as it progresses from left-to-right through a sentence. Let us examine how the SHRDLU mechanism might be modified so that semantic processing may be carried out as early in the analysis process as possible.

If we adopt the modifications presented in Section 3.1 and Section 3.2 then a first step has been taken. The parser (or 'analyser') is building a tree composed of semantic rules with their arguments inserted. To produce the semantic structures these semantic rules have to be applied. The question is — how early in the analysis can this rule-application be done? The dismantling of large semantic rules into separate autonomous rules, each having perhaps only two or three arguments, should facilitate early semantic processing, since the semantic rule does not have to wait for the accumulation of several constituents as its arguments. It might be possible to apply each semantic rule as soon as all its arguments have been found. Then semantic processing would occur every time a subtree (no matter how small) was completed.

A further extension might be possible. Instead of each rule waiting for all its arguments to be inserted before operating, a rule could operate incrementally. That is, rules could be subdivided into parts (call them 'rule-components'), one for each argument-place in the rule. The nth rule-component would represent whatever semantic computation could be performed when the nth argument was found. Hence each rule-component could be applied when the corresponding argument was inserted, causing a gradual building up of a semantic structure. (It might also be useful to include a 'zeroth' rule-component in each rule, to set up an initial blank structure for the other rule-components to work on.)

One experimental version of the MCHINE program (see Chapter 13) implemented such a system, and the grammatical rules were re-written accordingly. The system was soon discontinued, since it was very cumbersome in practice, but the short trial was enough to illustrate the limitations of such a scheme. Using rule-components is not impossible, but it is more difficult for the grammar-writer to design rules in the incremental form, and there seem to be few advantages. Two main problems arise.

In the first place, many of the combining rules are such that the first argument conveys little information about the final result. This is particularly true where the arguments are themselves being represented as an operator applied to an operand — both are needed to produce the final result. This problem also arises where the second (or later) argument supplies the main structure for the result, and the first argument fits into some slot or property-value on it. In some cases the rule had to be written so that the zeroth rule component set up a structure of type X, the first component of the rule merely stored the first argument in some arbitrary slot on the X (as a temporary store) and the second (final) rule-component took the first component out of its intermediate storage position so that all the computation could be done. These bizarre manipulations demonstrated how rarely any useful processing could be done without all the arguments.

Secondly, even if such partial building were possible, the semantic processing could not go very far unless the next rule up the tree could accept a partially-formed argument. That is, even if rule R1 (in (17), below) gradually built a semantic item X, the semantic consequences would stop there unless Rule R2 could accept the partially formed X as its argument.

(17)

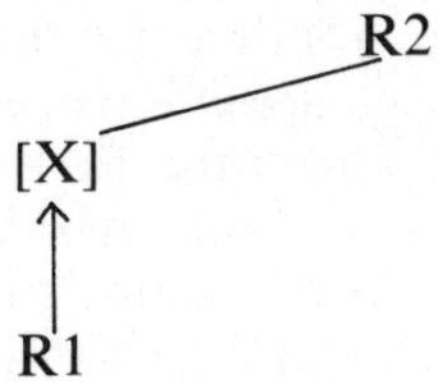

Possibly the only places where it was possible to segment the rules without losing anything were in the role-placement rules for verbs (see Sections 3.7 and 6.4). If there is a rule which arranges the object (and indirect object) into slots around the verb, then each rule-component can slot its argument in separately, and any restrictions (induced by the verb) on the slots can be checked immediately. The slight advantage of early checking of verb-restrictions has to be offset against the other difficulties created by having to write incremental rules.

(We have assumed here that any slot which may contain a value or structure, whether syntactic or semantic, can have a 'restriction' placed on it. That is, any data location may have an associated predicate which constrains the range of items which are allowed in that location. This is a common programming technique in artificial intelligence, and it has been adopted as one of the processing constructs in computational grammar.)

3.5. Separating Syntagmatic and Paradigmatic Information

Determiners ('the', 'that', etc.) are distributionally related to possessives ('my', 'Fred's', etc.). If we could arrange our semantic representations for referring expressions so that the combining process for <determiner> + <head noun> was the same as the combining process for <possessive> + <head noun>, then one SCR would do for both. This is probably not possible, for the following reasons. Determiners form a closed class, containing what are traditionally known as 'grammatical' formatives (see Lyons (1968)). Their function is to provide more detailed information about the semantic processing of the nominal provided by the head noun, regarding its definiteness, specificity, etc; they do not provide substantive semantic structure. Possessives, on the other hand, are an open class, and arbitrarily complex possessives can be built from noun phrases. These possessives contribute a substantial part of the meaning of the referring expressions, and supply a whole semantic structure which is to be combined in some way with the head nominal. The possessive construction is recursive (as will be discussed below) and structures can be built up within structures, whereas the determiner construction is not itself recursive. Two different SCRs are needed, say 'SCR-Possessive' and 'SCR-Determiner'.

Nevertheless, the distributional generalisation can still be captured in the recognition grammar, where the two categories (with features POSS and DET) appear as parallel options at the appropriate point of the ATN. A grammar which puts both classes of item into one category for all purposes would force the two levels of processing to be tied together. Here, we have managed to separate the level of SCRs from the level of ATNs.

Structural Combining Rules

Many adjectives have two uses as modifiers in a noun phrase, usually referred to as 'restrictive' and 'non-restrictive' (or 'defining' and 'non-defining' — Fowler and Fowler (1906)). Informally, the restrictive use is where the meaning of an adjective (usually denoting some property) is used to delimit the class of items denoted by a head noun, so that the combination of (adjective + noun) denotes some narrower class of objects, as in (18) (a) and (b).

(18)
(a) Pick up the *blue block*.
(b) The *male employees* should read this copy of the Sex Discrimination Act, and the *female employees* should read that one.

The non-restrictive use is where the class denoted by the noun phrase is not narrowed down by the meaning of the adjective, but the adjective conveys some property that the speaker wishes to attribute to that class. These are hard to illustrate, since most adjective + noun combinations can be understood restrictively, and there are few examples where only the non-restrictive interpretation is possible. (As Chris Mellish has pointed out (personal communication), there is a tendency in expository discourse to prefer the non-restrictive interpretation, as in (19) (d).)

(19)
(a) These *stupid* arguments do not concern me.
(b) Your *fickle* friends have deserted you.
(c) His *wealthy* parents have bought him a golf club.
(d) The mass is attached to a *light* string running over a *frictionless* pulley.

Since a wide range of adjectives can have either use, it seems better to describe these as two separate constructions, rather than having separate lexical entries for the two uses. (The latter could be done by having a feature [ATTRIBUTIVE] and a lexical redundancy rule stating that an adjective with that feature had two forms — [RESTRICTIVE] and [NON-RESTRICTIVE]. This would be possible, but inelegant.) SCRs provide an obvious mechanism for this, since there can be two SCRs for combining adjectives and nouns. One of these combines semantic properties in some way to yield a new class which has the properties of both items, and the other constructs an assertion which is to form part of the message conveyed by the speaker.

The non-restrictive SCR (call it SCR-NRAdj) has some interesting consequences for building surface structure.

Let us assume that the head noun generally provides some kind of predicate, denoting a class of items, and that a restrictive modifier can be combined with it to form a new, narrower class-predicate. This process can be applied repeatedly, so that the restrictive rule (call it SCR-RAdj) can take part in a right-branching structure like (20).

(20)

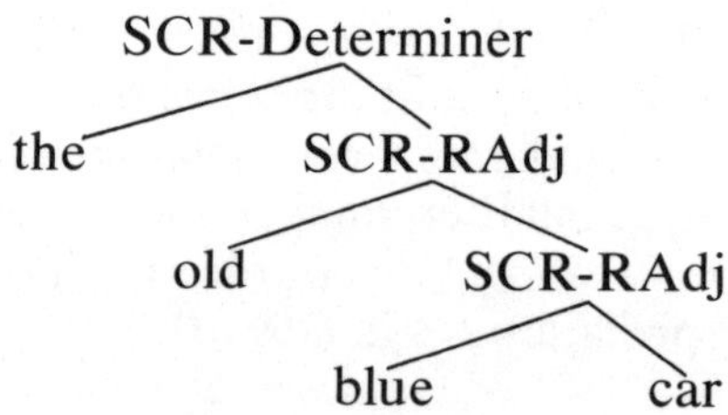

In this structure there are no discontinuous constituents — all the surface items which form a subtree are adjacent, and the restrictive adjective is always to the left of the item(s) it has to combine with. The non-restrictive case is not so simple. The non-restrictive adjectives acts not on a class-predicate (to form a narrower class-predicate), but on the final result of the SCR-Determiner (to form an assertion). In (19) (b) 'fickle' makes an assertion about 'your friends', and in (19) (c), 'wealthy' makes an assertion about 'his parents'. This seems to call for surface-tree of the form (21).

(21)

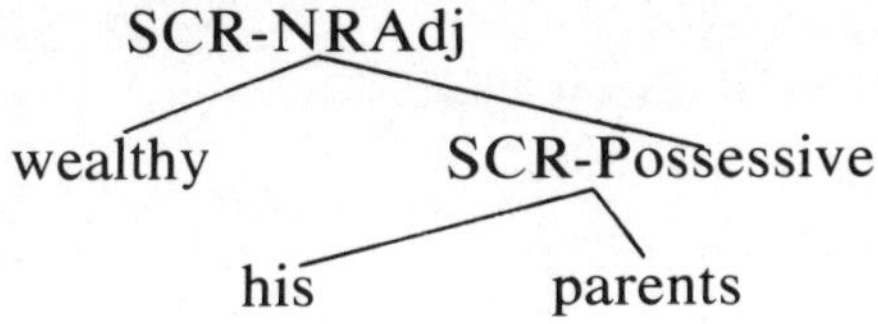

Remember, as outlined in Sections 3.1 and 3.2, that the surface-tree directly represents how the SCRs act on their arguments. There is no question of temporarily pasting together some 'syntactic structure' with different dominance relations and letting the SCRs sort out their arguments later.

Here there is a discontinuous constituent ('his . . . parents'). The non-restrictive adjective seems to act on the meaning of the (possessive + noun) and the subtree to the right of the adjective may be arbitrarily large. There are at least two ways of handling this.

One possibility is that the analyser could hold the possessive (or determiner — see above) in a temporary storage position (see Chapter 5 for details of this technique) until it had ascertained what adjectives were present in the noun phrase. Once all the non-restrictive adjectives had been built into a right-branching structure (there may be several adjectives, e.g. 'His kind, loving, wealthy parents . . .'), the possessive could be attached and the rest of the phrase analysed.

Alternatively, the analyser could build the possessive (plus a node with SCR-Possessive) on to the surface-tree at once. On encountering non-restrictive adjectives it could build branches on to the *top* of the subtree for the noun phrase. The stages would be as in (22).

The latter approach requires the subtree for the noun phrase to be built as a separate item before being attached to higher nodes (so that nodes can be inserted above the root of the subtree).

This structural aspect of SCR-NRAdj is related to the recursive aspect of SCR-Possessive mentioned above.

(22)
(a)

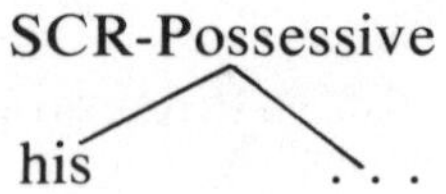

(b)

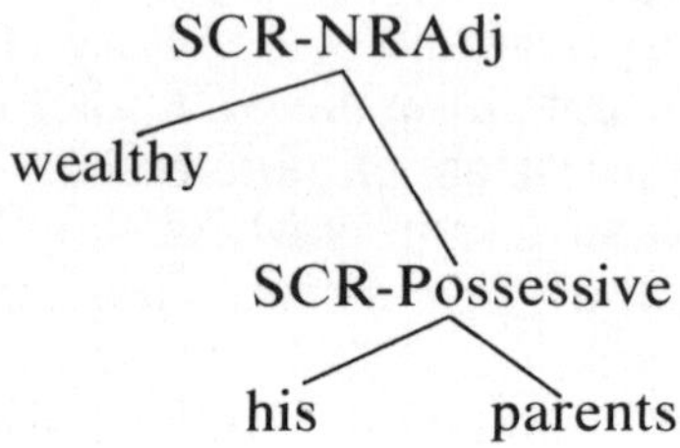

Possessives may be arbitrarily large phrases (e.g. 'the third old man's hat'), attached as constituents of other noun phrases. Let us assume that such phrasal possessives are processed initially as noun phrases, then (on encountering the ''s' at the end) attached under a SCR-Possessive node, with processing continuing on the main noun phrase. While processing the phrasal possessive the analyser may have no indication that this is not the main noun phrase and so will be building it as the subtree for the current constituent. On creating the SCR-Possessive node, some re-organisation is required, since the SCR-Possessive node becomes the new root of the main noun phrase, with the structure that formed the previous subtree as left daughter. Here is another situation where it is useful to have a temporary location for storing the root of the current subtree. Notice that these two manipulations of the location holding the subtree would not interfere with each other, although phrasal possessives and non-restrictive adjectives may occur in the same noun phrase. During the processing of the phrasal possessive the storage location contains the root of the possessive, and so any non-restrictive adjectives encountered (e.g. '[that *careless* man]'s motorbike') are inserted correctly above the possessive. Once the phrasal possessive has been completed, and the subtree restructured to allow the rest of the noun phrase to be processed, the location contains the root of the main noun phrase, and any non-restrictive adjectives will be attached correctly above this phrase, since they always follow the possessive. Even if a recursive left-branching structure occurs (as in the examples in Section 4.4 below), this re-structuring will occur in the same way at each embedding. The two potentially recursive constructions (possessive and adjective) will not interfere with each other, despite the fact that both re-allocate the contents of the location holding the subtree. (See Chapters 4 and 5 for the background to this informal discussion.)

It was observed above that several non-restrictive adjectives may occur in a single noun phrase. Careful examination of the two approaches outlined above (storing the possessive temporarily, or building a tree which is then re-rooted) will show that they will result in slightly different trees for such sentences. Holding the possessive in a temporary location will retain the surface order of the adjectives (see (23) (a)), whereas re-rooting re-orders the adjectives (see (23) (b)).

(23)
(a)

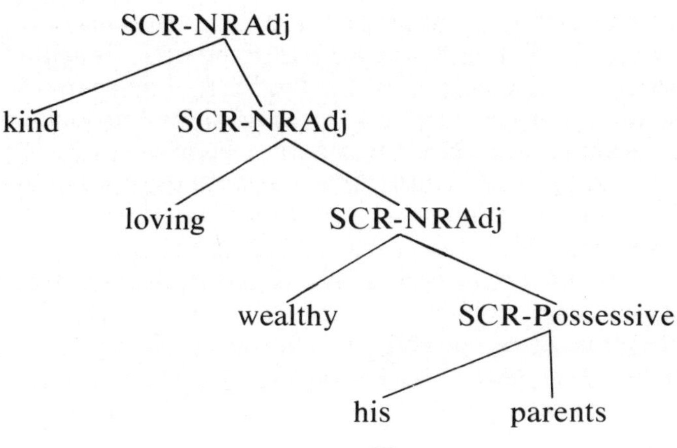

(b)

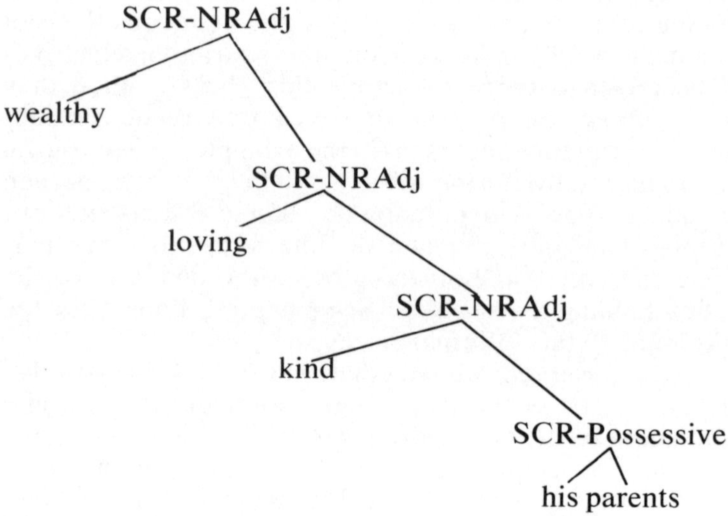

This does not give a way of choosing between the two methods, since both structures are suitable semantically, for the following reason. The inputs to SCR-NRAdj should be an adjective-meaning (say, a property P) and a noun-phrase-meaning (say, a description of a set S). The important question is — what is the output of SCR-NRAdj? Informally, the effect of the rule is to create an assertion that the set S described by the noun-phrase meaning has property P. However, this cannot be the *output* of the rule, since that would provide the wrong input for the SCRs higher up the tree. The noun phrase subtree as a whole should produce a set-description, since the constituent which includes the NP will use that set-description in some way; the containing constituent does not require an assertion to operate on. The best way round this is to have SCR-NRAdj pass up its second argument S unaltered as its output in the rule-tree, and do its work solely by placing the assertion (i.e. that P is true of S) somewhere suitable (e.g. in the 'world model' of the speaker). This allows SCR-NRAdj to apply to its own output, as is necessary in (23), since its second argument is a set-description and its output is a set-description. Since the same set S is being passed unaltered up trees like (23) (a) and (b), with various assertions being made about it on the way, the order of application of the different invocations of SCR-NRAdj is immaterial.

One advantage of separating out the non-restrictive semantic relationship into an SCR (instead of trying to build it into lexical entries), is that certain modifiers other than traditional adjectives sometimes occur with a non-restrictive type of relationship to the noun, e.g. (24).

(24) The *many* admirers of Shostakovich will be saddened by this performance.

The word 'many' occurs here after the determiner, and seems to express an assertion that there are many admirers of Shostakovich (it is certainly not restrictively distinguishing the 'many admirers' from the 'few admirers'). Such usage might be describable by using SCR-NRAdj to combine the meaning of 'many' with the meaning of the rest of the phrase.

This discussion has ignored the important question of how the analyser is to decide, while processing a sentence, whether a particular adjective is being used restrictively or non-restrictively. The decision seems to depend on factors which are impossible to formalise within the limited grammatical framework here — intonation, context of utterance, hearer's view of speaker's beliefs, etc., may all contribute. To test that the two surface structures described are practicable, the MCHINE program (see Chapter 13) was designed to allow either, but the choice of which to build was not made in a principled way — instead the adjectives were categorised into two disjoint subsets, with features NRA and RA to distinguish them.

3.6. Adjectives and Classifiers

So far the traditional term 'adjective' has been used quite freely, and the adjectives discussed in Section 3.5 have been regarded as expressing 'properties' that may be predicated of sets of elements. These oversimplifications aided the exposition (without affecting the relevant arguments), but they will now be examined in greater detail.

Bolinger (1967) discusses the wide variety of English adjectives, showing that it is not reasonable to describe all adjectives as denoting 'properties'. Examples like (25) are relevant.

(25)
(a) chief problem
(b) alleged thief
(c) former president
(d) possible problem

Montague (1970b) points out that describing the adjective-noun relationship as the intersection of properties (cf. Winograd (1972)) is valid only for a certain subclass of adjectives, and there is no reason to regard this as *the* adjective-noun relationship. He suggests that there should therefore be several adjective-noun combining functions; this proposal is easily re-phrased in terms of computational grammar as the need for different SCRs. If we could make the operations of the SCRs sophisticated enough, that might even allow for constructions like those in (26), where the way that the adjective modifies the noun depends in quite subtle ways on both the adjective and the noun.

(26)
(a) big flea
(b) small elephant
(c) good cook
(d) bad athlete

Further investigation shows that it is not very plausible to regard 'adjective' as a clear semantic category (although its pre-nominal usage gives grounds for a syntactic feature [ADJ]). Consider a phrase like (27).

(27) brass candlestick

Traditional grammar has two ways of describing this combination of words. Either it is an adjective-noun pair, like the rather heterogeneous examples in (25) and (26), or it is a noun-noun pair (sometimes known as a classifier-noun pair), like the examples in (28).

(28)
(a) donkey jacket
(b) soup spoon
(c) boiler suit
(d) monkey wrench
(e) gas stove

It is hard to define what criteria are used for sorting an example like (27) into either list. The main criterion seems to be that adjectives can be used to modify a wide class of nouns, whereas classifiers (i.e. nouns used as pre-nominal modifiers) are idiosyncratic. This generalisation is not strong enough to provide any real two-way classification, since some of the classifiers in the phrases in (28) can modify various nouns:

(29)
(a) soup plate
(b) gas fire
(c) soup kitchen
(d) gas mask

There does, nevertheless, appear to be a distinction between systematic modifier-noun pairs and idiosyncratic modifier-noun pairs, but it does not correspond to traditional adjective/classifier boundaries.

The relationship between the meanings of words in (29) (a) is (intuitively) very similar to the relationship between the meanings of the words in (28) (b). The same relationship seems also to occur in pairs like 'fish knife', 'dessert spoon', where the name of a kind of food is used to classify an eating implement. (29) (c), on the other hand, is different. Similarly, the relationship between the word-meanings in (29) (b) is like the relationship between the word-meanings in (28) (e), and this relationship also appears in phrases like 'coal fire', 'oil heater', etc., where a fuel is used to classify a fuel-using device. (29) (d) seems to be different. We could perhaps say that there are certain systematic modifier-noun relationships, which manifest themselves in phrases consisting of pairs 'X+Y' where both X and Y may vary over more than one item. There are also certain idiosyncratic modifier-noun relationships, which manifest themselves in phrases consisting of pairs 'X+Y', where X and Y do not vary (i.e. these are 'one-off' items). (28) (a), (c), (d) and (29) (c), (d) seem to be examples of these. Thus it appears that, while the traditional distinction between 'systematic' and 'idiosyncratic' modifier-noun pairs may well exist, it certainly does not correspond to the usual classification of 'adjective' versus 'classifier'.

It is worth digressing here to point out a simple linguistic test which distinguishes these two kinds of combination. In contrasting noun phrases with different modifiers, the head noun may be replaced by 'one' under certain circumstances, as in (30) (a). In this case the modifier-noun pairs are traditional property-denoting adjectives, which are highly systematic in the way they modify nouns. If the modifier-noun pairs are totally idiosyncratic, then the 'one'-pronominalisation results in oddity, as in (30) (b).

(30)
(a) This is a red ball and that is a blue one.
(b) ??? This is a monkey wrench and that is a pipe one.

This may be because the contrast which is being expressed includes the particular modifier-noun relationship involved, and if the two phrases have different internal relationships the contrast is difficult:

(31)
(a) This is a wine bottle and that is a whisky bottle.
(b) This is a red bottle and that is a blue one.
(c) ??? This is a wine bottle and that is a red one.

It seems that the contrast is being made between different

values for a particular property of the items, and so the same property must be referred to in both phrases. Systematic modifier-head relationships may be those where the modifier specifies some value for a particular aspect of the head, whereas idiosyncratic items are more like arbitrary labels. (There are borderline examples like 'ulterior motive', where the modifier seems to express some aspect of the head, but where there are no related phrases 'ulterior X' showing the same modification — ??? 'This is a worthy motive and that is an ulterior one'.)

This discussion has been somewhat vague, with frequent appeals to the reader's intuition. We hope it has been sufficient to make two points. Although there may be syntactic distributional grounds for grouping pre-nominal modifiers into adjectives and nouns, there is no useful semantic distinction to be made, since there are systematic uses of a wide variety of modifiers. Also, the aspect of modifier-head combinations which is semantically relevant is the way that the modifier modifies the meaning of the head; it may be possible to describe this by having many different SCRs for the vast number of possible relationships.

The latter proposal has unfortunate repercussions. Leaving aside the prickly question of whether we want to have a multitude of relationships like 'uses as fuel', 'is used to eat', etc., built into *linguistic* rules, there is still the problem of how an analyser is to choose the right SCR for a particular pair. It is rather implausible to have the analyser treat a pre-nominal modifier as n-ways ambiguous (where there are n SCRs which could take it as first argument), so the analyser will have to wait until the head of the phrase is found and then select a modifier-head SCR which will accept as inputs this modifier and head.

This may sound similar to the process described by Quillian (1969), where a semantic program examines the semantic structures of the modifier and head to work out the relationship between the two, but there is a slight difference. Here we are assuming that certain commonly-occurring semantic relationships are stored in standard modifier-head SCRs (instead of having to be computed each time). Thus, under normal circumstances, only the list of SCRs is considered, rather than all possible relationships. The Quillian process (which starts from scratch, with no standard set of relationships) would be useful for computing possible meanings of a hitherto unencountered pair, but even then it might be wrong if the newly encountered example is in fact idiosyncratic; consider what a productive process like that would have done with 'pyramid salesman' or 'battery hen' on a first attempt. While a heuristic process like Quillian's would generate guesses for unknown phrases, the suggestion here is to keep a set of standard relationships for systematic purposes, and enter idiosyncratic phrases directly in the lexicon as compound nouns. This also produces a problem for an analyser, since as well as searching the SCR list it will have to check whether the lexicon has a compound entry for the two items it is examining.

The process of searching a list of SCRs for one which 'matches' a pair of arguments is in fact required elsewhere in the grammar (see Section 8.5) so it is not necessarily a weak point of this description that it needs such a search process, but the search routine is not a well-developed concept at present and cannot be relied upon. None of the suggestions in the above argument were implemented in the experimental program (see Chapter 13), so this discussion can be regarded only as speculation on the possible uses of SCRs.

3.7. The Syntax of Verb Phrases

Another illustration of the way in which SCRs allow the separate description of patterns at different levels is given by English verb constructions.

Each verb has an associated semantic structure, with an indication of what semantic items are needed to complete this structure. This is similar to the Fillmore (1968) system of a verb having a 'case frame' which shows how the other constituents (subject, objects, etc.) are to be fitted into slots, but there are certain differences from the Fillmore 'case grammar' (see Section 6.4 for further details).

The semantic structure for the verb defines the possible

combinations at the level of semantic representation, but it does not indicate how these can be realised in syntactic structure. The task of getting surface constituents (e.g. subject, object) analysed and inserted around the verb is performed by the recognition grammar and the structural combining rules.

This has the advantage that the list of 'roles' (i.e. slots for other items for the verb) need not try to express, in one pattern, the necessary deep semantic pattern and the necessary surface syntactic configuration. All the roles are obligatory, in the sense that each role will be present in any given instance of a relation, even though the sentence analyser or semantic network processor may not have an item to fill it. This captures the point that if two relations have different sets of possible participants they are different relations. Fillmore's case frames allowed some cases to be 'optional' or to be classed in pairs one of which must occur. This attempted to record, in the deep semantic structure for the verb, information which was concerned with the surface realisation of the items. In computational grammar, the optional aspects are covered by the recognition grammar, using certain SCRs (referred to as 'role-placement rules').

The analyser uses information marked in the dictionary for the main verb to select a suitable 'role-placement' SCR (see Section 8.5 for further details). This SCR forms the basis of the subtree for the verb phrase, since its arguments are the main verb and the object(s) following the verb. The semantic structure built by the role-placement SCR for the verb phrase has the objects and the verb combined, with a further position in the semantic structure selected for the surface subject of the clause to fit into (see Section 8.5 and Sections 6.4, 6.5 for further details).

Passive constructions are handled quite naturally within this system. The role-placement SCRs are subdivided into 'active' and 'passive' (no good criterion has been found to characterise these two classes of rules, so at present the grammar writer has to mark the SCRs explicitly). When the analyser encounters a 'passive' verb configuration (auxiliary 'be' + perfect participle), it sets a restriction on the SCR entry for the verb phrase node, disallowing anything other than a 'passive' SCR to be put there. The appropriate SCRs (both active and passive) for a verb have to be marked in the lexical entry for the verb, along with a specification of what objects or indirect objects are needed; the grammar writer has to bear in mind that the 'agent' phrase (if it is included) has to be treated as an 'object' marked with the preposition 'by'.

There are several role-placement rules (SCRs) for single-object configurations, and several for two-object configurations. For example, the surface order of the items for the verb-roles is different in (32) (a) and (b).

(32)
(a) He said something to me.
(b) He said to me that you had left.

It might be argued that these could be handled by one SCR, with the analyser re-ordering the surface objects before putting them into the nodes for the SCR. This would have certain drawbacks. At present, the lexical entry for the verb has to specify only the SCRs to be used, the order of the objects, and their surface syntactic categories, thus providing a simple, extendible system (see Section 8.5). If we tried to economise by having a single SCR with different surface orderings the simplicity would be lost, since the grammar would have to incorporate some extra manipulation specifically for that verb. Also, it may be that the different orderings of the objects have some semantic content (e.g. concerning 'topic' or 'focus'); if so, we would want to be able to describe this difference by incorporating it into the different SCRs.

By having the SCRs perform the permuting of objects into the deep roles for a verb, and by separating the surface specification of a verb from the deep roles, we can avoid confusing the possible surface configurations with the set of relationships available at the level of meaning (unlike Fillmore's approach). Also, passive and active constructions are treated in a uniform, general fashion.

CHAPTER 4

PROCESSING LEVELS

4.1. PUSH and POP

The ATN notation (Section 2.9 above) and the PROGRAMMAR language (Section 2.10 above) have a mechanism for processing a syntactic constituent as a separate item. In this chapter we examine the details of this mechanism and illustrate its strengths and weaknesses. The ATN notation will be used since it makes explicit many of the aspects of the processing, but many of the points apply equally to PROGRAMMAR.

The ATN configuration for specifying where a particular constituent (phrase, clause, etc.) is to be processed is a network like (33), where X is the category name of the constituent.

(33)

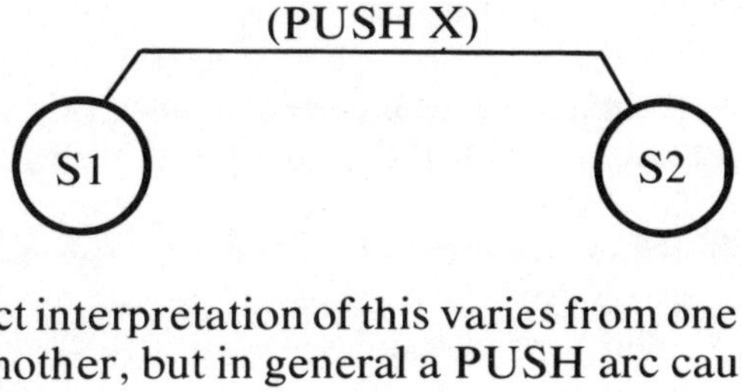

The exact interpretation of this varies from one implementation to another, but in general a PUSH arc causes several things to happen:

(34)
(a) The 'continuation state' (S2 in the above example) is saved somewhere (see Chapter 5 for discussion of storage). This is done because the path through the network is to continue from S2 once the item of

category X has been successfully processed.

(b) Separate storage space may be set aside (see Chapter 5) for the computation involved in analysing the item of type X.

(c) Processing continues from some state (not S1 or S2) which is the initial point of another network (or subnetwork) designed for type X constituents.

(d) A list of 'actions' (i.e manipulations to be carried out) is normally included as part of an ATN arc. In most versions the actions on a PUSH arc would be saved in much the same way that the continuation state is.

The sentence-analyser then continues through the incoming words, scanning the network appropriate to X items. Eventually, it should (if there is a well-formed X item) reach an arc labelled POP. This is the reverse of a PUSH arc and causes the following things to happen:

(35)

(a) The local storage space that was being used for the X constituent is relinquished.

(b) The continuation state that had been saved at the last PUSH arc is removed from storage.

(c) Processing continues from the newly-retrieved continuation state.

(d) If any 'actions' were preserved at the execution of the last PUSH arc they are now performed. (In some systems there may also be a need to pass up the result of the processing that has been done; this will depend on the exact details of the surface structure system.)

These self-contained periods of processing are normally referred to as being at different 'levels'. While one constituent is being processed another PUSH arc may be encountered (since a type X item may include a type Y item, or even another type X item — noun phrases can contain noun phrases). In this case the current level is temporarily suspended, just as the original processing had been, until this new, inner level can be completed. Such processing-within-processing is often referred to as 'nesting' levels, and a traditional syntactic parser using this technique often has the grammar organised so that the nesting of processing levels reflects the nesting of the syntactic tree being built (cf. PROGRAMMAR, Section 2.10).

(36)

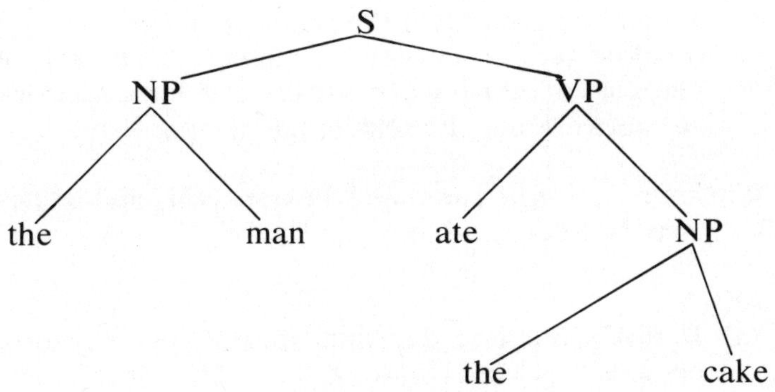

(37)

```
(  ( the man )        ( ate   ( the cake )      )      )

              NP                           NP   VP   S

---          -----                          -----  S

                    ----          ---              VP

    -------                -------                 NPs
```

4.2. Predictive Aspects of the PUSH command

The operations listed in (34) above determine where the use of the PUSH construct (i.e initiation of a new level) is appropriate in a grammar:

(38)
(a) It is necessary where separate working space is

needed to process a constituent without destroying information about partially-processed items ((34) (b)).

(b) It can be used only if the grammar-writer is prepared to specify what is to follow the constituent (i.e. the continuation state, (34) (a)), and what is to be done with it (i.e. the 'actions', (34) (d)).

(c) It can be used only if the grammar-writer can specify not just that some item is expected, but also what category of item it will be (in order that the appropriate subnetwork may be selected, (34) (c)).

Thus, the PUSH command has several characteristics which may be undersirable:

(39)

(a) It links into one decision several logically distinct choices ((38) (a), (b), (c)).

(b) It forces grammars to be written in a strongly predictive style ('top-down' — see Section 8.4), since a continuation state must be specified and the subnetwork is selected on the basis of the category which is expected. In some systems it may also be the case that different temporary storage allocation occurs for different categories; this would be further processing done in advance on the basis of the category prediction.

If we examine the decisions and operations initiated by a PUSH arc there seems to be a natural division into what might be termed 'global predictions' and 'local findings'. The former are based on, and are largely about, what is happening at the current level of processing (e.g. what continuation state will be relevant after the incoming constituent); the latter are based on what input comes in after the PUSH arc, and concern details of the constituent (e.g. what specific temporary storage to allocate). The global predictions are those aspects of the situation defined by the environment (in particular, the relationship of the incoming item to the existing structure) which are not inherently aspects of the category of item (e.g. NP) involved. The local findings are specific to the processing of the item itself and ignore how the finished item must be related to its environment.

We can therefore redefine the PUSH command so that it specifies just those aspects of the situation which will be predictable in advance (start state for constituent, what to do with constituent when found, continuation state if any), and use different commands for specifying those aspects which are better decided within the subnetwork (what structure to start building within the constituent, what storage space to set aside). Let us call the modified construct 'NEW-LEVEL', to distinguish it from the original 'PUSH'.

Although the name specified in a PUSH arc has always been looked on as a category label, its real purpose (in the interpretation of the network during processing) is to indicate a subnetwork for processing the incoming item. The information needed for this is the name of the initial state of the subnetwork. Hence, ATN grammars could be said to have a *state-name* (rather than a category name) mentioned in a PUSH arc, without affecting the meaning of the notation. (Presumably grammar-writers who used arcs like (PUSH NP) must have started their NP subnetwork with a state called 'NP', or else they incorporated a table to connect this category label to the appropriate initial state.) In what follows, therefore, we will refer to the NEW-LEVEL arc as specifying a state, rather than a syntactic category, but this is not different from the way that the PUSH arc worked. We shall allow the continuation to be unspecified, in which case the special blank marker 'NIL' will be written at the end of the arc.

Consider the configurations (40) (a) and (b).

(40)
(a)

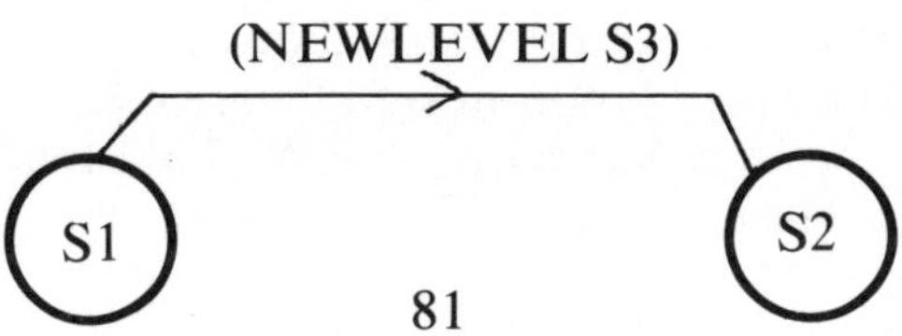

(b)

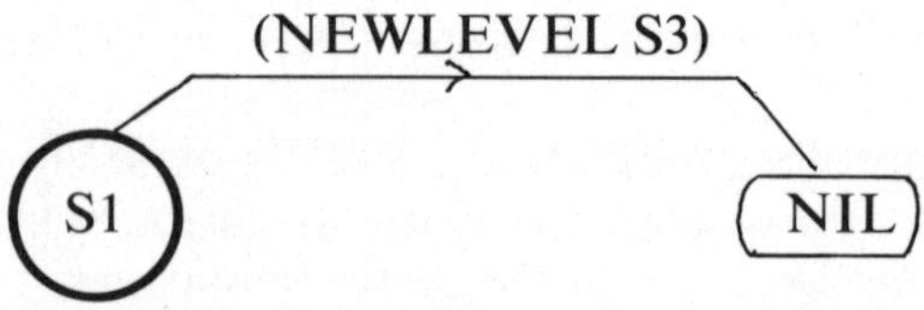

The operations to be carried out on encountering the (NEWLEVEL S3) arc are:

(41)
(a) Storage allocation which is required for any type of constituent (i.e. which is not specific to any one category) is carried out. If the continuation state is not NIL the allocation is done by saving the corresponding information for the current level so that it can be restored later; if the continuation state is NIL the allocation is done by releasing the corresponding space for the current level and re-assigning it to the new level so that the old values are lost.
(b) If the continuation state is not NIL (as in (a) above) it is saved and S3 is set as the next state to be processed.
(c) If the continuation state is NIL no state is saved but S3 is set as the next state to be processed.

This gives two ways of initiating new processing levels: *nested*, in which the current level is suspended, and *non-nested*, in which the current level is abandoned and the new level takes over entirely.

Any storage allocation or other computation which is specific to the category involved will then be done in the subnetwork for that category (i.e. it will be part of the grammar for that kind of constituent, not just part of the general NEWLEVEL mechanism).

Since processing returns to the higher level after a 'nested' level, a set of actions can be set aside to be performed after the constituent has been processed (as described in (34) (d) and (35) (d) above). A non-nested level does not return, so actions cannot be included on a NEWLEVEL arc that has a NIL continuation.

This revised mechanism has some interesting aspects. So far, the only advantage is that it makes certain predictive parts of the command optional, thus not forcing grammars to be predictive. As will be seen in the next few sections the concept of a 'non-nested' level seems particularly suited to certain aspects of English structure.

4.3. Complexity in Embedded Structures

It has often been noted (e.g. Yngve (1960, 1961), Miller and Isard (1964), Chomsky (1965)) that certain kinds of English sentence are hard to understand, although their grammatical structure seems to be similar to that of other, easily understood, sentences. Examples include centre-embedded clauses (e.g. (42) (a)) and verb-particle constructions containing 'heavy' noun phrases (e.g. (42 (b)).

(42)
(a) ??? The rat the cat the dog chased bit died.
(b) ??? He called almost all the thirty tourists he met on his holiday in France up.

Investigations of these phenomena sometimes seem to assume that such complexity will be accounted for by some single principle, and that the actual structure of the whole sentence will be the relevant factor in determining complexity. Neither of these assumptions is necessarily true — there may be several principles which contribute to 'complexity', and the most difficult examples may fall under more than one of these principles. Also, the relevant parameters for determining complexity may be within the processes of perceiving or producing the sentences, and may not be directly measurable in the final structure of the sentence.

One possible measure of complexity is the depth of the surface structure tree, defined as the longest path from the root to a tip. This does not account for all the data, as certain constructions appear to be easily comprehended despite great depth; left-branching or right-branching structures, such as (43) (a) and (b) respectively, are the usual examples (Yngve (1960), Chomsky (1965)).

(43)
(a) The emperor's wife's servant's room.
(b) The room of the servant of the wife of the emperor.

Yngve (ibid.) put forward a production model with a more subtle definition of 'depth'. His 'depth' was measured in terms of partially-processed surface structure nodes. This measure was more satisfactory, in that it did not rate right-branching structures as being complex (i.e. (43) (b) would not be classed as complex), but it did rate left-branching structures as complex, which is counter-intuitive. This resulted from Yngve's model being for production of sentences, rather than for analysis; the producing mechanism therefore started from the root of a subtree like (44) and began producing nodes down the left of the tree. The left-branching construction caused the nodes to be initiated in the order indicated in (44) (1-2-3-4), and completed in reverse order (4-3-2-1).

(44)

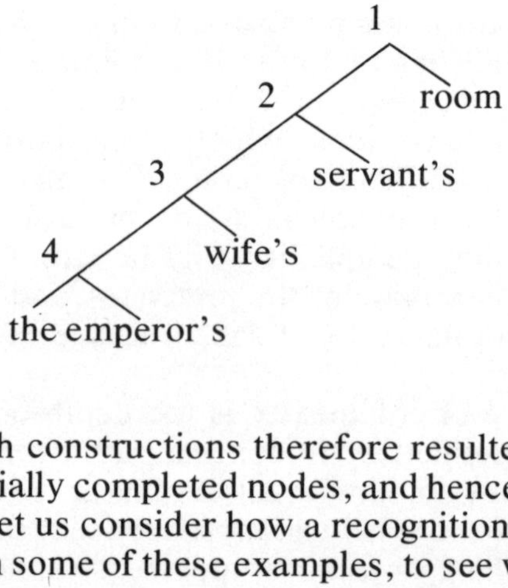

Such constructions therefore resulted in a large number of partially completed nodes, and hence had a large 'depth'.

Let us consider how a recognition mechanism might deal with some of these examples, to see whether the complexity might result from difficulties in the sentence analysis process.

4.4. Left-Embedding

We will now concern ourselves with left-branching structures like (43) (a). As observed before, Yngve's model predicted a large 'depth' for this construction, since his method was based on starting with the base of the complete subtree. The situation is different if we examine the structure in recognition terms. The analyser cannot know in advance that such a deep tree will be part of the input, and so it does not start by building a series of partially processed nodes. After processing the phrase 'the emperor's', a whole node (like (45)) will have been completed (see Section 3.5 above for more details).

(45)

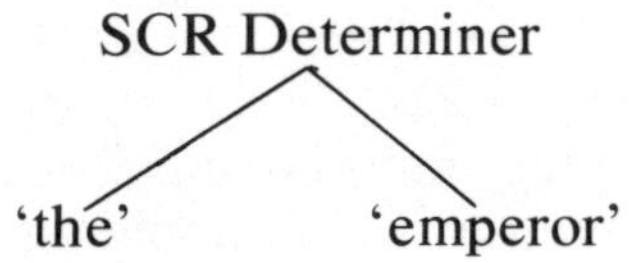

The ''s' signals that this whole node is to be subordinated to a new node that must now be commenced. Hence, only one of the phrase nodes is incomplete and being processed at any given time.

Consider how this processing can be described using the constructs defined in computational grammar. As discussed in Section 3.5, possessive noun phrases fulfil the same role (in the containing structure) as lexical possessives, and are paradigmatically related to articles. Hence, after the analyser has built a possessive node, it should process the containing phrase from the appropriate point; that is, as if an article or lexical possessive had been found. It should not try to process a whole noun phrase, since another article or possessive should not be present.

(46) *The emperor's a wife lives here.

Since the phrase forming the possessive has been completed, information held in temporary storage for it need not be retained, and some of the storage will be needed for the incoming phrase. The appropriate command to insert in the grammar at this point (as observed by Winograd (1972, p.93)) is a jump to the state following a 'determiner' or 'possessive', and a clearing of any storage. No new levels are created, either by nesting or by overwriting the old one.

Left-branching structures create difficulties for any simple recognition grammar, since there is a danger of infinite recursion. Some special modification is usually needed in a context-free parser which uses recursive left-branching rules. (See Foster (1970) for an explanation of this problem.) It should be emphasised that the above approach to the problem is just such a special-purpose modification and there is no claim that the ATN *interpreter* proposed here can handle *any* left-branching structure, as currently designed. In order to analyse left-branching phrases specific instructions had to be inserted in the ATN *grammar*. A similar method might be employed for left-branching structures (for example, in another language) but it would have to be included in the recognition *grammar* of that language.

4.5. Right-Embedding

In the standard ATN or PROGRAMMAR mechanisms each embedded constituent is processed at a different 'level', and these levels are organised in a strict hierarchical fashion, corresponding (usually) to the structure of the surface-tree. For example, in PROGRAMMAR, when a parsing procedure terminates normally it attaches its result to the current node of the syntax tree. Normally a tree with n embedded structures will have been processed at n different levels. Each level is initiated by a 'PUSH' arc and terminated by a 'POP' arc (in ATN notation), with information about higher levels being stored while lower levels are processed. The kind of information that needs to be retained will depend on the exact details of the theory of surface structure being used (see Chapter 5).

The information about a particular level has to be retained until it is finished, and the only way of finishing it is to 'pop-up'; this, in turn, can happen only when all lower levels have been completed and 'popped'. Hence information builds up in the temporary storage as levels grow downwards. It is quite plausible to suggest that this building-up is what contributes to complexity. However, embedded constituents are all treated similarly, whether embedded in the centre or at the extreme right of a clause. In either case all the information builds up for each level. Hence it is not simply that overloading storage causes trouble, for then both centre- and right- embedding would be perceptually difficult. It is more that overloading causes some kind of 'forgetting', and this lost information is not needed in right-embedded structures since no further processing occurs at the higher level.

If we were not interested in modelling linguistic behaviour in detail we could continue with the traditional approach of allowing the analyser unlimited storage space to process arbitrarily complex constituents (which might be incomprehensible to humans). However, since the aim is to restrict our model wherever possible and to reflect human linguistic ability as much as possible, it seems reasonable to investigate how the embedding facilities can be limited. The exact bound on storage and/or processing is possibly very subtle, but a crude approximation could be achieved by putting a limit on the storage in such a way that items inserted earlier are lost if overloading occurs. This still leaves various possibilities for using such storage in the ATN interpreter.

We could continue the traditional method of storing information even for right-embedded structures but organise the structure-building mechanism so that the surface structure tree would not be incomplete or ill-formed if certain levels were never re-activated by the parser.

Alternatively, we could have two different processes, centre-embedding and right-embedding, where performing the latter does not store away information and leaves the structure at the current level in good order before 'forgetting' its details. The main difference between these two is that the traditional method 'forgets' levels only when forced to and 'remembers' information at every embedding; in the second method, the analyser decides at the start of a constituent that it is not going to return to the current level again and abandons the information immediately. The latter approach was incorporated into the experimental program (see Chapter 13). Although there was little to choose between the alternatives, the second method was preferred for the following reasons. It fitted in well with the idea (Section 4.2) of not needing to specify continuation states on every PUSH arc. Also, it seemed easier to organise a structure-building mechanism where levels were abandoned deliberately, rather than being left to survive after being 'forgotten', and there were certain constructions (see below) where this decision method seemed very suitable. Moreover, it seemed an interesting idea whose feasibility should be investigated.

The right-embedding device has already been described in Sections 4.1 and 4.2, as it is the modified PUSH construct referred to as (NEWLEVEL . . . NIL). The interpreter should, on executing such an arc, create a new processing level without storing the details of the current level, as outlined in Section 4.2.

This device can be used quite neatly in analysing right-branching noun phrases like (43) (b). Suppose that the analyser has completed the phrase 'the room', and reads the word 'of'. (The traditionally intransigent problem of attaching prepositional adjuncts is ignored at this point, on the assumption that the argument offered here applies to at least one of the options facing the analyser.) If it decides that a right-branching prepositional adjunct is about to be processed the action it must take is exactly that of a (NEWLEVEL . . . NIL) arc. The analyser needs a new level to process the next NP, but it has no new information about what will follow the whole NP, since this second NP forms a structural subpart of the first NP. It has to assume that whatever was predicted to follow the original NP will now follow the total NP including the adjunct. It would just be an embarrassment to have to specify another continuation state when no further predictions can be made about the grammatical environment surrounding the NP. Since the first NP can be regarded as finished apart from the adjunct now being started, no interpreter information need be kept concerning it. (The first NP will have been attached to the surface structure tree and so will not be lost from the analysis.) Instead of the storage locations building up four nested levels to process (43) (b), only one level is used at a time. Hence no 'complexity' or unintended 'forgetting' is caused by processing a multiply-branching phrase like (43) (b) inside a clause. Using the more traditional methods, some continuation state (say, STOPNP) would have to be specified each time, and the location for storing the continuation state would pile up three copies of it.

4.6. Centre-Embedding

Intuitively, most (or all) of the 'difficult' sentences are cases where a large constituent (in some sense) has been inserted in a central position in the sentence. If a small constituent is inserted, or if the large constituent is at the right-hand end of the sentence, oddity does not occur.

(47)

(a) I told my story to the police.

(b) ??? I told the story that I had heard from a crowd of Arabian horse-thieves who were planning to set up a Citizens Advice Bureau in Friockheim to the police.

(c) ??? He said that he had an appointment to the secretary.

(d) ??? He said that almost all of his friends were founder members of the First International League of Bad Linguists to the secretary.

(e) He said that almost all of his friends were founder members of the First International League of Bad Linguists.

(f) I said that Bill knew that Harry thought that Fred was a crook.

Informally, what seems to be happening is that the analyser, while processing the embedded item 'forgets' some information relevant to the containing clause and so has difficulties when it attempts to recommence processing at the higher level. As Miller and Isard (1964) suggest:

> Let us imagine that anyone who knows English has something corresponding to a relative clause subroutine that can be called to process sentences containing such structures. When this subroutine is called, the main sentence-analysing routine is interrupted and the point at which it must be resume is stored temporarily until the subroutine has been executed . . . suppose that, while the subroutine is being executed, a second such construction is encountered, so the subroutine is required to call itself. If this recursive feature were not available, confusion would result; the temporary memory for the point of re-entry into the main routine might be erased, for example, so that when it is resumed, the main routine would have to treat subsequent words as if they began a new constituent of the sentence.

(Notice that this was written some years before the augmented transition network model was suggested for English.)

This would be compatible with the fact that larger constituents (which presumably require greater processing resources) cause greater difficulty, and with the fact that no difficulties occur in right-branching structures where no segment of the higher clause is left after the embedded item (e.g. (47) (f)). It is not plausible to suggest that it is the initial storing of information about the containing clause that goes wrong, since phrases like (47) (d) and (e) show that the trouble derives not from embarking upon an arbitrarily long constituent, but from trying to re-commence the containing clause afterwards.

Another classic case where an embedded structure is difficult to perceive occurs when there are relative clauses within relative clauses, as in (42) (a) above. It is interesting to assess what the computational analysis of relative clauses given in Chapter 11 suggests regarding the possible processing difficulties presented by sentences like this.

There are several aspects of the relative clause construction which lead to a great deal of storage space being used:

(48)

(a) The relative clauses are all attached to the *subject* of the containing clause. In writing grammars it has become apparent that the subject position is one of the few places in English grammar where a NEWLEVEL . . . NIL arc is not an adequate form of embedding, since some continuation state must be specified (for the start of the complement of the clause), and so the new processing level must be nested. Hence, the information for the containing clause is being saved while the subject phrase is being analysed.

(b) As will be argued in Chapter 11, the head of a relative clause is stored temporarily until the appropriate syntactic location for it is found. The relative elements in examples like (42) (a) are all to be located as *objects* of their clauses, so that they must be stored from the start of the clause until the end.

(c) The wh-clause uses all the storage for the clause network, plus a location for the head of the clause. This is more than any other class of constituent.

Also, a great deal of processing must be carried out at the end of the clauses, since three wh-clauses all terminate within a few words. At the end of each wh-clause the analyser has to tidy up storage at that level, fit the head phrase into surface structure and take relevant information (e.g. the continuation state) from storage in order to resume the higher level.

As can be seen from the points made in (48), the storage locations are more deeply piled with entries during the centre-embedded relative clause construction than in most others. Thus, if there were a limit on how many entries could be made in storage this could also create difficulties since earlier entries might be lost.

There are several factors which might be thought to contribute to complexity, e.g.:

(49)
(a) Total storage space required
(b) Total processing required (if this could be quantified)
(c) Depth of stored information
(d) Loss of information about a higher level (owing to (a), (b) or (c), or some other factor)

It can be seen from the points made here that the description of Chapter 11 will predict that multiply-embedded relative clauses are 'complex' whichever measurement is selected from (49). This is not very interesting since the same is likely to be true of almost any serious description of English relative clauses. However, there is one point worth noting about the version here, if our complexity measurement is based on (49) or related factors.

A more standard ATN analysis of relative clauses will also predict that *any* multiply-embedded structure is complex, since information builds up in store for every constituent processed, as outlined in Section 4.5 above. In computational grammar this is not the case, since the NEWLEVEL . . . NIL construct allows some constituents to be nested without loading up storage. Hence the discrepancy in complexity between a right-branching and a centre-embedding structure is much clearer in computational grammar than it would be in a standard ATN description. The self-embedded relative clause is one of the few cases where genuine nesting (as opposed to NEWLEVEL . . . NIL processing) has to occur to several layers. (One of the other examples is the embedding of a clause within the first of two objects in a clause, as in (47) (c) and (d).)

After the experimental program had been debugged on some target sentences and had carried out several simple dialogues (see Chapter 13), a test was carried out to see how the NEWLEVEL . . . NIL construct interacted with multiply-embedded relative clauses. There was a variable DEPTH in the program which recorded the maximum depth of entries allowed in store, and the program had been debugged with DEPTH set to 8. This allowed at least four self-embedded relative clauses to be processed successfully. With DEPTH altered to 3 the program could still successfully process non-centre-embedding sentences, but failed on triply-embedded relative clauses.

To summarise, the analysis of relative clauses to be presented in Chapter 11 indicates that multiply embedded relative clauses will be complex, if any of the factors in (49) are taken to determine complexity. To compensate for the vacuity of this observation it is worth making the point that a grammar with the NEWLEVEL . . . NIL device distinguishes more sharply the complexity of centre-embedded relative clauses from that of other embedding constructions. The idea of using a subroutine-like mechanism for embedded constituents is not new, but the NEWLEVEL . . . NIL construct introduces a modified form of subroutine which seems particularly useful.

CHAPTER 5

TEMPORARY STORAGE

5.1. Registers

In describing the analysis process for certain English constructions, it sometimes happens that the neatest arrangement is to store a partially-built structure temporarily until a decision is possible on what should be done with it (see, for example, Section 3.5 above). Also, some temporary storage may be needed by the analyser to keep track of its path through the grammar (see Chapter 4). The computational grammar device for temporary storage is the 'register', as described by Woods (1970) (see Section 2.9). A register can be thought of as a storage location which can hold a single structure or value for any part of the processing of the sentence. There are various operations that can be carried out on a register, such as inserting an item, removing an item, examining the register to see what is in it, etc. Using registers is not the solution to all problems of grammar-writing but it is a very useful technique. Since many of the grammatical devices use registers (e.g. the 'level' system of Chapter 4), and many grammatical rules will be phrased in terms of the way that they affect (or are affected by) the contents of registers, it is important to describe exactly how registers operate and what types of storage are available within computational grammar.

5.2. Different Types of Register

The first useful distinction is between *flags*, *structure-holding registers*, and *pointer-holding registers*. A flag is generally used as a location to test for some simple condition and holds one of a small, fixed set of values (e.g. 'TRUE', 'FALSE'). When some condition occurs during an analysis this fact is recorded for later use by setting the value of a flag; at some later stage(s), when the analyser needs to test this condition, it need not do any re-computing but can merely examine the current value of the flag. Some recognition grammars use a two-valued flag to record whether a passive or active verb-configuration has been formed; the analyser, on encountering a 'by'-phrase, can react differently according to the value of the flag.

A structure-holding register provides temporary storage for a piece of structure which has been built but not allocated to a position in some larger structure. For example, a register HEADNOUN might be useful for holding the head of a noun group while checking if any adjuncts follow the group. A pointer-holding register is used for keeping track of where, within some larger structure, a particular item is. For example, a register CURRENT-NODE might be useful for keeping track of the node currently being processed. If this distinction seems vague, consider the following. Failing to assign an item to a pointer-holding register makes that item difficult (but probably not impossible) to find, and does not alter the relationship of that item to any containing structures. Failing to assign an item to a structure-holding register loses it completely, since it is not yet attached to any other structure. (Those who are interested in the analogy between ATN grammars and ordinary computer programs may consider the following: if the ATN system had a garbage-collector, putting an unattached structure in a register would prevent it from being garbage-collected.)

Another distinction (independent of the three-way classification above) is between *interpreter registers* and *grammatical registers*. In the course of analysing a sentence it is necessary for the device which scans the input and the network (i.e. the ATN interpreter, as in Section 2.9) to keep track of where it is in the grammar and where it is building structure. For example, the CURRENT-NODE register mentioned above might be needed, and a 'continuation' register for holding states still to be processed. These interpreter registers are more or less independent of the transition network grammar being interpreted, although the linguistic theory within which the grammar was written will affect the choice of such registers. On the other hand, certain specific grammatical registers will be needed, according to how the grammar is written. For example, the HEADNOUN register instanced above might be useful in one grammar but irrelevant in another.

Generally, registers are used just like variables in a programming language, with each register having a distinct name to identify it. The analyser can examine specific registers by name and have separate registers for as many items or pointers as it needs. One possible variation on this is to have just one or two general purpose registers which are used for different purposes at different stages in the parsing. Call these *work registers*. Such registers are trickier to use since the parser has to keep track of what has been most recently placed in a work register and make sure that the stored values for one process do not interfere with those for another. The only advantage to be gained is the general methodological one of restricting the mechanism as much as possible. It would be interesting to construct a parser which requires only a very limited amount of storage space; using work registers instead of named registers is one way of investigating this. (It would also avoid the covert decision-making described in Section 8.6.)

As described in Chapter 4, constituents are processed in computational grammar by nested subunits. In the course of such processing, working space for the different constituents must be kept separate so that stored values do not corrupt each other. Suppose there is a grammatical structure-holding register HEADNOUN which is used to process a noun group. If several noun groups are nested within each other each different noun group may need a separate copy of HEADNOUN. Since the processing is hierarchically arranged, one way to achieve the integrity of working space is to allow certain registers to act like 'local variables' in block-structured programming languages (e.g. ALGOL, POP-2). That is, a fresh incarnation of a local variable is available to each hierarchical unit that requires that variable; these incarnations exist only temporarily, as long as the hierarchical subunit is processing, and then they vanish. One way to look on such a system is to regard the registers in question as push-down stores; the current value is kept on top of the store and the store can be pushed down on commencing a nested unit, thus providing a fresh value slot while storing the previous value temporarily. If we call such registers *stack registers* (or simply *stacks*), this gives another possible classification independent of the previously described distinctions.

In programming languages which use 'local variables' there is some way of associating sets of variables with processing units so that the same named locations are immediately available whenever that unit is activated. In ATN terms this would be like having a list of named grammatical stack registers associated with each sub-network. This device seems to be useful for certain English constructions (in particular, 'wh'-clauses, as described in Chapter 11), but computational grammar does not include an automatic way of associating lists of registers with subroutines; Ritchie (1977) describes some of the methods tried in the experimental program. At present, the grammar-writer has to specify explicitly (in the 'actions' part of the ATN grammar) which grammatical registers are to be altered, and when. Thus we can class a register as being: pointer-holding, structure-holding, or a flag; grammatical or interpreter; work register or named register; stack or non-stack.

Notice that this section has not suggested any concepts that are not already in use in existing programs; it has merely drawn attention to certain possible classifications, so that later sections can be described in a more precise terminology. This is necessary if we are to examine fully the linguistic formalisms being proposed. Hitherto, this level of detail has not been discussed but it is essential to the development of more complex (or more restricted) devices. Since most (if not all) of the operations carried out during sentence analysis use registers (and the transition network configuration merely expresses the list of options) elucidating the uses of registers is a central part of investigating the processing operations.

Chapter 6

SEMANTIC REPRESENTATION

6.1. Sense and Reference

The program of Winograd (1972) keeps a single data-base which describes the state of the BLOCKS world. No distinction is made between how the blocks are actually arranged and how the program 'thinks' they are arranged — since one data-base serves for both, no discrepancies are possible. Hence there can be no real distinction made between 'Is there a red block on the table' and 'Do you think that there is a red block on the table?'. There are two ways of regarding this single world model:

(50)
(a) It represents the 'real' state of the BLOCKS world, as a simulation of a physical system.
(b) It represents the 'mental' model of the BLOCKS system that the program (regarded as a simulated speaker) has.

The consequence of interpretation (50) (a) is that the program performs all its operations, including linguistic ones, by examining the 'real' world. That is, to work out exactly what the phrase 'the red block' refers to, the program must scan the world (not its memory of the world) to find such a block. Hence no provision is made in this model for talking about items which the hearer cannot currently perceive, which is rather a limited approach to language.

The consequence of interpretation (50) (b) is that any operations which the program is to perform on actual objects (e.g. 'pick up') must be carried out on mental constructs. In this approach actions are performed by fiat, analogously to a person playing chess without a board. This makes no allowance for the case where a 'real-world' interface is needed (e.g. playing chess *with* a board).

There seems to be a confusion in the Winograd model between two logically distinct processes which might be called 'reference evaluation' and 'referent recognition'. When someone attempts to understand a phrase like 'the President of the United States', there is no need for him to search the White House physically to 'find a referent' for the phrase. If the hearer has sufficient world-knowledge he will be able to work out that a particular person (probably not currently perceptible by any of the senses) is being described. To do this the hearer may need to scan his memory, but he can do this sitting down with his eyes shut. Let us call this mapping of a description to a particular object 'reference evaluation'. (It will be discussed in greater detail in Section 6.2.) On the other hand, if someone has to obey the command 'Shoot the President of the United States', some further processes are necessary. The person will have to get himself into a physical position where he can perceive the President and must be able to recognise the President (probably visually). The latter stage (perception and recognition) could be carried out by a deaf-mute to whom the assassination command had been conveyed by pictures, and is not essentially linguistic. Let us call this 'referent recognition'.

A brief digression here will show that this confusion is not confined to Winograd's program, and will suggest some possible consequences of this distinction. Some writers imply that a phrase will 'have a referent' if and only if it describes some real world object(s). For example: 'There are also clear advantages to a language that can employ expressions which have no referent or which have not been secured a referent . . . We surely want our language to leave open for its users the possibility of constructing theories which hypothesize the existence of such things as phlogiston, ether and animal spirits . . .' (Katz (1972, p.142)) 'The reference of a proper name is the object itself.' (Frege (1892, p. 60))

Brown (1958) uses 'referent' in a language-learning context to describe concrete objects. Russell (1905) uses the word 'denoting' to mean 'standing for real world objects', and says that the phrase 'The present King of France' does not denote since there is no such existing object. However, for well-formed, successful conversation, it is the reference evaluation step that is important, not referent recognition. As Russell (ibid.) comments: 'It often happens that we know that a certain phrase denotes unambiguously, although we have no acquaintance with what it denotes.' (p. 479)

Certain noun phrases in English are clear examples of a linguistic device for automatically providing referents for the hearer, although he may have no perceptual data from the associated real-world object (see Section 6.2 for further discussion):

(51) My oldest brother lives in Glasgow.
(52) His father gave him a cheque.

Here the term 'referent' will always be taken to refer to the construct that is determined by reference evaluation in some model of the world. The corresponding object in one particular model (known as the 'real world') will be referred to as the 'concrete referent'.

One advantage of making this distinction is that we can distinguish between the concrete referent of a phrase and different people's referents for that phrase. In the classic example, the phrases 'the morning star' and 'the evening star' have the same concrete referent; but someone who does not know any astronomy may regard the phrases as referring to different objects. Such a person can be said to have two different referents for the phrase (in his notion of the world).

When describing the semantics of phrases which refer to something (e.g. noun phrases) it is important to make a distinction between the 'meaning' of the phrase (usually described in some formal representation) and the set of things the phrase refers to (as observed above, these things are not usually in some absolute 'real' world). This is, roughly, the traditional distinction between 'sense' and 'reference' (Frege (1892)).

Montague (1968, 1970a, 1972) formalises this distinction in a rigorous way. His model uses the notion of a 'point of reference', which is used as a parameter in deciding what an expression refers to (see Section 2.6). The point of reference has a direct influence on how an expression refers, because Montague defines the meaning of a term to be a function from points of reference to functions which define sets of objects. A single meaning (i.e. the same function) may refer to different objects if it is evaluated at different points of reference.

There is an obvious analogy here with program-evaluation. A piece of program must be evaluated in some context (i.e. some state of the machine). Some recent developments in programming languages have allowed program-contexts to be manipulated as items so that a piece of program may be executed in different contexts on different occasions (McDermott and Sussman (1972), Stansfield (1975), Davies (1973)). Even a simple piece of program such as (A+B) will refer to different numbers depending on the values of A and B.

Expressions like 'I' and 'he', whose reference is entirely dependent on the context of use, are sometimes classed as 'indexical expressions'. Bar-Hillel (1954) gives an elegant treatment of such expressions in which he points out that to discuss reference we must always include the context of use in the calculations. Indexical expressions are merely those where the influence of context is very obvious — in principle, the context must always be taken into account. Sentences which are non-indexical (such as 'ice floats on water') are those whose reference is unaltered by changing the context. (Compare this with the program 'sin(0);', which should yield 0 no matter what program context it is evaluated in.)

If we let the 'meaning' of a noun phrase be a piece of program which, when run, will produce the set of objects referred to by the phrase, then the sense/reference distinction is automatically incorporated. Winograd uses pieces of program to represent the meaning of noun phrases, although it is not clear that they are used as systematically as Montague's intension functions (see Ritchie (1976)). There are certain difficulties involved in using pure programs for noun phrase meanings (see Section 6.2), but it is worth noting the analogy between program-evaluation in a program-context and determining the set of referents of a meaning. It seems desirable to retain this aspect of the Winograd representation in any modification.

6.2. The Semantics of Noun Phrases

The term 'noun phrase' can be taken to cover a wide range of forms, including nominalised clauses. For the purposes of this discussion we will focus primarily on the simpler forms — proper nouns, pronouns, and common nouns with optional modifiers before and after. Various classifications (e.g. 'definite/indefinite', 'specific/non-specific') can be made of such phrases, and these categories are generally treated as syntactic rather than semantic. The object of this section is to show that these traditional distinctions are better looked on as semantic regularities and to suggest how the patterns might be incorporated into a computational model.

The SHRDLU program (Section 2.10) translated English noun phrases into procedures which, when executed, found the referent(s) of the phrase. As observed in Section 6.1, this incorporated some aspects of the 'sense/reference' distinction, provided that we take 'referent' to mean some abstract construct rather than an external object. We will try to refine that approach, to see exactly what kinds of 'meaning-procedures' there are and what kind of operations can be performed on them.

Certain kinds of 'definite' noun phrase (using the usual classification) seem to have a fairly straightforward behaviour. They can be regarded as providing descriptions which, in a particular context, will identify a unique set of objects that the hearer knows about.

(53)
(a) The red block
(b) This man
(c) The farmer's wife

Even if we could formalise this way of describing the meaning of NPs, it would be neither a necessary nor a sufficient criterion for traditional 'definiteness'. It is not clear whether proper names and personal pronouns are traditionally 'definite', but they are certainly used to identify a unique set of objects that the hearer knows about. Winograd (1972) points out that it is odd to use a phrase like 'the pyramid' if the context does not make it clear to the hearer which pyramid is referred to. Compare this with the comment by McCawley (197lb) that (54) sounds odd if the context does not make it clear who 'he' is.

(54) He resembles Mike.

The further observation should be made that (54) also sounds odd if the context does not make it clear who 'Mike' is. This alleged similarity between proper names and descriptive phrases may seem dubious at first, but in fact proper names, as used in English conversation, are not 'pure names' in the philosophical sense; that is, there is not a one-to-one correspondence between names and objects. Names may be intended as an approximation to pure names, but the way that they are used is analogous to the use of identifiers in programming, where the value of an identifier depends on the context. The expression 'Mike' in (54) may have different referents in different contexts, since different people have different mutual acquaintances.

As Winograd points out (ibid., p 156), 'definite' cannot be identified with 'known to the hearer'. There are various kinds of 'definite' noun phrase which can be used to refer to objects not previously mentioned.

(55)
(a) My brother who lives in Chicago.
(b) The title of his new book.
(c) The tallest elephant in Indiana.
(examples from Winograd).

Winograd observes that (55) (b) is allowable apparently because the noun 'title' denotes, in some way, a function defined on the set of books. Similarly, (55) (c), by providing a full description, allows the hearer to assume that such an object exists. Sentences like (55) (a) are more interesting — 'brother' does not denote a functional relation (since a person can have several brothers), nor is there any guarantee that 'who lives in Chicago' provides a unique description in the way that 'tallest' does. If a speaker uses (55) (a) in addressing someone who knows nothing of his brother the assumption is that this description provides all the relevant information (for this particular conversational exchange). If the hearer does know all the details of the speaker's family, the phrase is once again like those in (53), and the sentence may be inappropriate if it does not sufficiently define a referent.

This raises a further aspect of 'definite' noun phrases — the adequacy (and relevance) of the information involved. There seems to be a general principle in using definite noun phrases that distinctions need not be made if irrelevant in the particular context. Oddity can result from not being consistent about what distinctions are relevant. (56) (a) sounds acceptable on the assumption that which 'end' is involved is irrelevant, but (56) (b) sounds odd, with the second clause suddenly introducing a contrast as being pertinent.

(56)
(a) I sat down on the end of a nearby log.
(b) ??? I sat down on the end of a nearby log, and Harry sat on the thin end.

When the program of Davey (1974) is constructing referring expressions it takes into account which distinctions are relevant to the context using various equivalence classes within the domain of discourse.

Let us try to cover these aspects of 'definiteness' by the following generalisation:

(57) A definite noun phrase is used by the speaker to provide the hearer with all the relevant information to produce a set of referents; the information may be inherent

in the description, as in the case of 'functional' words, superlatives, etc.

The main inadequacy of (57) is that it says almost nothing, as becomes apparent on considering the idea 'produce a set of referents' in more detail. In the case of some referring expressions (e.g. proper names, pronouns, certain phrases with 'the') the referents are to be found in the hearer's 'world model' since they are things which he should know about already. However, in the case of phrases like those in (55) there seems to be a process of generating a referent on the spot, given a description which it must meet. Hence 'produce' in (57) means 'find *or* generate'. At this point in the argument, (57) becomes so general as to cover many other kinds of referring expression. 'Indefinite' noun phrases can be used to provide a description of an object the hearer is not acquainted with and the speaker provides only the information he feels is relevant.

(58)
(a) A woman with a collecting can accosted me.
(b) Some vandal has wrecked this phone box.

The difference seems to be that 'indefinite' noun phrases can be used *only* to generate a set of objects — there is no possibility of 'finding' one automatically in the hearer's world model. (That is not to say that he could not infer, at some stage, who the subjects of (58) (a) and (b) refer to, but that would not be part of the information that the speaker is imparting in the noun phrase.)

This contrasts with certain other noun phrases which we have been classing as 'definite', where referents must be 'found', but cannot be 'generated' if the search fails. In particular, proper names, personal pronouns, and demonstratives all seem to require that the hearer can actually identify what objects are referred to — the meaning of the phrases allows no construction on the spot of a referent(s) to match the description. If we class these phrases as 'deictic', then the classifications so far are as follows.

DEFINITE and DEICTIC: find a referent.
DEFINITE and NON-DEICTIC: find a referent; if none, generate one.
INDEFINITE: generate a referent

(Rumelhart and Norman (1973) give a similar gloss for 'definite' but they attribute this behaviour to the article 'the' rather than to some more general property of definiteness which is possessed by various kinds of phrase.)

So far all the noun phrases have been regarded as referring to some set of referents in a given context. There are certain expressions for which this is not a very satisfactory way of describing the meaning. In particular, generic statements often do not have particular referents as their subjects or objects:

(59)
(a) Wolves eat meat.
(b) The wolf is a carnivore.
(c) A wolf is a carnivore.
(d) The monarch is the head of the Church of England.

The subject phrase sometimes does have a referent in a particular context, as in (59) (d), and there may be an interpretation of the sentence in which that is the best way to describe the contribution of that phrase. Nevertheless, in the cases being considered here, there is also a 'generic' reading of the sentence in which the statement conveyed is not about one particular referent in one particular context. Let us refer to the generic interpretation of the noun phrase as 'non-specific' and the other interpretation as 'specific'.

Noun phrases like 'the monarch' or 'a wolf' can have either a specific or a non-specific reading, depending on the context of use, but certain other kinds of expression are less versatile. For example, it is very difficult to find a generic (non-specific) use of a proper name or personal pronoun. The subject of (60) (a) cannot be interpreted as meaning 'anyone named Ed'.

(60)
(a) Ed drinks excessively.
(b) Anyone who protested was thrown into prison.

Also, some phrases (e.g. the subject of (60) (b) are wholly non-specific. It might be thought that the set of wholly specific phrases and the set of deictic phrases might be related since they clearly overlap. However, some wholly specific phrases are not deictic, e.g. 'Someone who protested was thrown in prison.'

Intuitively, the non-specific phrases are being used as patterns to make statements about any object(s) that match the pattern, whereas the specific phrases are being used to produce instances, in a particular context, which do match. It would be useful if we could find some single representation for the meaning of a noun phrase which could function in both these ways.

Noun phrases can be combined with the verb 'be' to produce a verb phrase which can form the complement of a sentence. It would be preferable if whatever semantic representation we can devise for referring expressions will also describe their behaviour when they combine to form predicates, as in (61).

(61)
(a) Bill is the owner of that Mercedes.
(b) Your landlord is a Marxist.

The two previous subsections have indicated that a suitable representation might be some kind of 'pattern' which can be used directly (non-specific), or used to find a set of referents (definite), or used to generate a referent set (indefinite). This suggests that we consider either using the referent set to form the predication (in effect, treating the phrase in the complement as specific), or using the pattern itself to convey the predication (in effect, treating the phrase as non-specific). If the phrase inside the complement is either wholly specific or wholly non-specific there will be no choice, but it remains to be seen which is better for those phrases which can take either interpretation.

If we are making the assumption that semantic processing is carried out locally as far as possible (see Section 10.9 for discussion of this), then the difference between using the specific and non-specific forms would be as follows. The specific form would produce a referent set for its semantic structure, whereas the non-specific form would produce a pattern. In the former case the subject-complement SCR would have to perform some kind of object identification process between the set of objects referred to by the subject and those produced by the complement. In the non-specific case the subject-complement SCR would have to assert that the pattern was true of the subject set. There seems to be no way to choose between these, other than seeing which integrates best with other rules and operations required. It would be extremely useful, for example, if the structure chosen for such complements was similar to that chosen for ordinary verb-phrases, since then there would only need to be only one subject-complement rule to cover both cases. A common structure does seem to be possible (as will be proposed in Section 6.5 below), but we will first have to outline the system of semantic representation (Section 6.3) and apply it to verb phrases (Section 6.4).

6.3. Semantic Representation

The emphasis of computational grammar, at its current state of development, is on the way that processing occurs during sentence-analysis rather than on the kind of structure eventually produced. However, it is impossible to study processing in isolation, particularly if a computer program is to be written. This section discusses some of the possible ways of representing 'facts' as a preliminary to defining a semantic system which is at least sufficiently valid to avoid vitiating the rest of the framework. Let us consider some of the criteria that a semantic formalism should meet.

It will have to be general in two respects. It must not be specific to the subject matter and it must not be specific to the language being described. It should allow the representation of any meaning that can be expressed on any subject in any language.

It should interface closely with other parts of the language model. That is, there should be ways of relating the semantic items systematically to the more structural (syntactic) aspects of language. This may seem an irrelevant comment, but it could be argued (see Section 2.8) that one deficiency of the work of Schank (1972a) is the lack of a clear theory of the relationship between surface form and conceptual meaning. Semantic structure should not exist in isolation, however splendid.

The representation system should provide some way of comparing or relating semantic structures, for example by rules of inference, so that 'meanings' of different sentences can interact in some way (although not necessarily in traditional syllogisms, for example).

Other desirable attributes of a representation system might be simplicity, perspicuity and having self-evident atomic constructs, but these are less important.

There seems to be a consensus forming within artificial intelligence and linguistics over semantic representation. The systems proposed by Wilks (1973), Schank (1972a), and Rumelhart and Norman (1973) have many similarities. All these systems are intended to be independent of subject matter, and Schank and Rumelhart and Norman claim that their representations are language-independent. (The latter claim is largely unproven since the systems are mainly illustrated with examples from English or related languages.)

Two kinds of device are used in these systems to express relationships between different meanings. There are rules of inference (which are generally discussed informally so that it is not obvious what canonical form(s) are being proposed, if any). Also, meanings (of particular words, etc.) can be decomposed into smaller units ('primitives') so that similarities in meanings can be displayed in the configuration of primitive elements. Both inference rules and primitive-decomposition are very difficult issues for which no one has found any good solutions (see the papers in Schank and Nash-Webber (1975)). The main problems are when to operate the mechanism and when to terminate it; that is, how many inferences should be followed up at any given point, or how much breaking down into primitives should occur.

There is another problem for a system which operates entirely in terms of primitive elements. Some information about particular meanings or concepts will have to be associated with the larger semantic items rather than with the component primitive elements. To take an example suggested by Wilks (lecture at Edinburgh (1976)), there is information about 'smoking' which cannot properly be tied to its representation in terms of 'drawing smoke into the lungs through burning tobacco'; also, Charniak has suggested that some aspects of the meaning of 'sweat' cannot be indexed under the component items like 'water' and 'skin'. A primitive-based system might associate such information with substructures made up of primitive elements but this would be to acknowledge the validity of these larger 'chunks' for some descriptive purposes.

There is an added problem for any system which describes all meanings by associating a static structure with each sentence. Some words or sentences may be better expressed in terms of something other than a simple relationship between the few items involved.

(62) John believes that Mary likes Bert.
(63) Does John think that Mary likes Bert?

For example, if we are to use the meaning of (62) to make any deductions concerning John it would be useful to have it recorded (somehow) that a particular proposition (namely, that Mary likes Bert) has a particular truth-value in John's model of the world. Then (62) could be related to (63), for example, without a specific inference rule relating 'thinks' and 'believes'. To designate a simple semantic network like (64) as the 'meaning' of (62) would not be very helpful (see Section 2.12 for an outline of this notation).

Rumelhart and Norman allow each relation in their semantic system to have an associated piece of program which can be executed under particular circumstances. This general facility allows the linguist or programmer defining the relations to include arbitrary special effects; in particular, the procedure could be used to re-express the

(64)

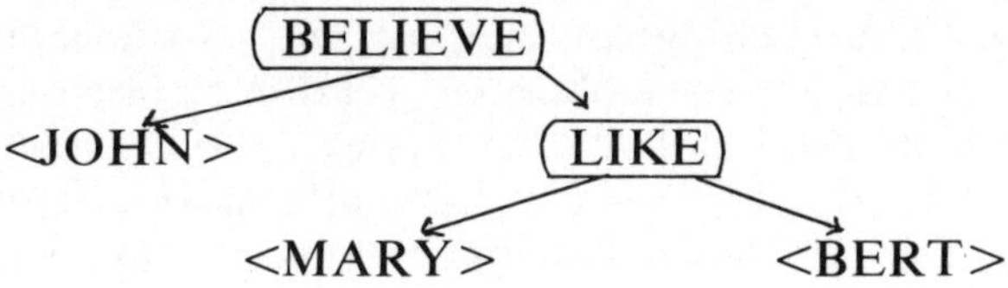

relation in terms of some other conditions on the semantic network.

The semantic system adopted in computational grammar is very similar to that of Rumelhart and Norman. There are 'relations', which can be used to form a general relational structure (a semantic net). Each relation has a fixed number of 'roles' which can be filled with other semantic items, each role having an associated 'restriction' which limits the kind of item which can fill that role (see comment at the end of Section 3.4). An example of a relation with some, all or none of its roles filled is referred to as a 'relation-instance'. That is, (64) depicts a semantic network containing two relation-instances, and any semantic network will be made up largely of relation-instances.

Facilities are provided for both primitive and procedural re-expression, as follows. Each relation can (optionally) have an 'expanded form' and an 'elaborated form'. The expanded form, if present, is a piece of semantic network which expresses the relation in primitive form. Some notational device is necessary to keep track of how the arguments of the main relation fit into the primitive network. The system thus includes both non-primitive and primitive relations, and the former may be re-expressed in terms of the latter.

The elaborated form (if present) can be thought of as a set of three procedures — a procedure for testing if the relation holds, one for making the relation 'true' in the main network, and one for making the relation 'false' in the network. (In the experimental program these three functions were fulfilled by a single structure, interpretable in three different ways — see Ritchie (1977).) When matching two pieces of relational network for similarity, or testing to see if a relation-instance is 'true' in the network, the expanded version can be tried as well. When testing or setting the 'truth-value' of a relation-instance the elaborated version can be used as well as the main relation itself. In this way the meaning of some relation (e.g. 'believe') can have alternative expression in terms of conditions on configurations of other parts of the network.

The interface with other aspects of the linguistic model is achieved by having the SCRs build up semantic networks gradually so that each subpart of a sentence has its own associated semantic structure. The semantic part of lexical entries for words are always pieces of semantic network. In particular, each main verb has an associated relation. This means that any idiosyncratic parts of the meaning of a verb can be associated with that relation, and its connection with other meanings can, if necessary, be included by using the expanded or elaborated forms.

6.4. Verbs and Cases

Winograd's syntactic system uses the features SUBJ, OBJ and AGENT to classify the groups which are directly related to the main verb of a clause. 'Subject' and 'object' are useful classifications for describing English surface structure, but their semantic relevance might be queried; Lakoff and Ross (1967) (in attacking Chomsky (1965)) claimed that 'subject' and 'object' cover no semantic generalisations and are purely a surface classification.

Different surface configurations may be used to express similar semantic relationships; for example, (65) (a) and (b) are very similar in meaning, and (66) (a), (b), (c) and (d) are also.

(65)
(a) John hates Mary.
(b) Mary is hated by John.
(66)
(a) Fred gave Mary the book.

(b) Fred gave the book to Mary.
(c) The book was given to Mary by Fred.
(d) Mary was given the book by Fred.

This could be expressed by associating with each verb a canonical set of object and subject slots, and classing together those sentences which are similar in terms of the items filling these places. That is effectively what Chomsky (1965) did, using 'subcategorisation rules' to describe the slots for main verbs, and having canonical deep structures (to which the subcategorisation rules applied) for superficially different sentences. The 'deep structures' for (65) (a) and (b) differed only by the presence or absence of a passive marker — they had the same deep subject and the same deep object. Similarly, all the sentences in (66) had a deep structure in which the deep subject, object and indirect object correspond to the surface subject, object and indirect object of (66) (b). Although Chomsky's subcategorisation rules did not use relations such as 'subject' and 'object' he pointed out that it might be possible to define terms like these at the level of deep structure. Chomsky's method is sufficient to capture the similarities in the sentences in (65) and (66). We could re-formulate the information by stating that verbs can have an 'AGENT', a 'PATIENT' and a 'GOAL' at some 'deep' level, and these may appear in various orderings at the surface, but this is more or less a notational variant of the 'Aspects' system. Let us call these deep canonical slots around the verb 'roles'.

A further elaboration of this description of verb meanings was produced by Fillmore (1968) who made the suggestion that there was a small fixed set of roles (more than just the three corresponding to 'subject', 'object' and 'indirect object') and that these deep roles were semantically significant. For example, there is a role AGENT, which various verbs have, which has some independent semantic content. He hypothesized that there was a small, universal set of roles which are used in deep classification of verbs, such that whenever a certain role appears it always expresses the same relationship between the verb and the term involved. If a term X has the role of INSTRUMENT in a verb V1 and a term Y has the role of INSTRUMENT in a verb V2, then Fillmore's hypothesis is that X and Y are serving the same semantic function, in some sense, in the structures containing V1 and V2. Fillmore called these semantically relevant roles 'cases'.

To account for the semantic similarities in sentences like (65) and (66) it is necessary to have some description of the main verb other than its surface behaviour. The most obvious way is to look on the verb as being a relation with a certain number of arguments where these arguments may appear in a variety of surface configurations. Some rules for showing how these surface configurations are related to the argument places in the relation would also be necessary in a complete description. This is very similar to what Chomsky proposed in 1965, if we avoid the confusion caused by the use of different terminology. Fillmore's main extension was to suggest that there could be some semantically interesting classification of the kind of roles that verbs can have. Some natural language systems in artificial intelligence (see Bruce (1975) for a review) claim to be using a 'case grammar' where in fact they are using a notational variant of Chomsky's system. A program does not really use a Fillmore-style system unless it includes some non-trivial categorisation of the roles used in verbs, and uses this categorisation in some way, for example to perform inferences. At least some of the inferences would have to be phrased solely in terms of the 'cases' involved, without reference to the particular verbs. If the verbs (or relations) concerned are mentioned at all times then the semantic content of the role has not been made independent of the verb and the inference is really referring to 'the nth argument of the relation R' as could be done without cases. 'Cases' in most artificial intelligence language systems are simply mnemonic labels for argument slots.

Verb constructions are handled in the following way in computational grammar. Each verb has an associated semantic relation and the set of roles for that relation fulfils the purpose of a 'case frame' for that verb. Some of the SCRs (which will be referred to informally as 'role-placement rules') take a relation as first argument, and build a structure based on a relation-instance using that relation (see Sections 3.7 and 8.5). A role-placement rule puts its other arguments (which will come from the object and indirect object of the verb) into roles of the relation-instance. It also marks, in a way which is described in Section 6.5 below, which of the remaining (unfilled) roles of the relation-instance is to be used for the subject of the sentence.

(67)

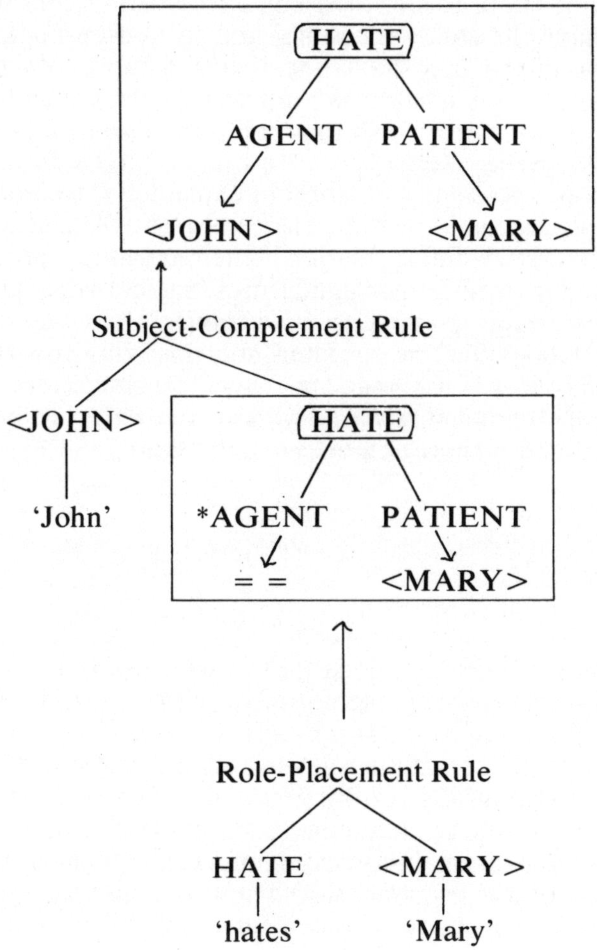

The subject-complement rule then fills out the relation-instance by putting the semantic item from the subject of the clause into the selected role. Diagrammatically, the SCR tree is like (67) (where the semantic item produced by each SCR in the tree has been sketched in, the symbol = = is a 'blank' marker, and the * marks the role allotted to the subject item).

This has the advantage that if we wish to represent the fact that two verbs have 'similar' meanings there are two ways of doing this. One crude way is to give the two verbs the same relation (with, consequently, the same role-list). Thus two verbs can have the same 'meaning' and still differ in their surface behaviours (since that is specified separately). In the experimental grammar 'address' and 'speak' were handled in this way. If we do not wish to identify the two meanings we may still represent some degree of similarity by using the facility for re-expressing a relation in expanded (primitive) form. Two verbs can have different non-primitive relations but have the same primitive relation in their expanded forms. Fillmore tried to capture such similarities (e.g. between 'kill' and 'die') by simply comparing case frames. As Charniak (quoted in Wilks (1976) has pointed out, this will show the similarity only if it is assumed that there is some common semantic 'core' of meaning paired with the two different case frames. The method here achieves exactly that.

6.5. Definers

There is one kind of semantic structure which is extremely useful in constructing representations for the meanings of several categories of item. If we take a piece of semantic network and select one of the roles (whether filled or not) as a 'focus of attention' the resulting structure can be used in various ways. (In the implemented version these structures were represented as a pair consisting of a semantic network and the name of the selected role.) These structures can be created during processing, if a semantic rule selects some role in a piece of network, or they can be entered directly in lexical entries with the role already selected.

Let us call such a structure a 'definer'. It can function as a predicate, which is 'true' of all items X for which there is a 'true' network matching this one, with X in the selected role. It can be used to find a particular spot in the overall semantic network by finding a piece of network to match and then singling out the selected role; thus found, any item located at that spot can be examined, or another item can be placed there.

Not all the roles in the piece of network in a definer need be filled for it to operate successfully. Suppose we have a relation FATHER, with roles 'SON' and 'DAD', which can hold between sets of items (classed in the semantic model as 'PEOPLE'). We could construct a semantic item for the word 'father' by a definer like (68) where = = is a 'blank' entry and * marks the selected role in the definer.

(68)

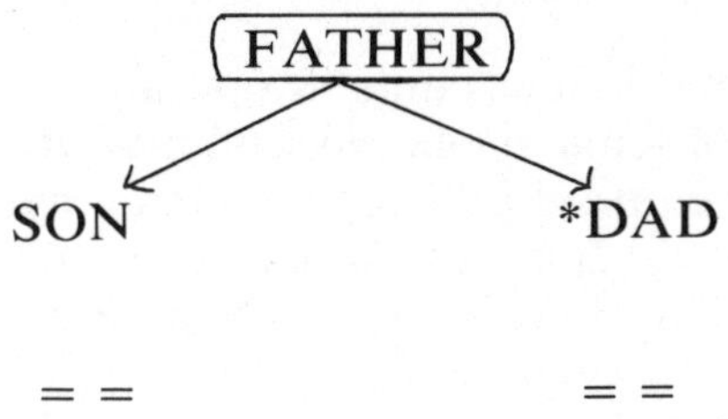

This will act as a predicate which is true of any item X for which there is a network like (69) recorded as 'true', where Y can be *any* item.

This allows for the use of 'father' without mention of the offspring, e.g. 'Harry is a father'. If the other role became filled (e.g. in the structure for the phrase 'John's father'), the semantic item would then look something like (70), where angle brackets enclose an item whose internal details are not important here.

(69)

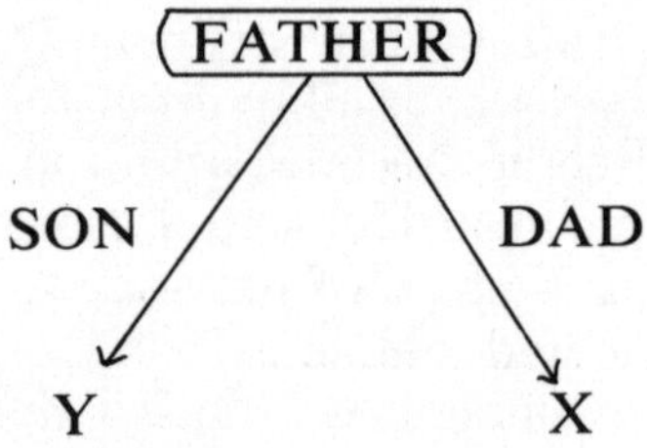

(70)

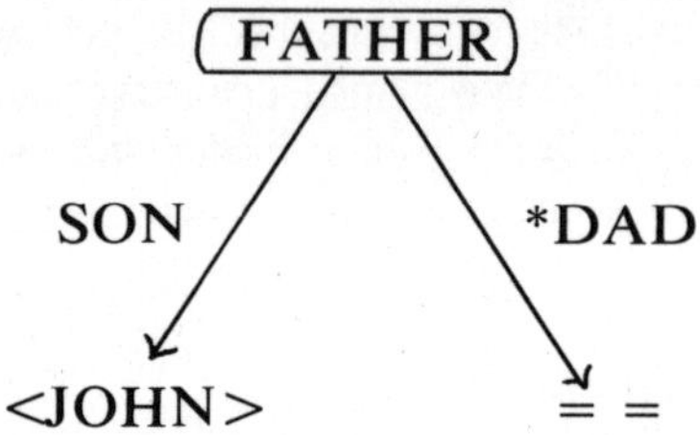

In this case, the definer can still operate as before, except that the range of semantic networks that it will match is much narrower (since one of its roles now must match a specified value <JOHN>). It could, for example, act as a predicate which is true of any item X for which there is a 'true' network like (71).

(71)

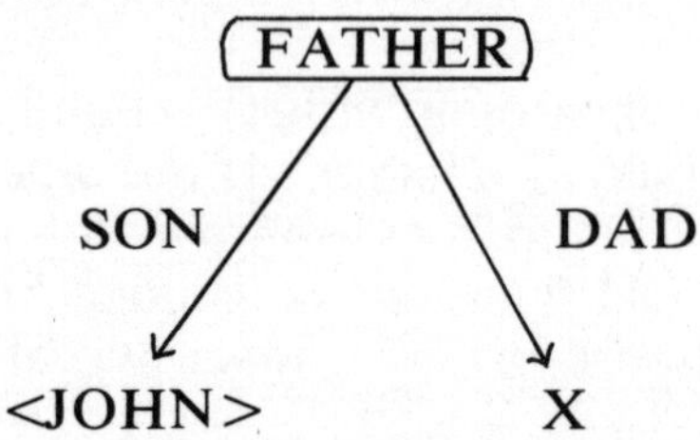

The same definer (i.e. (70)) could also be used to find a position in the network, and the item there (e.g. X in (71)) could then be accessed or replaced. That is, one representation for the meaning of 'John's father' can act as a predicate, a way of finding an item, or a path to some spot in the network where some item can be placed. (The latter might be useful for interpreting a sentence like 'Dave is John's father', for example.)

Notice that these are exactly the operations that are needed for the processing of simple noun phrases, as argued in Section 6.2. If we can arrange to represent noun phrases by semantic structures which are 'definers' then there is a natural way of having the same semantic item function in the various required ways. Markings such as 'definite', 'specific', etc. will have to be present on the definers in the lexicon (for one-word phrases) or be inserted during sentence analysis (by the noun phrase SCRs). These markings will then indicate to the semantic network processor which way to operate on the structure.

This means that we need *semantic* properties which classify meanings (not to be confused with syntactic properties — Section 3.3 — which categorise surface-tree structures). Let us call these markings *sense properties*.

The other versatile aspect of the 'definer' is the wide variety of grammatical categories for which it can be used to represent the meaning. Not only can a definer be used as the semantic item for a noun (as above), the fact that a simple regular adjective can be regarded as a predicate means that a definer can represent the meaning of an adjective, e.g. for 'blue' we could have (72), or even (73).

(72)

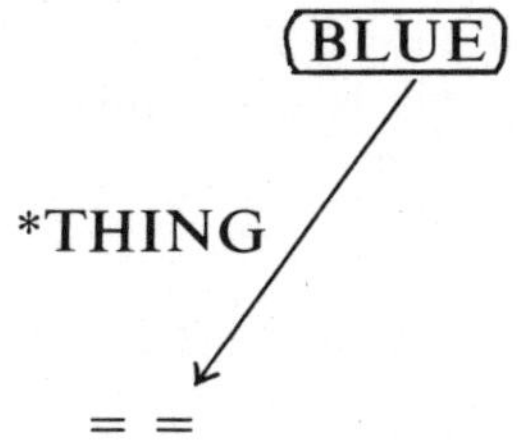

(73)

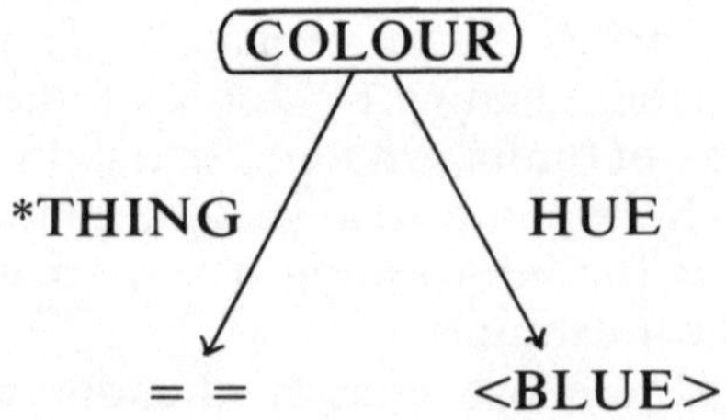

As outlined in Sections 3.7 and 6.4, verbs are represented by relations, and case frames by the roles of a relation, with role-placement occurring in what is traditionally called a verb phrase. The meaning of a verb phrase can therefore be represented by a definer, where the semantic network part has the selected role unfilled, so that the 'subject' of the sentence can be fitted in there, by the subject-complement SCR. A phrase such as 'likes John' would then have a definer like (74) as its meaning.

(74)

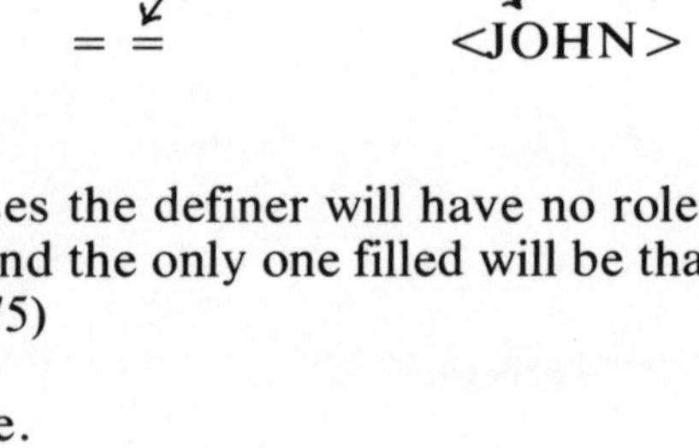

In some cases the definer will have no roles filled in the verb phrase, and the only one filled will be that used by the subject, e.g. (75)

(75) Fred ate.

This illustrates the need for a variety of role-placement

SCRs (see Section 3.7), since a single verb may have different combinations of subjects and objects. However, the way that the different surface configurations are permuted into deep roles is determined *within the verb phrase*. Compare (76) and (77):

(76) John was liked by Mary.
(77) The book was given to me by my brother.

That is why the definer is suitable for a verb phrase structure — it reflects that fact that the characteristics of the phrase (e.g. passive verb, prepositions) determine the role of an item outside the phrase (i.e. the subject).

This simplifies the subject-complement rules. Although (78) (a)–(d) have diverse surface structures, the italicised parts can all be represented by some kind of definer.

(78)
(a) John is *Harry's father*.
(b) John is *a doctor*.
(c) John is *stupid*.
(d) John *likes bananas*.

The subject-complement rule can be designed to insert the semantic structure for the subject into the selected role in the definer from the complement, thus producing a fuller relation-instance. (This assumes that 'be' would not affect the overall semantic structure of the phrase, but that is quite a plausible proposal; some transformational treatments of 'be' regard it as absent in deep structure and insert the surface form by a transformation.)

(Bach (1968) discusses certain semantic patterns which cross traditional syntactic boundaries and which seem similar to the generalisations that are attempted here.)

Several details have been omitted or glossed over here since they have not been fully worked out. The notion of a 'definer' proved very useful in writing the experimental program and its characteristics seem interesting enough to suggest its general applicability, but the details have not been perfected yet.

6.6. Semantic Categories

Semantic structures can be classified in many different ways and it is advisable (to avoid confusion in later chapters) to explain here some of the kinds of category used in computational grammar. (See Chapter 7 below for some comments on classification.) The system of semantic representation described here gives rise to three different kinds of semantic classification, as follows:

Referential Classes

The items in the subject matter of the discourse or dialogue can be classified according to their characteristics in the external world. This area was much debated within transformational grammar in the 1960s (under the heading simply of 'semantics'), and some of the more intransigent problems are summarised by Bolinger (1965). (See also Katz and Fodor (1963), Weinreich (1966), Katz (1967).) In computational grammar each referential class is represented by a predicate which tests for membership of that category (the predicates are represented as 'definers' — see Section 6.5 above). The referential classes are structured into a hierarchy of sub- and super-classes and grouped into antonym classes (as proposed by Katz (1972)) for the purposes of describing 'semantic anomaly'.

Sense Classes

The linguistic representations of meanings (that is, the semantic structures, not the referents) can also be described in terms of their semantic network structure. Different kinds of structure (e.g. 'relations', 'definers', etc.) have different capabilities for combining with each other, so it could be said that the sense classes describe the 'abstract syntax' of the linguistic items.

Sense Properties

As well as the gross network structure of a semantic item, the grammar may need miscellaneous information about how to process the item. For example, 'definer' is a sense class, but definers can be used (as described above in Section 6.5) to represent miscellaneous linguistic items and they may need different annotations to indicate how they are to be processed. Properties like 'definite', 'specific', are the clearest examples, giving details of the matching and instantiating which should be carried out on the semantic items on which they are marked (see Section 6.2). The meaning of a relative clause is also representable as a definer, but with different sense properties to record the fact that it must be used in slightly different ways in the semantic routines.

The MCHINE program (see Section 13.5) used various sense properties, including markings to indicate aspects of clause meanings such as tense, negation, etc.

CHAPTER 7

LEVELS OF DESCRIPTION

7.1. Syntagmatic and Paradigmatic Information

There are several ways in which a linguistic constituent could be classified: what its internal structure is, how it is related to other constituents, what steps are necessary to parse it, where it can occur in a sentence and what kind of meaning it has. These six criteria for classifying are logically distinct and might be called morphology, syntagmatic relationships, parsing steps required, distributional (or paradigmatic) behaviour and semantics. Traditional syntactic categories usually try to summarise some or all of these under one label (e.g. 'Noun Phrase') which makes an implicit claim about how these different factors are related. There are some interesting relationships between these classifications (e.g. the internal structuring of an item determines how it must be parsed) but it will lead to confusion if we assume immediately that all six factors give the same classification.

For example, consider articles and possessives in English. Articles ('a' and 'the') are paradigmatically related to possessive adjectives ('my', 'Fred's', etc.) in that they all occur at the beginning of a noun phrase and there cannot be both an article and a possessive in a noun phrase. This suggests we might simplify the grammar by creating a category or feature (say, DET) which includes both and not distinguish the two. However, this ignores the possibility that the syntagmatic relationship between article and head noun may be different from the relationship between possessive and head noun (see Section 3.5). If our grammar is to represent such relationships explicitly (as in Section 3.1) it may be necessary to distinguish the two subclasses in the syntagmatic representation even though they are treated similarly during parsing. Winograd (1972, p. 93) has his parser attach possessives under a 'DET' label on the syntax tree and has a class of 'determiners' which includes both articles and possessives. This is largely because syntagmatic relationships are not represented in his syntactic tree but are worked out later by the 'semantic specialists'. Hence his syntactic labelling need not be too fine. It might be asked what the criteria are for assigning different syntagmatic relationships to different combinations. The answer to this is that if different semantic operations must be performed on the combination then a different relationship is required. This begs the question until we have some clear idea of 'different semantic operation', but, as was argued in Section 3.5 there is a case for regarding possessives as semantically different from the other 'determiners'.

7.2. Different Types of Feature

Related to this is Winograd's all-embracing use of 'features' to classify every aspect of a syntactic unit, which is as confusing as the traditional packing of all characteristics into syntactic categories. Some features are distributional/paradigmatic and guide the parser, e.g. DET in the lexical entry for 'the'. Some features are morphological and describe the internal form of the unit they are attached to, e.g. NDET on a noun group node means that there is no determiner attached beneath that node. Some features are syntagmatic, e.g. AGENT, when attached to a 'Prep Group' node, describes the relationship of that node to the main verb; when attached to a Clause node, it describes the internal relationships between the items of the clause. Some features are both syntagmatic and semantic, e.g. NPL marked on a noun group node indicates its number. Some features appear to be wholly semantic, e.g. DEF or INDEF marked on a noun group. The major categories like NG (noun group) contain similar conflations — NG is the name of a parsing method (as in a command (PARSE NG . . .)); NG is a feature marked on a node; there are a particular set of semantic specialists associated with the category NG.

Marcus (1974) suggests that a 'feature' is any aspect of a

constituent that the parser may need to find out by a quick inspection. This sums up one important aspect of features in a recognition grammar (they are there to guide the parser) but it is not very perspicuous to use the same device for describing disparate aspects of structure without indicating the distinctions. This confusion is also present in other areas of grammatical classification, particularly around the boundary between syntax and semantics.

Consider the italic phrase in (79):

(79) *The man who you saw last night* rang up.

There are several statements that might be made about this phrase or its meaning. It is a noun phrase. It is made up of a noun group and a relative clause. It is made up of a nominal and a modifier. It is a referring expression, and is definite and specific. It is the subject of the verb in the sentence. It refers to a human, animate thing (or should do, if used appropriately). These make seven different classifications and cannot be covered simply by providing one set of 'syntactic' categories and one set of 'semantic' categories. Strangely enough, the hardest classification to make firm is the traditional 'noun phrase'. All of (80) (a)–(f) could be classed as noun phrases, and they differ in many respects.

(80)
(a) *The dog* attacked him.
(b) *Flying kites* can be tricky.
(c) *To have been loved* is better than to have been lost.
(d) I don't like *what you did*.
(e) It amazed me *that you arrived here*.
(f) I will ignore *anything you may do*.

7.3. Some Grammatical Classes

It is very hard to lay down levels of classification in isolation from an overall model since different descriptive frameworks may make different distinctions (e.g. the 'deep structure' of Chomsky (1965) is a disputed level). Computational grammar includes various concepts and rules which can be used to induce classifications of linguistic structures at various levels. Some of these categories fit easily under the headings of syntax and semantics, but others are less easy to allocate. The kinds of categories and rules available are the following, grouped under headings that may help to indicate the level at which they operate.

(81)

(a) Concrete Syntax: syntactic properties, syntactic features (see Section 3.3).

(b) Abstract Syntax or Intensional Semantics: Structural combining rules (see Chapter 3), sense classes, sense properties (see Section 6.6).

(c) Referential Semantics: referential classes (see Section 6.6).

Notice that the only categories which may vary with a change of subject matter are those at level (c) — all other classifications should be general linguistic statements. It is not the case that all semantics is dependent on the domain of discourse — the level of intensional semantics ('sense' as opposed to 'reference') should be domain-independent.

These ways of describing items take on meaning only in the context of the full framework. Drawing attention to these distinctions should clarify the expositions here and may avoid the need to class every concept as either 'syntactic' or 'semantic'. Traditional concepts (e.g. 'noun phrase', 'subject') could be defined in this framework by fitting them into this system. For example, computational grammar does not use the concept 'subject' as such, but certain SCRs could be classed as 'subject-complement' rules, and an item could be said to be a subject if it is the first argument of a subject-complement rule.

CHAPTER 8

DECISIONS, MISTAKES AND PREDICTIONS

8.1. The Methodology of Mistakes

If we are to examine sentence processing in detail one notion that needs some clarification is that of a 'decision'. A sentence-analyser makes, as it processes a sentence, various choices and performs various operations — attaching pieces of structure, developing one analysis path but not another, pushing down registers, etc. When we talk of an analyser making a 'mistake' or a 'wrong decision', which of these actions are relevant? For example, Marcus (see Section 2.11, and below) bases much of his argument on the need for a parser that does not make 'mistakes', and he claims that a human hearer is normally aware when he has made a mistake in understanding the structure of a sentence. If we are to rely on these conscious judgments about 'mistakes' (as one source of 'oddity', as in Section 1.3), then we must be explicit about what actions in the formal model constitute 'mistakes' or else we cannot relate anomaly (mistakes defined by the model) to oddity (mistakes detected by a hearer). It conveys very little to say that an analyser makes very few mistakes during parsing if there is no clear notion of what constitutes a mistake; similarly, it is not a restriction to specify that an analyser should not make any wrong decisions if we do not specify what counts as a decision.

As a preliminary let us now review some of the general techniques commonly used in sentence analysers for controlling the search for possible analyses.

8.2. Exhaustive Strategies

Owing to the ambiguity of natural language an analyser is frequently faced, in the course of analysing a sentence, with several possibilities at once. There are two standard strategies that a parser can use to follow up multiple options. A program is said to use a *depth-first* strategy if, at each choice point, it chooses one of the options and follows it up fully, to the exclusion of others. If a choice proves to be wrong the program 'backtracks', i.e. it returns to the most recent choice point, undoing all or most of the processing performed since that point, and tries another option. When all the options at a choice point have been tried unsuccessfully, the program backtracks to the previous choice point. This has the advantage that there is only one partial analysis being maintained at once (with choice points recorded in some way), and (if the program makes the right choices) the correct analysis is found very quickly. One disadvantage is that if the program makes the wrong choices it has to do a great deal of backtracking and this may involve undoing processing which will have to be repeated when other options are taken. A drawback to having only one partial analysis in existence is that there is no way of comparing several possibilities so that the 'best', in some sense, may be chosen. Several analyses can be compared only by producing complete analyses. That is, instead of the analyser stopping when it has found one successful path, it continues to explore systematically all the other choices that it has not yet tried (in the same way that it would if it were backtracking because of failure).

A program is said to use a *breadth-first* strategy if all the options at each choice point are developed simultaneously. This has the advantage of finding all the possible analyses in one scan of the sentence, and it allows (in principle) the program to compare several different partial analyses, selecting the better ones for consideration. In a pure breadth-first system such a selection facility would not be used, since all analyses are developed regardless of merit, but a natural development would be some form of 'pruning' of the set of analyses (if some principled method could be found). The main disadvantage is that several analyses must be maintained simultaneously even although many of them will prove to be transient.

The augmented transition network formalism is neutral

between depth- and breadth-first exploration. A particular network provides the arrangement of the choice points, but these may be explored in either fashion. The program of Thorne, Bratley and Dewar (1968) used a pure breadth-first approach, and the LSNLIS system (according to Marcus (1975)) uses the depth-first approach.

If we wish to examine the details of how decisions are made in sentence-analysis (with an eventual aim of constructing a plausible model of human processing), then pure depth- or breadth-first systems are not very helpful. The reason for this is that both methods have inherent inefficiencies which are overcome by brute force. These are exhaustive strategies in which the grammar does not have to be particularly clever, elegant or carefully constructed in order to succeed. If parsers are justified solely on the grounds that they 'work' with sufficient computation then we are left with no means of comparing rival recognition grammars. With a suitably large computer one could write a parser which would produce any desired analyses for sentences just by putting suitable (*ad hoc*) markings in the dictionary and by making the parsing strategy exhaustive. The whole point is that we want to be able to say something about *how* the parser operates and whether one program is neater than another — the fact that it eventually produces the analyses is not a sufficient condition for adequacy. We need to refine our notions of parsing strategies, simply because, as commented in Section 1.1, one of our main criteria in a scientific investigation is that we should try to find the neatest solution.

This is not to say that all parsers that use exhaustive strategies are alike. The parser for the IBM REQUEST system (Plath (1973), Petrick (1973)) used a reverse transformational derivation which resulted in a large combinatorial explosion. Quite short sentences had so many possible surface groupings that even with several 100K of machine space the parsing was difficult (or impossible). On the other hand, the program of Thorne, Bratley and Dewar (1968), using a breadth-first exploration of an ATN grammar, was able to parse comparable sentences quite quickly using only 16K of store. It is implausible to suggest that this difference could be due solely to implementation details. The radically different analysis procedures must account for some of this discrepancy — but that is a direct admission that we can appraise a program in terms of *how* it works. Once this criterion is allowed the obvious step is to try to refine the brute force exhaustive strategies into neater, more elegant devices.

A more specific objection to exhaustive processing strategies is raised by Marcus (1974). He points out that there exist 'garden-path' sentences (like (82) and (83)), where people (usually) make a mistake in perceiving the structure of the sentence on first assessment, and hence need more than one attempt to 'understand' them.

(82) I told the boy the dog bit Sue would help him.
(83) In the book the girl took the basket had magical powers.

In such situations people are conscious of making a mistake and having to re-assess the sentence. Marcus argues that if the normal processing method is depth-first (where automatic backtracking is part of the process), then people must be making continual 'mistakes' while processing ordinary sentences, without any disruptive effect. If that is the case, why should the 'garden-path' sentences not be handled smoothly by this automatic, unconscious, backup method? This argument can also be applied to exhaustive breadth-first systems. If people normally consider all partial analyses simultaneously (and throw away those that go wrong without being aware of any oddity), why should they see only one analysis for 'garden-path' sentences? Marcus concludes that people do in fact process just one of the possible analyses (and hence can be 'wrong' in a garden-path sentence), but that they choose this analysis very carefully, rather than relying on automatic backtracking to allow an arbitrary blind choice. He suggests that a recognition grammar should proceed deterministically (i.e. not maintaining multiple analyses), building structure only if it will not have to alter it later, and holding partial structures in temporary storage (cf. Chapter 5 above) until they can be attached in their final position. This matter will be discussed in greater detail in Section 8.4.

8.3. Weighting and Preference

Both Woods (1970) and Winograd (1972) suggest the use of a numerical 'weight' which can be associated with different analyses in a parse, indicating which of the analyses is the 'best'. As observed above, partial analyses cannot be compared in a depth-first system, so if Winograd's parser were to make use of the weighting (the SHRDLU parser does not), it would have to compare alternative complete analyses. Woods says that the weight allows one 'to suspend unlikely looking paths in favour of more likely ones' (ibid. p. 605), which suggests that partial analyses are being compared. Wilks (1975) suggests a totally different framework which uses a more sophisticated 'preference' system (see Section 2.7), and presents semantic arguments for using such a device. (His preference measurement is not used in a gradual left-to-right analysis, so many of the comments here do not apply directly to it.)

The question of how to use 'weighting' or 'preference' is not simple. There are two main issues — relative versus absolute failure, and local versus global assessment. A facile approach to the idea of preference might abolish the notion of 'discarding' a partial analysis in favour of some mechanism of 'reducing preference'. Although superficially plausible, that would be unworkable for the following reasons. At any given stage in an analysis there are certain options available and 'failure' occurs when the input word does not meet the conditions for any of these. If we no longer discard failed analyses we would have to follow up every option regardless of the input. Leaving aside the problem that the structure-building might be unmanageable if, for example, a preposition has to act as a surrogate for a verb, we have created a severe combinatorial problem, since the input would not be constraining or guiding the analyser at all. In ATN terms, the ATN interpreter would have to pass through the entire network, keeping different preference counts, with no search paths being terminated by 'failure'.

Another suggestion might be to assign each option at any stage (each arc in ATN terminology) a value, depending on how well the input word matches the corresponding condition. The arc with the 'best' value would be the only one to be explored. There are two main problems with such an approach. For one thing, it is a form of 'depth-first' searching and hence does not allow the comparison of more than one partial analysis (thus losing one of the advantages of a preference system). Also, the initial choices in the analysis process will be made on the basis of the 'best' options at that early stage, thus discarding any analyses which might prove 'better' later.

These two hypothetical set-ups illustrate an important point regarding 'weighting': the weighting system must discriminate sufficiently to ignore some possibilities, otherwise the search space is absurdly large; on the other hand, it must not discard for local reasons possibilities which might later prove valid, and it should not always concentrate on just one analysis.

A working system seems to need the notions both of 'discarding' and of 'reduced preference', with different kinds of 'failure' invoking the two reactions. The system described in Chapter 13 operated with the following division of mechanisms. Each analysis path had a numerical value (the 'tension') which could, in principle, be incremented by any part of the program (the 'tension' was set initially to zero, and the lower the 'tension' the 'better' the analysis). Failure in arc tests and surface structure building caused the analysis to be discarded, but failure in applying any of the semantic rules (or in 'reference evaluation' — see Section 6.3) merely caused the 'tension' to be increased. (This demarcation seems to be similar to that which is implicit in the programs of Wilks (see Section 2.7).)

The above discussion has been aimed at establishing two points concerning search strategies in parsers. First, exhaustive strategies, in which arbitrarily many erroneous paths may be followed are both theoretically uninteresting and intuitively implausible. When a recognition grammar is written the linguist should not just specify all the alternatives. Moreover, where multiple analyses have to be considered, some notion of 'preference' would be useful so that the 'best' of several alternative analyses may be chosen. This entails simultaneous development of a few paths, with some part of the program having access to all the partial analyses.

8.4. Top-Down and Bottom-Up

Another way of classifying parsing strategies depends on whether the parser searches for some specific configuration in the input ('top-down') or whether the input is examined first and then arranged into successively larger structures ('bottom-up').

The breadth-first/depth-first classification is logically independent of the top-down/bottom-up distinction, but the combination of top-down with depth-first is quite common (what Marcus calls the 'Guess-and-Backup Principle'). Purely bottom-up parsers for natural language are rare in the artificial intelligence literature, and many of the devices currently in use are hard to classify firmly as either top-down or bottom-up.

For example, the notion of a 'demon' (as described by Charniak (1973)) has been used as a sentence-analysing device by Marcus (1975) and by Riesbeck (1974) (under the names 'module' and 'expectation' respectively). A demon consists of a *pattern* and a *body*. At any given point in the execution of a demon-based program certain demons are deemed to be *active*. If a demon is active, and some item(s) in the input match its pattern, then the body (a piece of program) is executed. In a sense this is a bottom-up device, since the body of the demon will be performed only if the input triggers the demon via the pattern; however, the demon-based program as a whole is somewhat top-down in that only the active demons are available for triggering. To some extent the list of active demons defines what the program is 'looking for' in the input, but it will react only to those items which are actually present. The options specified by the arcs in an ATN state are similar in this respect to a small list of demons which may be activated together (like a 'packet' in Marcus' terminology). The state suggests what few options to look for (top-down), but only those arcs whose tests are satisfied will be explored (bottom-up). (This does not apply exactly to PUSH arcs, as discussed in Chapter 4.)

ATNs are often regarded as purely top-down, and demons as bottom-up, but this is slightly misleading. It is also not very illuminating to try to put every mechanism wholly into one of these categories, particularly as the most appropriate method for certain tasks may well be some mixture of the two. Also, the ATN mechanism can easily be embellished to incorporate various bottom-up devices along with the usual network grammar. Some of these, which were tried out to varying extents in the program described in Chapter 13, are described below.

8.5. *Bottom-up Devices for ATN Analysers*

Pre-tests in PUSH or NEWLEVEL arcs

Marc Eisenstadt (personal communication) has made the following observation regarding ATN grammars describing embedded constituents. Suppose that a grammar defines one of the possibilities for 'sentence' to be a 'question'; one of the possibilities for a 'question' is a 'wh-question'; a 'wh-question' starts with a 'wh-phrase'; a 'wh-phrase' starts with a 'wh-word'. In analysing the first word of a sentence, such a grammar might go through the following sequence of arc-conditions:

```
PUSH <Question>
    PUSH <WH-question>
        PUSH <WH-group>
          PUSH <WH-phrase>
            FEATURE WH
```

At this stage the input word is tested; if it turns out to be 'does' (in keeping with the hypothesis of a question), this analysis path fails — but it has to nest several levels just to achieve this. The recognition rules have decomposed the initial task very straightforwardly into simpler subtasks, so all the subtasks have to be initiated, even although the input word is unsuitable. This extra work could be avoided if the grammar-writer was able to include pre-tests in some of the PUSH arcs. Instead of a simple (PUSH WH-QUESTION) indication, ordered conjoined tests could be included, e.g. ((FEATURE WH) (PUSH WH-QUESTION)). Thus, the full search would be made only if the initial word is suitable.

Notice that this is slightly different from the device used in the program of Thorne, Bratley and Dewar (1968), where the ATN *interpreter* automatically carried out a form of pre-testing for any subnetwork, as a form of optimisation. Here, the grammar-writer can include an explicit pre-test in the ATN *grammar* in cases where he requires some very specific check. It is worth noting that simply by allowing conjoined tests (i.e. adopting the convention that a list of tests is interpreted as a set of conditions which must *all* be met), a pre-test can be incorporated anywhere in a grammar.

Some difficulties still remain. It will not necessarily be easy to find a simple pre-test which is appropriate for a particular kind of constituent, although (FEATURE WH) and (FEATURE VB) are obvious examples for wh-clauses and verb phrases. Ordinary noun phrases seem to have no natural class of initial words, since, for example, 'any', 'black', 'bananas' and 'Harry' can all start a noun phrase. (In the grammar for the experimental program, the rather dubious feature 'STARTNP' was included for this purpose, but that is not very satisfactory. Dewar (personal communication) has stated that the automatic pre-testing in the Thorne-Bratley-Dewar program relied on the presence of suitable category markings, and this also led to some otherwise unmotivated category assignments.)

Dynamic Grammar-building

It may occur that a part of the recognition rules of a grammar shows some internal pattern with certain clearly-defined variations. What is needed is some way for such generalisations to be extracted, thus simplifying the specification of the grammar. One example of this occurred while designing the MCHINE grammar for verb phrases, and the solution adopted has the consequence that the analyser is strongly guided, when analysing verb phrases, by the properties of the input. The situation is as follows.

Verbs in English may have two, one or no object(s), where 'object' is used loosely to mean, roughly, 'any post-verb constituent whose meaning is to be considered as an argument for the main verb-relation'. (See Sections 3.7 and 6.4 for a fuller discussion of English verbs.) This could be described by allowing three options in the grammar, and analysis paths could branch depending on whether the verb required two, one or zero objects. However, the situation is slightly more complicated. The surface forms that the objects may take can vary greatly and will usually depend to some extent on the particular verb involved. If this information were to be incorporated directly into the grammar the number of options (arcs) would expand excessively. On the other hand, the information concerning the quantity and surface form of the objects can be stored in the lexicon for each verb, and the grammar need only contain actions which extract this information and use it to build, in the course of the analysis, a section of transition network which sets out the relevant objects.

The sentence analyser processes verbs as follows. On encountering the main verb it accesses various syntactic properties (see Section 3.3 above) in the lexical entry which tell it how many objects there may be and how to process them. This information is conveyed by three lists (any of which may be empty). One list indicates the possible SCRs if no object is present, the second list contains pairs of SCR and ATN state-name (for single object processing), and the third list contains triples of SCR and two state-names (for double-object configurations). The analyser uses the state-names, if given, to process the object(s), if any, and uses the corresponding SCR given to build a structure round the meaning of the verb. This has the advantage of allowing the individual behaviour of verbs (in terms of how their objects are expressed and how they fit into the verb roles) to be specified separately in the lexicon, rather than itemising every possibility in the grammar. New verbs, with idiosyncratic surface constraints, can be added simply by writing an appropriate lexical entry. Role-placement SCRs do little (in the MCHINE grammar) apart from permuting objects into the deep roles and setting up the selected role which the subject of the clause, if any, will fill. Prepositions can act as clues to the analyser in processing the objects, since a verb can be marked (using the state-names in its lexical entry) as having a particular kind of prepositional phrase as an object (e.g. 'speak' takes an (indirect) object starting with 'to'). This illustrates the case-marking function of prepositions to some extent.

The construction illustrated in (84) can be included for the verb 'address' by including (85) among its single-object specifications in the lexicon, where SCR4 is some suitable role-placement rule marked as 'passive', and STPRPBY is the ATN state which 'expects' the word 'by'.

(84) I was addressed by the chairman.
(85) [SCR4 STPRPBY]

For example, in the MCHINE program (Chapter 13) the lexical entry for a verb includes (as a syntactic property) a list of object-information lists. An object-information list gives the name of the structural combining rule and the names of certain ATN states — one state for each object involved. The analyser, on encountering the verb, consults this part of the lexical entry; a surface subtree is established using the combining rule, and the states are used to construct the ATN which is then used for the next part of the analysis.

In this way the pattern (that the verb idiosyncratically determines the number and form of the objects) has been extracted and built into the actions which perform the grammar-building. As a consequence, the verb can guide the analyser more strongly than if all possible object configurations had to be tried.

Processing units triggered by words

Winograd suggests that certain words could be regarded as 'demons'. That is, instead of the recognition grammar having rules stating what to do with a particular word, the lexical entry for the word should specify an action to be performed on encountering that word (see Section 2.10). In the examples he gives (conjunctions) the actions involved are quite sweeping since they radically alter the flow of the analysis process. Winograd observes that such a mechanism is not allowed in the ordinary ATN formalism, but that is slightly misleading. The PROGRAMMAR system in which SHRDLU's parser is written allows two varieties of input analysis — (PARSE X . . .) statements and demon words — and the PROGRAMMAR interpreter must be written to handle both. In the same way, an ATN interpreter could easily be written which would examine each input word to see if it was a 'demon' before passing it on to the arc-testing routines. Such an interpreter would increase the similarities between the ATN and PROGRAMMAR methods.

Many English constructions have the consequence that an initial substring of a sentence will itself resemble a complete English sentence, e.g. (86) and (87).

(86) *He wrote several letters* after eating.
(87) *I saw the full moon* when I was in the garden.

One way to allow for this in the grammar is for such constructions to be sought explicitly in a two-stage top-down manner — find a clause, then find the second constituent. This has the slightly inelegant consequence that every sentence is ambiguous right to its clause end. That is, when analysing (87) the analyser has to consider several possibilities (one for each possible optional constituent at the end), including the case of the full sentence being (88).

(88) I saw the full moon.

What seems to be needed is some way for the analyser to process the initial clause on a single path and then consider the second clause only if it in fact is present.

An interesting approach to this problem is to let the opening word of the second clause directly influence the way that the analyser restarts its processing in the following way. Syntactic features appear in various word-tests in the recognition rules, and hence any set of syntactic features implicitly defines a subset of rules (of arcs, in an ATN grammar); namely, the set of rules such that some feature from the set appears in the condition. Hence we can define a 'restart' mechanism for the ATN interpreter: on reaching the sentence-final point in the grammar, if there are still input words to be processed, the interpreter should use the feature-list of the next word to construct a set of appropriate rules (the set of arcs associated with the feature-list constructed in the way described here) and continue processing using these rules.

Notice that this is different from Winograd's 'demons' and is aimed at covering a different set of phenomena. A demon word takes over the analysis process wherever it occurs and supplies all the necessary actions. The 'restart' facility is used only when there is no currently active set of rules (i.e. no non-trivial arcs in the current state) and there are more words to be processed; under any other circumstances the implicit mapping from words to rules is ignored.

It might be interesting to try to generalise the 'restart' mechanism so that words can select rules in situations other than clause-endings (e.g. at the start of the sentence), but this has not been explored here. A simplified 'restart' system was incorporated successfully in the experimental program.

Selecting Structural Rules by their Arguments

If a recognition grammar searches directly for two related constituents the recognition rules can specify directly what building rule should be used to combine the meanings of the two items once found. However, if the constituents are found by some less explicit method (e.g. analysing a clause, doing a restart as described above, then analysing a time-adjunct clause), there may be nowhere in the recognition grammar to specify which combining rule to use.

This deficiency can be overcome partially by having a technique which can select a combining rule on the basis of what potential arguments have been found so far. (The crudest way to implement this would be to have the analyser search the whole set of combining rules in order to find one for which the found items would be suitable inputs.)

This still leaves some difficulties. For example, if the combining rules have an input specification in terms of a list of simple predicates, a list of potential arguments may satisfy the input conditions of several different rules, particularly if some rules have very broad input conditions. This could lead to multiple ambiguity at the stage of rule-selection. This problem can be reduced by refining the classification of semantic structures so that each rule specifies as narrowly as possible what its inputs should be. However, in any real grammar several combining rules will have overlapping input specifications to an inconvenient extent. Ritchie (1977) gives a more detailed description of the problems which arose as a result of these difficulties when debugging a particular grammar. The whole question of determining inter-constituent relationships on the basis of the semantic structures of the constituents needs much more investigation.

8.6. Decisions within an ATN analyser

Let us now turn in more detail to the question of what constitutes a 'decision' during sentence-processing. One kind of action which is a definite commitment by the analyser is the building of surface structure (as described in Chapter 3). The rule-tree directly determines the final form of the analysis without any further manipulation by the analyser of the particular item involved. Also, any storage allocation which is specific to a particular grammatical category (i.e. setting up local grammatical registers, as in Chapter 5) is a prediction, since it is a step which will be inappropriate if the input turns out not to be of that type. That is why, in Chapter 4, this was classed as something which should be extracted from the PUSH command, as it was not part of the general preparation for processing any kind of constituent.

Two more confusing questions are 'look-ahead', and the use of registers to postpone decisions. Sometimes it is the case in a recognition grammar that a particular decision will be resolved completely once the next input word has been processed. A look-ahead of one word would thus avoid making an unnecessary branch point in the analysis. (The TESSA parser (Soul (1975)) includes a one-symbol look-ahead.) If the information to be extracted from the next word can be simply expressed (e.g. 'is it the word "not"?'), then the necessary look-ahead can be easily programmed in as an extra condition on an arc. However, in many cases the information required is exactly a complete parsing of the next word in context (e.g. 'can this word start a suitable noun phrase?'). This could also be directly programmed in, but it would require applying a full set of arc-tests, for some state in the grammar, to the word. This would be slightly redundant, since, if the test succeeded, the parser would then proceed to exactly that state and carry out all the processing again. Also, to be certain that the look-ahead processing was valid (in terms of the context it was performed in), it would be necessary to make all the modifications (e.g. movement of the sentence pointer) which are part of jumping to the state in question. It might be better just to allow the parser (in these more complicated cases) to continue processing, but not to regard this as non-determinism. That is, branches which last for only one word are not to be looked on as 'mistakes'.

Storing a structure in a register might seem not to be a decision, since one of the advantages of using structure-holding registers is supposed to be that structure-building decisions can be postponed. However, this depends on how the registers are used. Woods (1970, p. 601) states that using registers enables the postponement of decisions until the relevant information is available, instead of guessing and then altering the situation later. In fact, in the examples he describes, the decisions *are* made at an early stage and then changed if wrong. The grammar he gives makes quite specific initial hypotheses by placing structures into particular registers, then alters these decisions if necessary by moving the structures to other registers. There are several labelled registers, one for each aspect of the syntactic analysis being produced, and the contents of these registers at the end of the parse define the analysis constructed. That is, the assignment to structure-holding registers is effectively structure-building, since no separate tree needs to be built out of the contents of these registers later. Hence the sample grammar *does* make premature guesses about the sentence structure and revise them later — using labelled registers instead of an explicit tree-structure does not alter this fact. Registers could be used to postpone decisions by having them fulfil genuinely temporary roles but regarding them as labelled slots in the final analysis does not do this.

As discussed in Chapters 5 and 11, computational grammar uses all registers as purely temporary storage, but some of the registers may have specific names in a specific grammar (e.g. 'HEADNOUN'). Storing an item in a named register is a form of decision, but the grammar writer should employ such storage only where the decision is itself a postponement. That is, where the reason for storing the item is that only partial information is available, and where the real destination of the item, within surface structure, will be determined later.

(Ritchie (1977) contains a slightly more technical discussion of these issues, in terms of ATN mechanisms.)

8.7. Specifying Structural Locations in Advance

One further elaboration of the PUSH construct was incorporated into the MCHINE program to see what consequences it might have for the sequence of predictions and decisions during sentence-processing. NEWLEVEL arcs contained, as well as the state-names described above, a specification of where to insert the item built at the lower level. The specification could be:

(89)

(a) the word IN — meaning 'attach constituent to the surface node currently being built'.

(b) the word HOLD — meaning 'insert the constituent in the HELDSLOT register'.

(c) the name of any register — meaning 'insert the constituent in the named register'.

It was necessary to have some way of specifying where the substructure was to go, since a NEWLEVEL . . . NIL arc would not allow any 'arc-actions' to be performed at the end of the lower level, and hence the structure could not, in such cases, be put in place afterwards. Even in the cases where a later arc-action was available to manipulate the item (i.e. after a nested level), it was interesting to see if the location could be specified in advance.

In most cases the 'IN' option was the appropriate one, since the natural way to build surface structure trees was to proceed from left-to-right with most branching occurring towards the right (see Section 4.5). The 'HOLD' option was used in only two places — the noun phrase in the subject position of the sentence was not allocated to a node immediately, since the correct node was not available at that stage of the analysis; this use of the 'HOLD' option could probably have been eliminated by a more careful organisation of the structure-building at the start of the clause. Also, the 'wh-phrase' at the start of an embedded 'wh'-clause (as in 'He told me *what* you wanted') was put in HELDSLOT until it could be allocated correctly; this was because the node had to be put into two positions (i.e. in the surface structure tree and in the WHSLOT register — see (Chapter 11), but perhaps a better designed grammar could eliminate this. The power to name an arbitrary register as the destination of the structure was never used in the experimental grammar.

These findings are compatible with the use of NEWLEVEL (or PUSH) as a predictive device — if the grammar can predict that a noun phrase is about to occur it should be possible to predict where that phrase should go.

CHAPTER 9

CONVERSATIONAL STRUCTURE

9.1. The Need for Dialogue Procedures

Winograd's SHRDLU program (Section 2.10) did not include any systematic treatment of how one utterance relates to others in a conversation. A question from the person talking to SHRDLU was translated directly into a program for producing an answer and the reply was given immediately. The only example in the sample dialogue where one conversational exchange (question + answer) seems to be inserted inside another is example 22 (Winograd (1972, pp. 12–13)) where an ambiguous phrase is queried before the original question is given a reply. In this case, a stereotyped form is used, and the human's reply must be not another English sentence but an integer. Hence this is hardly a 'conversational exchange'. Pronoun reference in the program uses preceding utterances, apparently by consulting a list of the most recent sentences. Presumably, the program has a repeating sequence of instructions, so that each sentence is processed on its own with the program re-starting the process anew for the next sentence. This has the following disadvantages.

A human hearer can generally choose to answer a question or not. Although this is difficult to simulate in a program without including a set of 'beliefs' or 'goals' which might influence this choice, it is reasonable to have this decision made at an appropriate level in the model. Winograd's approach builds the choice into the semantic interpretation of the sentence, so that 'understanding' a sentence includes deciding to answer it. It seems more plausible to have some level of description of conversational behaviour at which such decisions (relating to the type of 'speech act' of the utterance (Austin (1962)) can be handled.

Also, we need to make a distinction between the

sentence-type of an utterance (declarative, interrogative, or imperative) and its illocutionary force (a statement, a question, or a command). For a simple conversation there may be a simple one-to-one relationship between the two and the distinction may be overlooked. However, they are logically separate categories — interrogatives can serve as commands and statements can be orders:

(90)
(a) Can you pass me the fingerbowl?
(b) You are not going to the party.

It might be argued that requests (e.g. (90) (a) are idioms, but that would not alter the fact that the intended response by the hearer is not the supply of information, despite the fact that the surface form of the utterance is interrogative. This suggests the need for separate levels of description which separate the hearer's reaction to the utterance from the semantic/syntactic form of the sentence. (Winograd's sample dialogue includes one command starting 'Will you please . . .', but it is not clear how it is handled by the program.)

If utterances are processed on a one-off basis, then there is no way in which different exchanges between the interlocutors can be nested inside each other. To generalise Winograd's *ad hoc* mechanism for resolving ambiguity we need some way that the hearer can suspend his reaction to a question while he seeks further information from the questioner. This may not be a simple clarification of the question, but may be, for example, information about what would constitute an adequate answer for this particular questioner, e.g.

(91)
A: Where is the Bionics Research Laboratory?
B: Do you know Sandy Bell's pub?
A: Yes.
B: The Bionics Lab is behind that.

Another related improvement that is desirable is some

way of relating utterances to higher goals. If a sentence is treated as an isolated string of words there is no way of describing how it fulfils a function in a dialogue. If a person wants to find out information he has to ask a question and know how to use the answer. He must also have some idea of what constitutes a suitable answer and how to react if this is not given.

To sum up, an adequate description of the conversational use of language will not treat a dialogue as a disconnected series of self-contained utterances.

9.2. Conversation Games

Conversational structure is not the main focus of computational grammar, but it is desirable to sketch some general environment within which sentence-processing rules operate, to ensure that the sentence analyses proposed are not based on faulty assumptions about what is needed. (Also, it was necessary in writing the computer program described in Chapter 13 to implement some form of dialogue system to allow the whole program to run.) The ideas used (as a preliminary version) are borrowed from Power (1974), but we do not follow his notation or all the details of his rules.

Dialogues are structured into instances of 'conversation games'. Each game is supposed to be a stereotyped sequence of conversational actions and reactions, with each game being associated with some purpose or task (cf. Schank (1975)). This association is wholly in the mind of the dialogue grammar-writer (or programmer) and in the way that the games operate; there is no mechanism for choosing which game to initiate by some general description of the task involved (as, for example, in the 'goal-directed invocation' of Micro-Planner, Sussman *et al*. (1972). For example, we may need an 'answering game' for replying to a question, and a 'clarification game' for seeking more information about some item referred to. A game can be thought of as a procedure, in the computational sense, i.e. a group of steps which may be regarded as a unit. One game can initiate (or 'call', to borrow the computational term) another game, so that the structure of a dialogue is built up as a sequence of sections, either consecutive or nested within each other, corresponding to invocations of games.

In most programming languages a procedure cannot, at the point where it finishes, initiate another procedure — either it terminates or it calls another procedure nested within itself, but not both simultaneously. This arrangement would be rather restrictive for conversation games, since it is desirable for one game to be able to specify what game is to be called next without having to build up a deeply nested structure for the whole conversation. For this reason, the control sequence for conversation games has been designed to allow three ways of initiating the next routine, as follows:

'nested call': suspend current game, initiate new game, but return to the suspended game when the new game terminates.
'exit-call': terminate current game and commence new game.
'exit-all-call': terminate all currently active or suspended games and commence new game.

The function of conversation games is to act as an interface between the sentence-analyser and its surroundings. That is, the currently active game initiates the operation of the sentence analyser, and, on the basis of what the analyser produces, either operates appropriately on the 'world knowledge' of the model hearer (e.g. to find the answer to a question) or moves on to a suitable game. Each game can maintain its own local information (in the same way that an ATN subnetwork can have 'local registers' — see Chapter 5), which may affect the behaviour of the sentence analyser. For example, the game could specify, when invoking the analyser, which ATN states to start at; in this way, the conversation game can influence the initial 'expectations' of the analyser, by using predictions about whether a question, statement or command is imminent to select a suitable starting state.

9.3. Some Typical Games

The details of the steps in various games will depend on the various analyses made by the linguist. Conversation games are the dialogue counterpart of ATN grammars — they merely define a mechanism which can be used to express various descriptions, providing the descriptions conform to the (very loose) definition of conversation games. It may be useful to give, as elementary examples, an outline of some of the conversation games which were incorporated into the MCHINE program (Chapter 13). They will be referred to here by the mnemonic names that were used in that program.

Initially, a game called CGREET, which expects a ritual greeting, is started up. This game does not invoke the sentence analyser, but compares the input string with a pre-set list of greetings. If no matching entry is found in this table the game CGBAFFLE is started (as an 'exit-call' — see Section 9.2 above) to convey lack of comprehension by uttering the fixed string 'Pardon?'; on the other hand, if the incoming string does match one of the entries in the greetings table CGREET makes the appropriate response, as entered in the table. It then performs an 'exit-all-call' of CGREADY.

CGREADY is an all-purpose game which applies the sentence-analyser to the next input string, starting from a neutral ATN state which will allow any sentence or phrase to be analysed. On the basis of the illocutionary type of the analysed form (interrogative, imperative, etc.) a more specialised game is then 'exit-called'.

Whenever the analyser fails to produce a result the game CGADIEU is invoked (by an 'exit-all-call') and this attempts to match the unanalysed string against a pre-set list of 'farewell' utterances. If this fails it 'exit-calls' CGBAFFLE, which in turn 'exit-calls' CGREADY; on the other hand, if it succeeds in finding a matching 'farewell' the appropriate action from the 'farewell' table is executed and the conversation is terminated.

In most dialogues the games would be invoked consecutively (i.e. using 'exit-calls') with 'exit-all-call' being used only for greetings and farewells. 'Nested calls' are used only when the current game is to be temporarily suspended while some conversational exchange takes place. This is a useful facility, since it allows the hearer to seek information from the speaker at any stage without abandoning the current exchange completely (cf. comments in Section 9.1 about the Winograd program). The only place where this was tried in the MCHINE program was in the reference evaluation of definite expressions (see Section 6.2 above). If no referent set could be computed for a definite expression the reference evaluation routine made a 'nested-call' of CGQUERY. This game put out the query 'Which . . . ?', inserting a crude English description of the item being evaluated, and then set the initial ATN state to be a state suitable for starting phrases, instead of the usual one for starting sentences. The program's interlocutor could then type in a noun phrase which would be analysed and passed up to the routine which was evaluating the definite expression. CGQUERY would terminate *without* calling another game, and the game which had been suspended at the 'nested call' would resume where it had stopped.

The other games used in the program were:
CGANS: finds out answer to a question
CGTELL: express a statement (usually an answer to a question)
CGOBEY: carry out a command
CGAWAIT: expect a command

As the above descriptions indicate, these routines are fairly primitive (and *ad hoc*). However, they serve to illustrate the kind of conversational unit which is being proposed here.

CHAPTER 10

SUMMARY OF THE FRAMEWORK

10.1. The Story So Far

Chapters 1 to 9 have provided the background to computational grammar in terms of assumptions, influences from other sources and arguments in favour of various facilities. We can now provide a summary of the whole computational grammar framework. First, it is useful to give a brief recapitulation of the points covered so far.

The aim is to examine the structure of the English language and the way that this structure could be used by a hypothetical hearer. The research strategy is to write a recognition grammar for a subset of English (or several fragments of grammar). Sentence processing proceeds in a strict left-to-right order and as much semantic processing is carried out at each stage as seems feasible. The analyser attempts to make only those decisions which are justified at any given point at the input, rather than using exhaustive, mistake-driven techniques. To achieve this, registers are used to avoid premature decisions. In describing grammatical phenomena a clear distinction is made between syntagmatic, paradigmatic and other types of description, so that these dimensions may be treated independently if necessary. No separate syntactic structure is built, but a tree structure based on hierarchically organised structural combining rules is used instead. There are many different structural rules as they have to make all the distinctions previously made by syntactic rules and semantic rules. Where the analyser encounters possible ambiguity, it develops both paths in parallel, but there is a provision for ordering the paths relative to each other. Constituents are processed at separate levels, with independent local register space, in a way that avoids the creation of too many different levels. The semantic system includes some form of sense/reference distinction and allows expressions to refer to non-existent objects. Syntactic classification is in terms of binary features aimed at guiding the analyser explicitly, and syntactic properties to guide the structure building routines. A system of conversational rules is used to describe certain aspects of sentence usage which are inappropriate to include in the sentence-grammar.

The framework will be described in eight sections, as follows:

10.2 Structural Combining Rules
These combine semantic items to form other semantic items.

10.3 Recognition Rules
These direct the flow of input-processing.

10.4 Semantic Representation
This defines the constructs available for building meanings.

10.5 Syntactic Properties and Features
These markings allow arbitrary processing information to be marked on structures.

10.6 Analysis Procedure
This sets out how the sentence interpretation proceeds.

10.7 Registers
These are the facilities for storing information during sentence-analysis.

10.8 Conversational Routines
These have not been greatly developed but are included to provide a level of description outside the sentence.

10.9 Guidelines for Analyses
Some informal rules are provided for applying the apparatus of Sections 10.2–10.8.

No formal definitions are presented here and all the concepts are described in an informal way. The outline is brief but Chapters 1 to 9 present the arguments in favour of the various methods and the program described in Ritchie (1977) (which is summarised briefly in Chapter 13) offers a possible elaboration of the details.

10.2. Structural Combining Rules

These rules are on the conceptual boundary between 'syntax' and 'semantics' and so are hard to allocate to either category. They are very similar to the 'projection rules' of Katz and Fodor (1963), or the 'semantic specialists' of Winograd (1972), since they combine semantic items to form other semantic items. On the other hand, the gradual setting up of rules and arguments while processing a sentence (see Section 10.6 below) results in a tree-building process like a traditional syntactic parse. One way to look at a structural combining rule is to regard it as the pairing of a Montague syntactic rule with its corresponding semantic rule (Montague (1970a, b)).

A *structural combining rule* (SCR) consists of:

(92)

(a) Rule body: the operations to be performed on the inputs. At present, these can be any manipulation, and there is no basic set of 'primitive semantic operations'.

(b) Input specification: a list of semantic predicates, one for each argument-place, which states what kind of items are allowable as arguments (like type restrictions in some programming languages). The semantic predicates will be composed from sense classes and sense properties.

(c) Output specification: this allows the result produced by the rule to be explicitly labelled with some semantic classification. The output specification will be either a referential class or a function which produces a referential class by combining information about the inputs to the rule in some way. (See Ritchie (1976) for some of the reasons for this.)

(d) Property inheritance rule (optional): for each argument place, a list of syntactic property names. This is used for handling temporary structural information during the sentence analysis process (see Section 10.6) and does not directly affect the semantic structure produced by the structural combining rule.

The way that structural combining rules are used will be explained in more detail in Section 10.6.

10.3. Recognition Rules

The linguistic model will use the concepts of an ATN/ PROGRAMMAR system subject to the modifications described in earlier chapters. The exact notation is not important but the ATN terminology is adopted here for ease of exposition. This is not a formal mathematical definition but it is intended to be clear.

A *recognition grammar* is defined to be a set of *states*. A state is an (unordered) set of *arcs*. Notice that 'state' has a very specific use here (meaning 'set of arcs') and is not exactly synonymous with the general notion of 'machine-state' or 'computational context', although a 'state' does represent part of the computational state of the ATN portion of the analyser. Since an augmented transition network is based on a directed graph the term 'node' could have been used, but this would be excessively confusing since 'nodes' are used elsewhere in the model. Notice also that the notion of 'subnetwork' does not need to be defined since the notion of 'jumping to' or 'activating' a subnetwork uses just the first state of the subnetwork. The interconnected aspect of states in a subnetwork is never used directly by the interpreter when making the jump to its initial state. The reason that a state is not defined as an *ordered* set of arcs is that no principled way of ordering the arcs has been found; if some use could be made of a 'priority' rating for each arc, that would have been included.

An arc consists of an *arc-head*, an *arc-action* and a *state-specification*. An arc-head can be any truth-valued function of one argument, but certain classes of tests are particularly useful, as follows:

FEATURE: gives a list of features which must be present on lexical entry for input word.

CATEGORY: gives a predicate which must be true of the entire lexical entry for input word.

PROPERTY: gives a syntactic property name and value that must be present on lexical entry for input word.

SEMANTIC: gives a predicate that must be true of the semantic item in the entry for input word.

WORD: specifies exactly what the input word must be.

RUN: provides a piece of program to be executed, leaving no result, but having side-effects.

TEST: provides a piece of program to test arbitrary aspects of the environment.

NEWLEVEL: gives a state-name to activate at the new level and a place to put the item found at the new level (see Chapter 4).

Obviously this set of tests is redundant — all possible testing could be done with just TEST. However, this subdivision makes the content of the tests more obvious to the grammar-writer and highlights what different types of tests are being used — RUN is a particularly undesirable trick and should not be allowed to hide. Any of these tests can be logically conjoined or negated thus allowing arbitrary Boolean combinations.

An arc-action is any operation (taking no arguments) which returns no result. A state-specification consists of either a special null marker or a pair comprising a state and a *tag*. A tag can be one of two indicators, signalling one of two possible options to the interpreter of these rules — whether or not the next word is to be taken in before moving to the specified state.

10.4. Semantic Representation

The semantic system is discussed at greater length in Chapter 6, so just an outline is presented here.

There is a set of *relations*. Each relation has associated with it:

(93)
(a) A set of *roles*
(b) A set of *role-restrictions*

(c) An *expanded form*
(d) An *elaborated form*

Semantic structures are constructed from relations in the following way. A *relation-instance* consists of:

(94)
(a) A *relation*
(b) A list of *role-values*
(c) A *truth-value*

(See Section 6.3 for examples.) A role-restriction is a truth-valued function of one argument which limits what items may be associated with that role. An expanded form is a relation-instance, with certain special role-values; these are needed to indicate how the entries in the expanded form correspond to the entries in the main relation (see Section 6.3). An elaborated form is a triple of procedures — two have side-effects but no result, and the other produces a truth-value.

A *semantic network* consists of a set of relation-instances with truth-values either 'TRUE' or 'FALSE'.

A *definer* consists of a pair comprising a relation-instance and a role, where the role is one of the roles associated with the relation in the relation-instance (see Section 6.5).

There are various *sense properties*, each with a set of possible *values* (the 'range' of that property) and a sense-property *name*. A *sense-property list* is a set of pairs, each pair comprising the name of a sense property and a value from the range of that sense property. While being processed or constructed a semantic structure may have associated with it a sense-property list which indicates how the structure is to be processed.

There are certain operations which can be carried out on semantic structures. These include matching one piece of semantic network against another, setting the truth-value of a relation-instance to 'TRUE' or 'FALSE', using a definer to produce an item from a network and inserting an item in a network at a point indicated by a definer. As in the case of structural combining rules (Section 10.2) no particular primitive set of operations has been found.

10.5. Syntactic Properties and Features

Each grammar contains a set of *syntactic features*.

Every lexical entry has a set (possibly empty) of features which is a subset of the full set of syntactic features.

An arc-head (see Section 10.3) may stipulate presence or absence of any set of syntactic features.

The *associated arc-set* of any feature is the set of arcs which include that feature in their arc-heads. The associated arc-set of a set of features is the union of the associated arc-sets of the members of the set of features.

The *associated state* of a list of features is the state composed of the arcs in the associated arc-set of the list of features.

Syntactic features do not appear anywhere else in the recognition grammar and are not used at all by any of the structural combining rules or the semantic network system.

Each grammar contains a set of *syntactic properties*.

Each syntactic property has an associated set of *values*, known as the *range* of the property, and a *syntactic property name*.

Each lexical entry has a *syntactic property list*, which either is empty or is a set of pairs of the form (<syntactic property name>, <value>), where the <value> comes from the range of the syntactic property associated with the syntactic property name.

Each node (see Section 10.6) may have a syntactic property list, which is defined in the same way.

Syntactic properties may be included in arc-heads, arc-actions or any of the node-manipulating routines. They are not used by the structural combining rules (except via the property inheritance rules, where these exist) or by the semantic network system.

10.6. Analysis Procedure

There is a device called an *analyser* which takes as input a string of words, a context and an *initial state* (i.e. one of the 'states' of the recognition rules). There is a slight redundancy here in that the context could be taken to include the other two inputs, since the context represents a global computational environment. However, it is clearer to phrase it this way so as to emphasise that these two inputs are essential for the analyser, whereas extraction of information from the context may not always occur. The definition of 'word' is not relevant here — we will assume an adequate definition can be given at some stage — but each word has an associated *lexical entry*. A lexical entry consists of a triple — a semantic item, a syntactic property list and a syntactic feature list (see Section 10.5). Any of these parts of the triple may have a null entry but no lexical entry may have all three null. For each substring which starts at the beginning of the input string (i.e. each 'initial segment') the analyser has a set (possibly empty) of *partial analyses* (sometimes called 'partial paths'). If the segment is in fact the whole string the set is referred to as the set of *complete analyses of the string*. The last word in the initial segment concerned is referred to as the *current word* of the analysis. An analysis (partial or complete) consists of a state, a context and a *weight*. (Again, this is a redundant description, in that both the state and the weight could be included in the context, but the presentation here seems clearer.) The weight is a number greater than or equal to zero. The context includes the value of all registers (interpreter and grammatical) and the state of the main semantic network, and so can represent any structuring or side-effects. The state is referred to as the *current state* and is originally set to be the initial state. That is, the list of partial analyses associated with the empty initial segment is set to be the input context, the initial state and the weight zero.

The analyser makes one scan through the input string keeping a list of partial analyses which is altered as the analyser processes progressively larger initial segments. For each initial segment (i.e. for each current word) the analyser performs the following procedure on each partial analysis on the list. It finds all the arcs in the current state for which the test in the arc-head yields true if applied to the current word. For each of these arcs a new partial analysis is created (from the one being processed at the moment), the arc-action is executed in that analysis and the state-specification is used to select a new current state for the new analysis (except in the case of NEWLEVEL arcs — see below — where the state is selected in a different manner). The new list of partial analyses is made up of all partial analyses produced in that way.

There is one special type of arc, the NEWLEVEL arc, and one special action, POPUP, which must be described in detail. Processing occurs in the analyser at various *levels* only one of which is current (in any given partial analysis) at one time. Different levels have their own workspace, in terms of both interpreter registers and grammatical registers, and therefore the analysis can use a new level to process a constituent independently, using information distinct from that at a previous level. Levels are created when the analyser encounters a NEWLEVEL arc, using the information in the arc. The arc-head in a NEWLEVEL arc does not contain a test but indicates some state in the recognition rules, and the state-specification may be null. When a NEWLEVEL arc is processed the state given in the arc-head is set as the new current state and the registers are modified in the following way. If the state-specification is null then the structure for the old level is attached to its appropriate destination in the surface structure and all the interpreter registers (apart from the one which keeps track of the grammatical registers) are cleared. If the state-specification is not null it is pushed on to the continuation stack (see Section 10.7), the arc-action is pushed on to the action stack and all the interpreter registers are pushed down. Thus there are two ways of creating new levels — destructively, with all processing information from the old level being discarded, and by embedding, with all processing information from the old one being stored on stacks.

The POPUP action is, in a sense, the reverse of a NEWLEVEL arc. It causes the current level to be left and processing to return to the last level which has been saved; if none has been saved, special action is taken (see below). When POPUP is executed the structure built at the current level is attached to its destination, the grammatical structure-storing registers currently active are tidied up (see

Section 10.9) and the interpreter registers are popped up. Processing continues from the state given by the state-specification popped off the continuation stack.

If no previous level has been saved on stacks and there are still words to be processed the analyser performs a *restart* (see Section 8.5). That is, it sets up new structures on which to build, and computes a new state from which to process, using the associated state of the syntactic feature list of the next word (see Section 10.5). If no such state can be found the analysis is terminated (i.e. removed from the partial analysis list). On the other hand, if no words are left the analyser winds up the analysis by checking that all the structural combining rules so far built into the tree have been applied (see below).

The semantic structure produced by the analyser is the result of applying structural combining rules to combine the semantic entries for the lexical entries of the input words, and applying further combining rules to combine the semantic items thus formed, and so on in a hierarchical fashion. The analysis process consists of working out which lexical items to use as inputs to which combining rules, and which combining rules to use thereafter. The input-output relationships operate hierarchically (see Section 3.1, 3.2), and the lexical entries are examined in a left-to-right order, so the whole process can be looked on as building a tree from left to right. The analyser keeps track of this building up of rules and arguments by creating structures called *nodes*. A node contains a structural combining rule, a list of the nodes which will contain its arguments and a place for the result produced by applying that rule to those arguments. Each node can have syntactic properties (see Section 10.5) associated with it to help the analyser connect nodes correctly. When a node containing a rule is created, nodes are built below it to carry the argument values that will subsequently be inserted. These nodes are constructed using information in the rule (e.g. how many arguments it needs) and are called *dummy nodes*.

A dummy node contains restrictions for some or all of its entries, constraining what items can later be filled in on them. These restrictions will come from various sources during the analysis, including the semantic rule on the node immediately dominating the dummy node. (In some ways, dummy nodes are like the complex symbols of Chomsky (1965).) *Evaluating* a rule-node consists of applying the semantic rule at that node to the semantic items on the daughter nodes. A lexical entry is allocated to an input slot in an SCR (structural combining rule) by creating a rule node for the SCR, creating a node which contains the semantic part of the lexical entry (and has the syntactic properties of the lexical entry), and inserting the latter node as one of the 'argument nodes' of the former node. The syntactic properties of lexical entries can be passed up the nodes if the SCR has a property inheritance rule (see Section 10.2). A property inheritance rule for an n-argument SCR will be of the form (L1, . . ., Ln), where each Li is a list of syntactic property names. For each value of i between 1 and n the specified property values of the ith node will be entered on the syntactic property list of the dominating SCR node (and should not then be altered). Evaluating a SCR-node consists of applying the SCR to the semantic items contained in the argument (daughter) nodes. If the daughter is also a rule-node a check is made first to see that it has been evaluated and the property inheritance rules (for the daughter) are applied at that stage.

At the end of the sentence the topmost node in the SCR tree is evaluated and hence the whole tree of rules is evaluated (by the recursive system just outlined). The analyser associates with each complete path a list of *result-pairs*. A result-pair consists of the semantic item from the root of the rule tree and the corresponding context. (The latter can then encode, for some higher level process, any alterations to the 'world' which have resulted from the process of analysing the sentence.) The list of result-pairs is chosen by scanning the complete analyses for the sentence and selecting those which have the lowest weight. (There should be only one result-pair in this list unless the sentence is 'ambiguous'.)

This description does not describe every detail of the analysis process but it should be sufficient to integrate the descriptions in earlier chapters (which may themselves elucidate the mechanisms), and it covers most of the important points. Ritchie (1977) describes one particular implementation of this kind of analyser, and that may give some indication of how some of the vaguer aspects of the outline here can be realised.

10.7. Registers

There are certain *registers* which are used in the sentence-analysis process. The *interpreter registers* (i.e. those which are part of the framework — see Section 5.2) are as follows:

Continuation stack: holds the state to be used on terminating the current level (see Chapter 4).

Action stack: holds the action to be taken (if any) on leaving the current level.

Register stack: holds the list of grammatical registers in use at current level.

Holding register: can be used to hold the structure being built at a lower level, prior to attachment to the main surface structure (see Section 8.7).

Temporary register: a single slot for temporary work-space.

Shelf: a slot which can hold input words temporarily on a last-in-first-out basis. This is not referred to as a 'stack register' since its storage space does not 'pop' up or 'push' down with changing processing levels.

Current node: pointer to surface structure currently being worked on.

Top node: pointer to topmost node of subtree being worked on at this level.

Top nodes: list of subtrees so far built at this level.

Treetop: the overall result of the analysis.

In addition, the grammar-writer can define any register he wishes, designating them as either 'structure-holding' (i.e. to be included in the 'tidying-up' process — see Section 10.9, below) or 'pointer-holding'. There are constructs available for activating registers at the current level and for performing arbitrary manipulations on them.

The three stack registers above (continuation, action and register) always stack or unstack together when level-changes occur, so it would be possible to replace them with a single register (a 'control stack') which contains composite items recording all the information. This would not be a significant change.

10.8. Conversation Routines

As commented in Chapter 9, conversational structure is not a central part of computational grammar, but it was necessary to implement some dialogue system to test out the experimental program (Chapter 13). This outline is based on Power (1974) but does not follow his notation closely. The main points of the system are as follows.

Dialogues are structured into instances of *conversation games*. A game is simply a procedure, with various properties, that performs certain tasks.

A game is essentially an ordinary procedure, except for some unusual ways in which it can be invoked. When any game is in progress another game can be initiated in any of three ways — a 'nested' call, where the current game may be continued when the new game is finished; an 'exit' call, where the current game is immediately terminated before commencing the new game; an 'exit-all' call, where all games currently in progress are immediately terminated before commencing the new game.

The tasks performed by the games are not restricted, but they are mainly intended to furnish the interface between the sentence analyser and the 'world knowledge' of the hearer. A game initiates sentence-processing by providing the appropriate arguments (string, context and state) to the sentence analyser (see Section 10.6) when an input utterance is required. A game also uses the result-pair from the analyser to modify the world model of the hearer in a way defined by the details of the particular game. The operations carried out by various games will depend on the conversational analyses made by the linguist.

10.9. Guidelines for Analyses

As observed in Section 1.1, linguistic theories generally have a collection of techniques and concepts which are employed in applying the theory. Many of these are not explicitly stated and linguists may sometimes not be aware that they are making implicit methodological assumptions. This section outlines those aspects pertaining more to the application of the devices outlined in earlier sections of Chapter 10, rather than to the formal properties of those devices. To some extent the rules-of-thumb here characterise the notion of '*ad hoc* solution' for a computational grammar.

One question that has to be considered is where in the model to describe particular patterns. In a description which uses several syntactic and semantic mechanisms it may not be obvious where a given generalisation should be located.

Generally, the role of the SCRs (structural combining rules) is to separate out any syntagmatic regularities. If there are several examples X1Y1, X2Y2, . . . XnYn, where the relationship between constituent Xi and constituent Yi is the same in each case, this relationship can be most economically represented by putting it in the SCR used to combine the Xi Yi pairs, rather than trying to build this syntagmatic pattern into either the Xis or the Yis. On the other hand, if we have examples X1Zi, . . . X1Zn, where there seems to be some semantic similarity between the pairs, and no examples Y1Zi with this semantic property, it is neater to try to capture this pattern in the representation of X1. Some kind of balance must be struck between these two approaches — an SCR which only ever occurs with one particular value for its first argument is slightly *ad hoc*; conversely, a whole battery of semantic items with some common property directed towards syntagmatic combination suggests that a generalisation is being missed. (This principle underlies the arguments in Section 3.6 concerning modifier-head relationships.)

Related to this is a need to avoid proliferating lexical items. We do not want to describe different usages of a particular surface word by producing a different lexical item for each use. As far as possible we should account for different nuances of meaning by having the same item interact in different ways with the context (both linguistic and situational). This last point is an example of a fairly general principle which might be termed *localised semantic description*. The idea is that for ease of semantic computation in the surface structure tree all decisions are carried out at an independent, local level as far as possible. If we can arrange our semantic description so that each noun phrase, for example, constructs its own semantic representation without much reference to its surroundings, the rules can be written in a more modular fashion. Different uses of a noun phrase would then have to be described by appropriate differences in the SCRs that combine them with other structures, or in the way that they react with other structures once combined.

If some aspect of a constituent cannot be processed within that constituent, but has to be held until some more global information (either higher up the SCR tree, or in the conversational context) is available, then the way of representing this aspect may change. When the processing happens locally it may be possible to describe this property as a function acting on an argument, for example. If the property is uninterpretable locally its contribution cannot be expressed as a function-application occurring at the local level, and it must be held in some static form which a higher semantic item can react with later, or which can be manipulated by a higher SCR.

Section 3.6 gives some examples of situations where a generalisation can be extracted into an SCR. The assumption of localised semantic description underlies several of the analyses in earlier chapters, particularly Section 6.2. Chapter 12 includes examples of information which cannot be integrated at a local level but must be interpreted by a higher rule.

As stated earlier (Sections 1.3 and 1.6) computational grammar assumes that sentences or dialogues which sound 'odd' must contain (or result from) some anomalous structure or process. This criterion has not generally been used in artificial intelligence language programs. For example, recognition rules are sometimes given which will accept uncritically an endless stream of auxiliary verbs. The justification is that these rules will work correctly on correct input and their behaviour on ill-formed strings is completely irrelevant. However, if we adhere to the principle of relating oddity and anomaly (subject at least to a partial specification of what constitutes anomaly), then grammars must be more carefully constructed.

Since the focus of this investigation is on the sentence-analysis process, the guidelines for writing the recognition rules are important. As discussed in Chapter 8, grammars should not be allowed unlimited power to revoke decisions once made. Unlimited look-ahead should be avoided for the following reasons. The computational grammar model uses strict left-to-right processing, taking in one word at each stage. If the analyser requires to test a word somewhere 'ahead' in the input it should explicitly store the intervening items somewhere and process them later. If this can be managed then the look-ahead is permissible — the analyser is 'remembering' the string of words before starting to process them. However, if the look-ahead is a hidden way of parsing a later item before the current word, it is obscuring the true flow of decisions and should be avoided. (Martin Kay (at the Workshop on Theoretical Issues in Natural Language Processing, Cambridge, Mass., June 1975) commented that look-ahead could often be backtracking in disguise; look-ahead, he suggested, moved the sentence-pointer forward but left the label 'YOU ARE HERE' behind.) The exception to this is the 'one-word look-ahead' discussed in Chapter 8; this is not so much look-ahead as delaying, until the next word is taken in, all the actions that might have to be performed at the current point. Since the actions will be performed (or abandoned) immediately there is no need to store anything.

As commented in Chapter 5, it may be possible to use unnamed, general purpose registers for storage during sentence-analysis ('work registers'). There is no clear criterion for when these can or should be used, although it seems appropriate to use them when the item in question has not been analysed and so cannot be allocated to a very specifically named register (e.g. if indulging in explicit look-ahead in the way described above). In the interests of seeing how far this concept can be taken two work registers have been included among the interpreter registers — TEMPORARY and SHELF.

It seems plausible to suggest that a structure stored in a grammatical register must eventually be used, either by being incorporated into a larger structure, or by being discarded after some information has been extracted from it. Let us assume that the interpreter can distinguish pointer-holding registers from structure-holding registers. An intuitively attractive principle is that all structures built at a particular level should be explicitly used before leaving that level. That is, all structures which have been temporarily stored in structure-holding registers should be removed from these registers and either attached to some larger structure or else explicitly discarded (perhaps because all their information has been recorded in some way, as with an auxiliary verb). This is not to say that structures cannot be left lying in a register while a *lower* constituent is processed; it is just that such items should not be lost when the interpreter exits to a higher level and restores all the stacks. The grammar-writer should discipline himself so that any operations which use items from registers to build structure (as opposed to merely examining the registers) simultaneously remove those items leaving the registers empty. Then the interpreter, before leaving a given level, can check that all the structure-holding stacks that it is about to pop are empty. If any are not, it should try to use up the left-over items before leaving that level. This 'using-up' process will have to be fairly general and based on formal properties of the current surface structure, since it will have to be programmed into the interpreter, not the grammar. A first approximation might be to attempt to attach the spare structure on the bottommost empty node (cf. Kimball (1974)). Uses of this *tidying up principle* will be discussed in Chapter 11.

As defined in Section 5.2, a 'flag' is a register with a small, fixed range of values used for recording the presence or absence of some condition. These can be very useful devices allowing the same analysis network to be used for two similar phenomena with minor differences recorded in flags (Bobrow and Fraser (1969)). However, they should not be allowed to obscure the real relationships between various conditions and operations in sentence-analysis. For example, the fact that a clause has a passive verb form conveys information about the way that deep semantic roles (or 'cases' — see Section 6.4) will be arranged in that clause. Using a two-valued flag at various stages during structure-building is one way of handling this, but it may not be the most transparent. If possible, the consequences of a particular construction occurring in a sentence should be recorded or carried out as directly as possible. This complaint about arbitrary flags is analogous to the criticism of using arbitrary syntactic features to record (temporarily) a particular fact which is later decomposed into heterogeneous consequences (Section 3.1).

As discussed in Chapter 8, an analyser which handles decisions by exhaustive exploration is less interesting than one which manages to postpone decisions until sufficient information is available to resolve them. Ideally, an analyser which only ever maintained one (correct) analysis throughout the parsing of an unambiguous sentence would be extremely elegant. It therefore seems desirable to write grammars in such a way that the analyser has to 'branch' as rarely as possible.

So far, all the points mentioned in this subsection have been fairly peripheral to computational grammar. Most of them are not hard rules but rough guidelines. Some of them suggest ways of 'keeping the grammar clean', others are suggestions for ideas to try out. The points which follow may be slightly more important, since they serve to clarify the notion of a 'structural combining rule'.

In transformational grammar (at least in the 'Aspects' model) most phenomena were handled by one mechanism — the transformation (see Section 2.2 for a discussion of that approach). In computational grammar there are various ways to handle grammatical constructions. Descriptions previously formulated in terms of transformations can largely be replaced by descriptions employing two techniques — using structure-holding registers or defining several different SCRs.

For example, there were good syntactic arguments for the transformation of 'Subject-Verb Inversion' (Chomsky (1957), Burt (1972)), whereby the auxiliary verb at the start of a 'yes-no' question was described as part of the main verb phrase of the sentence. When writing a recognition grammar this notion again arises. It is rather clumsy to have to specify all the possible auxiliaries at two points in the grammar and use elaborate interconnections to relate the auxiliary at the start of a question to the following verb phrase. It is much simpler to store the question-auxiliary in a register (without recording all the information from it, but noting that the sentence is interrogative), and extract it later when commencing the verb phrase. This seems to be a very direct expression of the Chomskyan transformation. Although the phenomena which supported this strategy are the same as those used in a transformational argument, the justification comes from the *simplification of the parsing rules with no allied complication of any other part of the grammar*.

On the other hand, the different surface configurations of deep semantic roles (Sections 3.7, 6.4) are not amenable to such obvious re-ordering manipulations. Transformations such as 'Dative Movement' and 'Passive' were intended to shuffle subjects, objects and indirect objects into a canonical structure, resulting in a simpler statement of co-occurrence relations. However, co-occurrence relations are based on semantic properties (Lakoff and Ross (1967), McCawley (1968)) rather than on surface syntactic form. Hence such re-ordering would not simplify the recognition rules, since these handle the structural options available at surface level; this is not where the generalisation is. It might be, however, that the set of SCRs could be simplified using re-ordering operations; for example, we might need only one two-object rule instead of two separate rules if we replace Dative Movement by a register manipulation at the surface. As was discussed in Section 3.7, there are various factors which suggest that it might be better to use separate SCRs rather than re-ordering using registers. Given this, there is no motivation for attempting to include a re-ordering operation.

Generally, it is the overall simplicity of the grammar that decides whether to multiply the set of SCRs or to re-order constituents directly. Re-ordering is usually appropriate where the generalisation is describable in surface syntactic terms, since then (and only then) it should simplify the recognition rules. Where the pattern is semantic, the decision will depend on whether re-ordering would greatly complicate the recognition rules and whether the SCRs can be significantly reduced or simplified.

This brings up another point concerning the ordering of arguments in SCRs. The SCRs are functions whose arguments must be ordered so as to distinguish them, as with any mathematical function. Complications can arise when the same notational device (namely, left-to-right order) is used to represent this arbitrary ordering as is used to represent temporal ordering in the words of a sentence (see, for example, the chaotic arguments of McCawley (1970)). The crucial point seems to be this. Since the SCRs are used to process a temporally-ordered sequence, there is an ordering imposed on the SCR argument-slots, other than just the arbitrary order used to distinguish them — namely, the ordering determined by the order of processing of the individual arguments. 'First argument' in an SCR effectively means the 'first to be allocated to a slot in the SCR'. (This temporal ordering can then be used to distinguish the argument places, since any ordering achieves that.) A definition like this restricts SCR surface-trees to being built in a particular order (notationally, left-to-right) with no 'gaps' being left to be filled later. (In fact, the experimental program did use strict left-to-right building as this made it much easier to keep track of the structure being built.) So far no examples have been found which are difficult to handle in this way. Therefore we can adopt the principle that the ordering of SCR argument-places is significantly related to surface ordering and that arguments must be inserted in left-to-right order. (See Isard (1974) for some related comments on trees and processing order.)

CHAPTER 11

ENGLISH WH-CLAUSES

11.1. The Surface Structure of Wh-clauses

English relative clauses, and certain question-forms, share a common surface structure consisting of a sentence (or partial sentence) with a 'wh-word' ('who', 'what', etc.) at the beginning.

(95)
(a) *What did you use?*
(b) The car *which is parked outside* has a flat tyre.
(c) The man *who you sold the book to* wants his money back.
(d) *When did he leave the house?*

This formal similarity suggests that these clauses ('wh-clauses') may be describable in similar terms. This subsection examines how a recognition grammar can handle the surface form of wh-clauses, and later subsections will examine the semantic regularities involved.

The way that wh-clauses have been described in transformational analysis is as follows. The clause is regarded as a complete sentence where one constituent (usually regarded as a noun phrase) has been converted to a 'wh-phrase' (either a wh-word or a phrase starting with 'which', 'what', or 'how') and moved to the beginning of the clause from some position within the clause. This way of looking at the structure has certain advantages, since the relationships between the wh-phrase and the rest of the clause are generally the same as those which would hold between an NP in the 'original' position and the rest of the clause. Semantically, the wh-phrases in (95) can be regarded as displaced versions of the object, subject, indirect object and time-adjunct, respectively. Syntactically, subject-verb agreement seems to occur between the wh-phrase and the main verb of the wh-clause if the 'original' position is that of subject (cf. (95) (b)). Fuller arguments for this way of describing wh-clauses can be found in Kuroda (1966), Burt (1972), Chomsky (1964) and Ross (1967).

In the framework being used here there are two ways to describe wh-clauses. One way would be to accept the spirit of the transformational analysis and write a recognition grammar which attempts to locate the wh-phrase in its 'original' place in the clause. Alternatively, we could postulate a wh-clause SCR which takes the meaning of a wh-phrase as its first argument, and the meaning of a sentence (or partial sentence) as second argument, and produces a suitable semantic form. The former approach has been adopted here because of the following difficulties with the latter method.

Firstly, the wh-clause SCR would have to duplicate all the semantic intra-sentential relationships (e.g. subject-to-verb, time-adjunct-to-main clause, etc.) since these can all be used between wh-phrases and their associated clauses.

Secondly, the wh-clause SCR would have to include subject-verb agreement as a special case, since it would be treating an 'object' wh-phrase and a 'subject' wh-phrase as merely two possible options in a list of relationships.

Thirdly, the criteria for deciding which intra-sentential relationships to use are not primarily semantic (i.e. they are not based on the semantic structure of the two arguments for the putative SCR) but are surface syntactic. If the wh-clause sentence lacks a *surface* subject then the wh-phrase can be used regardless of what deep roles (in the terms of Section 6.4) are filled.

Fourthly, if the sentence-part of the wh-clause is a sentence-fragment (i.e. lacking a subject or object), then this cannot be analysed correctly by the simple sentence recognition procedure. For example, if we assume that 'say' must have a surface object, then (96) (a) is an acceptable sentence, but the sentence fragments (b) and (c) are not.

(96)
(a) What did you say?

(b) *Did you say?
(c) *You say?

Hence some recognition procedure is needed for the second part of a wh-clause which is different (albeit in some minor fashion) from the simple sentence grammar, and which takes into account the fact that a wh-clause is being processed.

Both SHRDLU and LSNLIS parsers (see Sections 2.10, 2.11) adopt this approach, using structure-holding registers to perform the task. On encountering a wh-clause, the opening wh-phrase is processed and stored temporarily in a register. The rest of the clause is then processed by a procedure which is similar to the sentence procedure, except that it may use the item stored in that register as part of the surface structure. This general strategy was incorporated in the grammar referred to in Chapter 13, but some interesting questions still remain. In particular, how do we ensure that the analyser processes the sentence successfully, and uses the stored wh-item in a suitable place?

Consider a sentence like (95) (d) above. The sentence part of the wh-clause ('did he leave the house') constitutes a complete clause, and so the analyser should find the right surface structure for it without failing. On attempting to leave the level at which the wh-clause has been processed, the tidying up procedure (see Section 10.9) will cause the wh-phrase left in WHSLOT (the register allocated to this purpose) to be found. Suppose we incorporate into the tidying-up procedure the option of performing rule-selection (see Section 8.5) to combine the left-over item with the current subtree. If this works, the Time-Adjunct SCR (see Chapter 12) should be selected, and the wh-phrase attached as a time-adjunct to the sentence part of the wh-clause. A similar analysis might work for place adjuncts, e.g. 'Where did he see you?'. However, wh-clauses in which the wh-phrase has to be treated as an obligatory surface structure constituent (such as subject, object or indirect object), cannot be handled in this way. Consider (95) (a). If the grammar requires 'use' to have a surface object, and the analyser does not find one after the verb, it may discontinue the analysis (since we are assuming that the analyser will not treat strings like 'Did you use?' as acceptable sentences). The tidying-up process is invoked only on leaving a level (at a 'POPUP', in the ATN terminology), so it would not help here, unless we introduced the additional principle that, before abandoning an analysis, the analyser should first try to leave the current level. Even if this could be made to work it would be suitable only for situations where the wh-phrase has to be located at the end of the sentence fragment. If the wh-phrase has to be put in subject position (as in (95) (b)) the lack of a constituent will show up long before it is feasible to leave the level of the wh-clause. One solution might be to have another general principle that, if a failure is about to occur, the analyser should try to use any structures in the current set of grammatical registers to fill the current structural requirement, and, if successful, continue. This is unattractive, for two reasons. It is introduced simply to patch up this problem, with no other justification. Moreover, it needs a clear definition of what would be regarded as the 'current structural requirement' and where (in the recognition rules) to re-commence if the structure-filling process succeeds.

It turns out that there is one quite neat way to ensure that the stored item is available exactly as needed. Notice that the wh-phrase can be regarded as a form of 'noun phrase' (cf. the transformational version of this phenomenon) and wh-phrases will always be allocated to a position that a 'noun phrase' could have filled. We can therefore write the noun phrase grammar (i.e. an ATN subnetwork) so that one of the options is to look in WHSLOT for a stored structure. Then, at any point where the analyser is looking for a noun phrase, it can fulfil this expectation by using the stored wh-item, if one is present. Using this trick has certain advantages. It means that the sentence fragment in a wh-clause can be processed using exactly the same network as is needed for an ordinary sentence — the insertion of the stored wh-item will happen if and only if it has been stored. Also, it allows the wh-item to occupy any position that a noun phrase could have occupied, without separate rules for each case. In particular, since a prepositional phrase includes a noun phrase, dangling prepositions (e.g. (97) (a) and (b)) will be automatically covered.

(97)
(a) Who did you speak to?
(b) The man that I was addressed by is here.

This will not interfere with the method already outlined above for optional adjuncts. By virtue of being optional the adjunct wh-phrase will not be sought by the sentence grammar (via the NP network) and so should still be in the WHSLOT at the end of the level.

11.2. The Complex Noun Phrase Constraint

If we adopt the above description of wh-clauses there are some interesting consequences. Since WHSLOT is a grammatical register associated with the level processing the wh-clause, it behaves like a 'local variable' in a programming language (see Section 5.2). That is, each time the analyser initiates a wh-clause a new version of WHSLOT is set up at the current level; hence, only one incarnation of WHSLOT can exist at each level, and so only the contents of the *current* WHSLOT are accessible. If one wh-clause is processed inside another (e.g. in (98)) the inner wh-clause will not be able to use the contents of the WHSLOT register for the outer clause, since that register is at a higher level, for which the processing and register contents are temporarily suspended.

(98) What did the man who you saw say?

Consequently, the analyser will become confused if two wh-phrases are associated with one wh-clause, both at different levels, as in (99).

(99) *What did the man who bought arrive?

(Where the intended interpretation is that 'what' represents the object of 'bought'.) This is not to say that two wh-phrases cannot be associated with one relative clause — cf. (100).

(100) What did you say to whom?

Here, both wh-phrases are located at the one level and can both be processed by the one use of WHSLOT. The two wh-phrases will occupy the single incarnation of WHSLOT at different times (if in fact the second one ever has to be stored). Also, there is nothing to prevent the wh-phrase appearing in a containing clause being used in a lower clause, provided it does not, as in (99), become entangled in another wh-clause.

(101) What did Mary think Fred liked?

In (101) the 'what' is intended as the object of 'liked', but appears at the opening of the clause 'did Mary think . . .'. This creates no problems, since no other use of WHSLOT occurs, and so the one version of WHSLOT established at the start of the sentence will still be untouched when needed at the end. Several wh-clauses may appear in the same sentence, provided the wh-phrases are kept adjacent to their associated sentence parts, allowing the WHSLOT register to be used properly.

(102) Where did the man who you mentioned bury the treasure which he stole?

This pattern (i.e. the acceptability of sentences like (98), (100) and (101), and the oddity of sentences like (99)) has been documented in the transformational literature. The best known description of the phenomenon is due to Ross (1967), who formulated it as a constraint on alterations to deep structures:

(103) *The Complex Noun Phrase Constraint*
No element contained in a sentence dominated by a noun phrase with a lexical head noun may be moved out of that noun phrase by a transformation.

The procedure outlined in Section 11.1 was based on providing a simple and effective way of locating wh-phrases in wh-clauses. The notion of a register being local to a level was not constructed solely for this analysis, being an obvious computational technique for processing constituents as embedded units. Nevertheless, this procedure (based on surface analysing procedures) appears to embody Ross's constraint insofar as it applies to wh-clauses.

The Ross rule (103) also covered complex noun phrases (CNPs) other than wh-clauses, so it is natural to examine these other cases to see how the procedure here relates to them. The other form of CNP was that where an ordinary noun phrase (NP) and a clause (S) were in apposiition:

(104)
(a) You believed *the claim that he was an agitator for a washing machine firm*.
(b) *The fact that it was Tuesday* was overlooked.

Let us investigate what similarities there are in surface structure between relative clauses and appositional CNPs. A sequence of the form 'NP + that' may be the start of either of these:

(105)
(a) I didn't believe the claim that he made.
(b) I didn't believe the claim that he made a mess of things.

A possible way for the analyser to handle this potential ambiguity is to consider both possibilities in parallel. This has no particular drawbacks apart from the general unattractiveness of exhaustive searching, as discussed in Section 8.2. However, let us consider one way in which the decision could be postponed by using a register. Let us assume that, after getting the intitial 'NP + that' sequence the analyser decides that a CNP (of some type) is to be processed, but it does not know what the relationship between the head NP and the sentence-part will be, since it is either apposition or one of the relative-clause possibilities.

(Perhaps the relevant sequence is NP + that + NP, since criteria for recognising the beginnings of relative clauses are difficult to state, but this is not crucial here.) The analyser therefore does not build the head NP into the surface SCR tree, but holds it in a register, and goes on to process the sentence part of the CNP. This shows the similarity between the appositional CNPs and relative clauses — they consist of a head phrase and a sentence-part, where the semantic relationship between the two parts is unknown at the start of the clause; the head phrase can be stored temporarily until the end of the clause. The appositional relationship is not intra-sentential, like subject or object, but is extra-sentential, like the optional time and place adjuncts. If we assume that there is an SCR for apposition the relationship will be found at the same stage as one of the adjunct relationships would be found in a relative clause, namely, during tidying up. The wh-clause strategy will then serve for both types of CNP and the limits on registers discussed above will apply equally to both. Hence Ross's constraint (103), in its full form, will be incorporated into a single method of dealing with appositional and wh-clauses and one more case of breadth-first searching has been avoided using registers.

Unfortunately, there are certain problems with this approach. In some sentences (as noted by Ross) the CNP constraint appears to be inapplicable:

(106) What did you make the claim that you liked?

(If (106) is unacceptable in some dialects then presumably what follows here does not apply to the grammars of those dialects.)

In (106) the object of 'liked' has been given a surface structure position outside the CNP which contains it. By Ross's constraint, and by the analysing strategy given here, this should result in an odd sentence. What seems to be happening is that the sequence 'make the claim' is being treated as a single verb (roughly synonymous with 'claim'), and the 'that + S' sequence is treated as the object of this 'verb' (cf. 'What did you claim that you liked?'). It is not at all clear how this could be handled in either a transformational or a computational account, and it is slightly obscure even how to treat it as an exception. Perhaps the neatest solution would be to enter 'make the claim' as an idiom or compound verb in the lexicon. The analyser would then be faced with two possible analyses for sentences beginning like (106). There would be one analysis where 'the claim' is part of the verb and one where it is the head of a CNP. The latter analysis would eventually fail, since the displaced wh-phrase would cause problems; that would leave only the analysis where 'made the claim' is a compound verb. Since computational grammar has, at present, no way of treating idioms or compound lexical entries, this suggestion is not very enlightening.

David Kilby (personal communication) has observed that in some examples the ambiguity between relative clause and appositional CNP is not resolved even at the end of the sentence:

(107) Did you consider the claim that he made an oversimplification?

The two interpretations of (107) are describable as follows. The relative clause interpretation results from the head NP 'the claim' being taken from the WHSLOT and inserted as the object of 'made', with the NP 'an oversimplification' being processed as the second object of 'consider'. The appositional CNP interpretation results from 'an oversimiplification' being inserted as the object of 'made', with 'the claim' being left in the WHSLOT register until the end of the clause.

Whether a particular grammar would find both these analyses or not would depend on the finer details of the mechanism for getting an item out of the WHSLOT. If we introduce some form of ordering between options (i.e. between ATN arcs in each state) then the analyser will get only one of the analyses. That is, if the grammar specifies that stored wh-items are to be used in preference to looking for an input noun phrase (where both are available) then only the first interpretation of (107) will be found. This would be a rather awkward ordering as it would empty the WHSLOT into the subject position of every wh-clause. On the other hand, if input phrases have priority (i.e. WHSLOT is searched only if a gap is found) then only the second interpretation will be found. In fact, it seems better not to order these two options, since either ordering will cut out possibilities that we need to include in the grammar. Sentence (107) is a special case of the fact that certain wh-clauses may present the analyser with a choice of using a stored wh-item or analysing the next part of the input string:

(108)
(a) What did you give your father?
(b) What did you give to your father?

For example, assuming that the SCRs used within wh-clauses are exactly those used in ordinary clauses for combining verbs and objects, (108) (a) and (b) differ in the order that 'what' and 'your father' are to be placed in the SCR tree.

11.3. Semantics of Wh-Clauses

It was suggested above that the best surface structure for a wh-clause was one similar to that of a sentence, but with a wh-phrase as one of the constituents. This assumes that the SCRs for combining the constituents of a sentence will function equally well with either a wh-phrase of some other item (such as an ordinary NP). This would be desirable, since otherwise we would need a duplicate set of SCRs for all the cases where one of the arguments was a wh-phrase. Now it is necessary to consider what the semantic representation of a wh-clause should be and whether the representation will allow such assumptions about the surface structure.

Consider the various uses of a wh-clause (exemplified in (109)). In a question it acts as a pattern to single out some set of items about which the questioner requires further information. In a relative clause it acts as a predicate to convey more information about the antecedent noun phrase (apart from the separate construction described in Section 11.4 below). In a relative clause without an antecedent it acts as a descriptive term to refer to some item.

(109)
(a) What did you buy?
(b) The book which you stole is boring.
(c) What you did was wrong.

If we simply let a wh-clause meaning be a clause-meaning (i.e. a relation-instance) with one component marked as the 'wh' part, all the semantic rules for handling semantic structures would have to check every relation-instance to see if it had a 'wh' component, since the behaviour of an ordinary relation-instance is completely different from this multi-purpose structure. On the other hand, one semantic structure which is ideally suited to this multiple role (as a pattern, a predicate or a term) is the 'definer' (see Section 6.5). If we can arrange our rules so that wh-clauses are a form of definer we may be able to capture all these uses in one structure. This will require some extra SCRs to construct these wh-clause definers, since at present we have assumed that only the ordinary clause SCRs are necessary. It may seem that what we need is a unary SCR which acts on a wh-clause (represented as a relation-instance) to produce a definer, e.g.

(110)

<definer>
↑
SCR Wh-clause
↑
<relation-instance>
↑
SCR Subject-Complement
'you buy what'

However, if we make the rule binary, with the wh-phrase forming the first argument (e.g. (111)), certain advantages accrue.

(111)

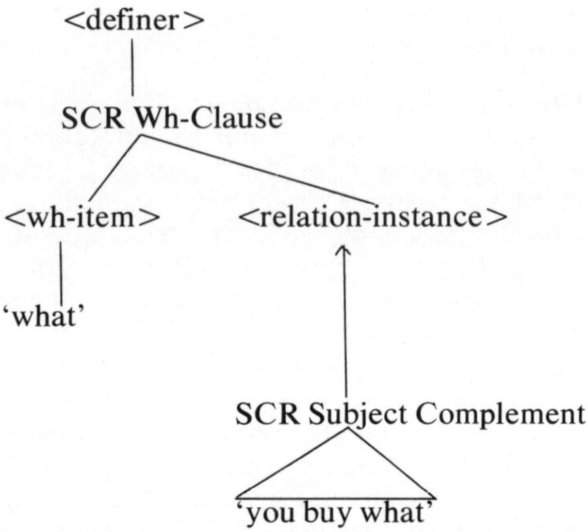

In particular, it allows for the fact that in ordinary relative clauses the semantic content of the wh-item is spread between the antecedent nominal and the relative pronoun. For example, the information that the relative clause in (109) (b) refers to a book derives from the antecedent 'book'. Therefore we might want to have some way of incorporating the semantic content of the antecedent into the overall meaning of the wh-clause. The phrase in (109) (b) might have a tree like (112).

If we have organised the representation of referring expressions so that they are normally represented as definers (see Section 6.5) then the two descriptions will connect quite well, since relative clauses (both with and without antecedents) will produce the same sort of structures (definers) as ordinary noun phrases. The only other interface to be arranged is for the question wh-clauses. The conversational routines will have to be able to

(112)

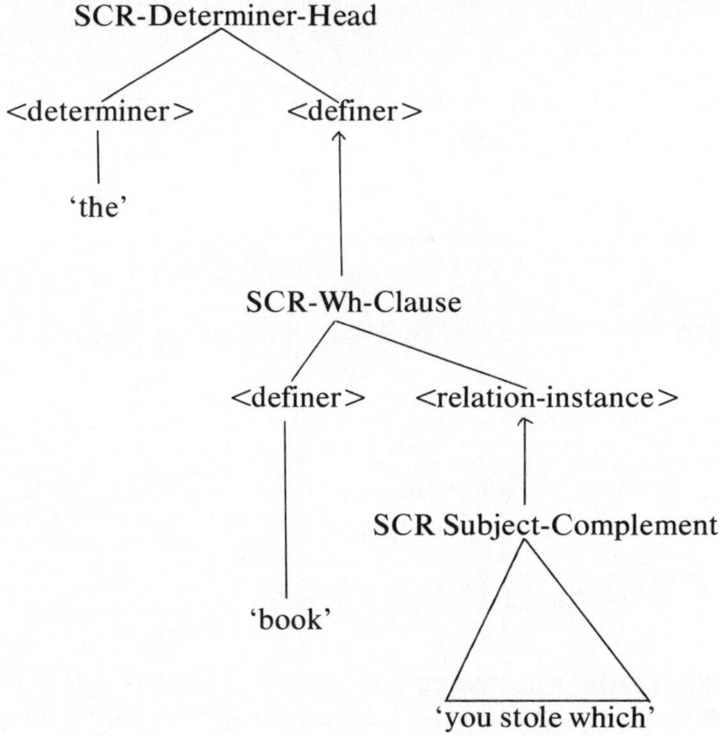

manipulate a definer (suitably marked) at any stage where a question might occur. This can be achieved by appropriate instructions within the conversation routines — see Chapter 9.

The way of converting a relation-instance with one component holding a wh-item into a definer is straightforward for simple examples. The wh-clause SCR has to find the component with the wh-item, mark it as 'blank' and select it as the selected role when constructing the definer. That is, a relation-instance like (113) (a) would become a definer like (113) (b).

(113)
(a)

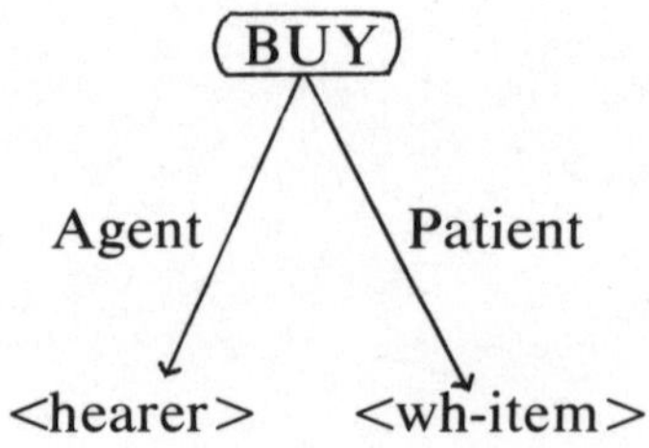

(b)

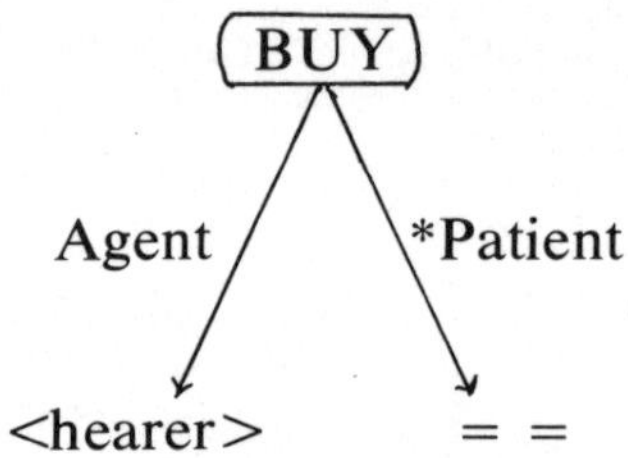

Marking the selected component as blank has one undesirable consequence — the information in the wh-item is lost. This information constrains the class of items that the definer refers to, and may be quite rich, as in (114).

The information can be retained, in quite a natural way, by transferring it to the *restriction* for that component in the definer. Then the definer will denote only items which match the description originally specified in the wh-phrase.

(114) Which large green furry object did you buy?

11.4. Non-restrictive Relative Clauses

There is yet another way in which wh-clauses can be used. Corresponding to the distinction between restrictive and non-restrictive adjectives (see Section 3.5 above) there is a distinction between restrictive and non-restrictive relative clauses.

(115)
(a) The girl who you met last night rang up.
(b) Alice, who I cannot stand, rang up.

Some relative clauses (e.g. (115) (a)) act as modifiers to restrict the scope of the antecedent phrase, thereby constructing a more narrowly referring expression. Other relative clauses (e.g. (115) (b)) do not restrict the range of items specified but add incidental information about the item(s) that the speaker wishes to convey. (See Smith (1964), Thomson (1971), and Ross (1967) for some comments on these clauses from a transformational standpoint.)

The other main difference between the two types of relative clause is that the restrictive relative clause combines with the head nominal of the antecedent to create a more complex nominal (which other items such as determiners can interact with), whereas the non-restrictive relative clause makes an assertion about the semantic item produced by the entire antecedent phrase. Hence restrictive relative clauses cannot be appended to proper names unless the name is treated as the head nominal of the noun phrase, e.g.

(116)
(a) Alice, who you like, has arrived. (Non-restrictive)
(b) The Alice who you like has arrived. (Restrictive)

The only problem in incorporating these clauses into the wh-clause grammar outlined above is finding some way that the analyser can distinguish between the two. As Smith (1964) comments, non-restrictive relative clauses often have 'comma intonation' surrounding them, and commas are the usual device for indicating the usage in written English. The grammar for the experimental program could analyse relative clauses as non-restrictive if and only if they were surrounded by commas, since its ATN included an explicit test for an opening comma at the start of the network for non-restrictive relatives.

The rest of the grammar is fairly straightforward. There is an SCR 'NRel-Clause' which takes any item and a wh-clause meaning as its arguments, makes an assertion about the item, using the wh-clause, and then returns the item unaltered as its result. The latter stage may seem redundant, since the main purpose of the SCR is merely to make the assertion, but the analysis process has been designed on the assumption that the SCRs will form a tree (with results from lower rules forming arguments for higher rules). Hence every rule must return one result. (See similar comments in Section 3.5.) The trees for non-restrictive relative clauses will be as in (117).

(117)

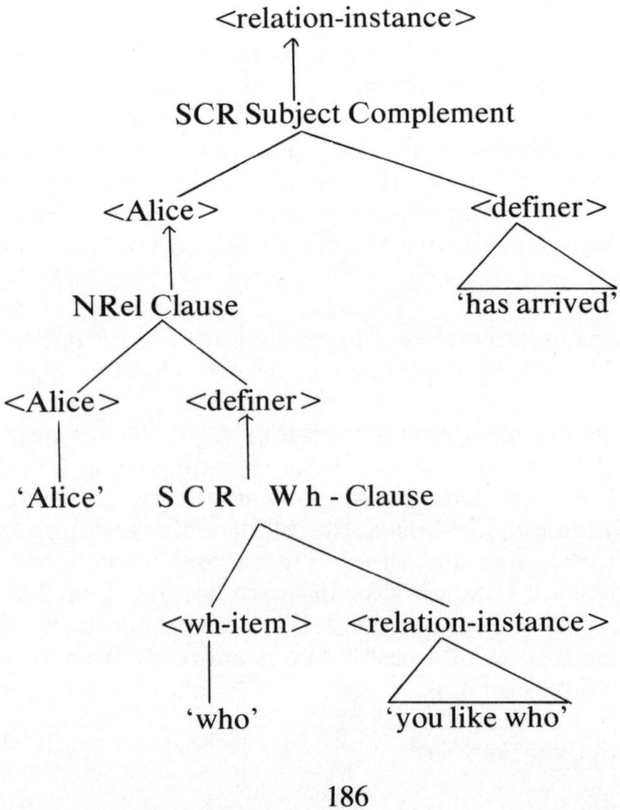

Notice that we have ignored, in all the above discussions, relative clauses which have no 'wh'-word in surface structure, such as 'The man you want is here'. As commented previously, it is not clear what sequence of categories signals the start of a relative clause, and clauses like this further complicate the problem. However, they should not affect the main arguments of this chapter.

CHAPTER 12

TENSE AND TIME IN ENGLISH

12.1. The Previous Descriptions

Although the concepts used in computational grammar have been in use for many years, there are relatively few examples of these computational devices being used for linguistic description in the traditional, semi-formal manner. One example of this approach is the work of Isard and Longuet-Higgins on tense, time and modality (Isard and Longuet-Higgins (1973), Isard (1974)). This chapter discusses that work and attempts to develop it further within the overall framework of computational grammar as defined.

In conversation we frequently indicate when (approximately) an event occurred by relating it to another event, as in (118).

(118) When I arrived, he had already left.

The 'when'-clause can be regarded as setting up a 'reference time', with respect to which the main clause is interpreted. We can talk of earlier events either by using past tense or perfect aspect, or both. Isard and Longuet-Higgins (following Reichenbach (1966)) distinguish:

(119)
(a) the time at which the sentence is uttered
(b) the time of reference
(c) the times at which the events in the sentence occurred

Thus, in (118) 'I arrived' gives the time of reference, which is before the time of utterance and after the time that 'he left'. That is, there are two event times in this example, one of which supplies the time of reference. Isard and Longuet-Higgins offer the following 'rule of thumb':

(120)
(a) past tense will be used when and only when the time of reference precedes the moment of speech
(b) present tense indicates that the two coincide
(c) the presence of 'have' (perfect aspect) signifies that the time of the event in that clause precedes the reference time
(d) the absence of 'have' indicates the coincidence of reference time and event time.

The idea of distinguishing event time, reference time and utterance time seems intuitively useful for describing tense, but the 'rule of thumb' is slightly misleading on points (b) and (d). Present tense can be used (as Isard (1974) points out) to refer to events in the future, and so reference times which succeed the utterance time can be set up using present tense, as in (121).

(121) When he arrives in London, he will have spent four hours on the train.

Regarding (120) (d), the exact relationship between reference time and event time (in the absence of 'have') is unclear:

(122)
(a) When they built the fifth bridge, they took several estimates.
(b) When they built the fifth bridge, they used the best materials.
(c) When they built the fifth bridge, there was a gala opening.

'Approximately coincide' seems the best summary of examples like these. When the data include clauses referring to intervals of time (which Isard and Longuet-Higgins were specifically excluding) even 'approximate coincidence' is not a very good description. Nevertheless, (120) (a) and (c) seem to be generalisations which are worth retaining.

Isard and Longuet-Higgins also observe that it is not necessary for the reference time to be established within the same utterance as it is required — it may be a previously mentioned reference time:

(123)
Was he there when you arrived?
No, he had already left.

The reference time for the answer is that set up by the 'when'-clause in the question.

McCawley (1971b) suggests that a past tense sentence (such as 'the farmer killed the duckling') is ill-formed unless the context provides a time-reference point for it. This is true only as long as 'context' is taken to mean the entire knowledge of the hearer of the sentence. Certain historical statements do not need such explicit reference times, as the events themselves are well known. Similarly, a sentence like 'Angus went to school in Edinburgh' does not sound odd if the hearer knows that Angus is educated, and hence probably went to school at some time. This is relevant to the use of 'when'-clauses, since it would be very difficult to carry on a conversation if some events or states were not already self-supporting; the whole point of a 'when'-clause is to use such an event or state to set up a reference time.

Isard (1974) develops these ideas further. He proposes two slots, PRESENT and REMOTE, into which reference times can be put. These slots maintain their values between utterances (to account for dialogues like (123)) unless either they are obliterated by some new value being put in the slot or the conversation switches to using some other slot. That is, (123) establishes the reference time referred to by 'when you arrived' in the REMOTE slot; later utterances which use remote tense will automatically refer to that reference time unless some new remote reference time has been specified, or some utterance in the present tense has been interposed. Isard suggests that it is the task of the 'time-binder' 'when' to get the reference time from the subordinate clause and put it into the appropriate slot. The main clause then uses the slot which corresponds to its own tense — the 'when'-clause should have filled this. The problem of 'approximate coincidence' of events is simplified for the Isard program by interpreting 'when e1, e2' as either 'e1 is coincident with e2' or 'e2 immediately follows e1', both of which are clearly defined in the domain he is using — events are moves in a noughts-and-crosses game.

12.2. Nested Tense Settings

The rules suggested by Isard and Longuet-Higgins for maintaining reference times between utterances seem to cover many cases. However, there are examples which seem to escape these constraints.

As commented above, an utterance may contain two event-times, one of which forms the reference time for the utterance. Sometimes this gives the next utterance in the dialogue a choice of two possible reference points — the already-used reference time or the event-time of the other (main) clause:

(124)

A: When I was at university, the Duke of Friockheim visited us.
B: Was there a big reception?

(125)

A: When I was at university, the Duke of Friockheim visited us.
B: What other exciting events occurred?

This seems to suggest that the conversational reference points are set up retrospectively, or else that some notion of 'potential reference time' is needed, or some combination of these two modifications. In such cases, selecting one of the two candidates for reference time sometimes eliminates the other candidate from later use, and sometimes does not. Consider a dialogue consisting of (124) followed by (126). The other reference point ('I was at university') seems to be still available for use in the last question.

(126)
A: Yes.
B: What other exciting events occurred?

However, if we append (127) to (125) the resulting dialogue does not flow smoothly.

(127)
A: Nothing much.
B: Was there a big reception?

The ducal visit seems to have been lost as a possible reference point in this case. This may be describable, like the previous set of examples, in terms of conversational structure divided into subsections. It may be that in the well-formed dialogue (124)+(126) the centre question and answer constitute a nested subsection of conversation using a different reference time; the previously-established reference time is saved for use at the outer level of conversation. The slightly odd dialogue ((125)+(127)) may result from there being no embedded section where a different reference time can be used. These comments are lamentably vague. One possible way to formalise this description might be to have a more precise notion of a subsection of conversation (e.g. as in Chapter 9 above) with the slots PRESENT and REMOTE being local to each subsection.

Alternatively, it may be that the tense slots are not single slots but are more like push-down stores where items can be heaped up in a 'last-in-first-out' basis. Finding the relevant reference time for an utterance may consist of searching back down the stack for an appropriate reference time and removing all potential reference points above it. That is, every tensed clause in the dialogue causes a potential reference point to be placed on the appropriate tense stack, but once a reference time is adopted it causes later entries on the stack to be lost.

These two 'solutions' are not just alternative re-wordings of the problem but differ in their effects. If we segment conversations into nested subsections (e.g. as described in

Chapter 9) then we may wish to associate various characteristics with each section. For example, each subsection might achieve some particular purpose in the dialogue, or there might be a whole range of 'local' information (other than just tense settings) which is specific to each subsection. To say that the tense settings are determined by the successive sections (nested or sequential) is to say that the patterns which occur in these other characteristics follow the same behaviour as the tense patterns. On the other hand, if we just say that the tense values are stacked and unstacked it says nothing about the way that such storing will relate to other aspects of the dialogue.

There seems to be a very low limit on how many reference times can remain accessible, whether the 'stack' or the 'subsection' approach is used. It is quite difficult to construct a fluent dialogue where the speakers use a succession of reference times and and then re-use previously mentioned reference times. The following exchange (128) has used five different reference times at the point marked — >. The subsequent utterances attempt to re-use several of these (in a last-in, first-out basis). The last utterance (*) seems to be slightly odd — a puzzled comment such as (129) seems as appropriate.

(128)
A: While I was a student, I lived for some time in France.
B: Did you visit Paris?
A: Yes.
B: Did you go to the Eiffel Tower?
A: Yes, we had a picnic at the top.
—>
B: What other towns did you visit?
A: Bordeaux.
B: Where else did you live?
(*) A: Italy, for a few months.
(129)
A: What, when I was a student, you mean?

Although the above discussion has been based on past

tense examples most of these patterns appear in present tense sentences as well. For example, the following dialogue uses two present tense time references, with the 'storing' effect described above.

(130)
A: When he is staying in London, his relatives will visit him.
B: Will they annoy him?
A: No.
B: Will he be working during the day?

If a retrospective selection of time-references is used then this provides another analogy between the behaviour of tense markers and that of pronouns (cf. McCawley (1971b)).

12.3. The Function of Time-binders

Isard (1974) suggests that most of the systematic allocation of reference times inside a sentence can be performed by the 'time-binder' word 'when' in the subordinate clause. That is, executing the semantic part of 'when' does the following in his program:

(131)
(a) it locates the event time of the subordinate clause
(b) it sets this event time into the appropriate slot (PRESENT or REMOTE)

The interpretation of the main clause then uses for its reference time whatever has been loaded into the slot that its own tense refers to. There are slight problems with this analysis. Other tense manipulations may be necessary within the sentence; also, it may be inappropriate to have all the manipulations performed by the time-binder.
Compare (132) and (133):

(132)
(a) Before I arrived he sent off the letter.

(b) When I was opening the window, he left the room.
(133)
(a) At five o'clock, he left the room.
(b) On Tuesday, he sent off the letter.
(c) Yesterday, all my troubles seemed so far away.

Although time adjuncts in the form of a clause contain a time-binder word (which can be given the responsibility of setting up the reference time) there are very similar sentences (e.g. (133)) where there is no single time-binder to which this task can be allotted. These sentences may need a separate SCR for time adjuncts, which takes the meaning of the adjunct (a time structure, whatever that will look like) and slots it into an appropriate tense slot. Thus the time-binder can be relieved of the task of setting up the tense slot — it has just to operate on the clause (or its meaning) to produce a time structure for the SCR to act on.

In the Isard program the meaning of 'when' operates on the meaning of a clause to produce a reference time — namely, the time of the event referred to by the clause. The difference between 'when' and other time-binders like 'before' and 'after' seems to be in the structure that this conversion produces. Compare the sentences in (134).

(134)
(a) When the sun was shining, I could see Ben Nevis.
(b) Before the sun was shining, I could see Ben Nevis.
(c) After the sun was shining, I could see Ben Nevis.

The relationship expressed by these sentences, between the time of one state and another differs as the time-binder is altered. Rather than postulate that the time-binders operate on two clauses, it might be better to have the different time-binders construct different reference times from the subordinate clause. Once this time-structure is inserted in the appropriate slot the procedure for interpreting the main clause can act differently on the different structures. If this conversion from clause-meaning to time-structure is the task of the time-binder then 'when' may in some sense be the most basic example. Whereas other time-binders may operate on the event or state referred to in the clause to produce some time structure not coincident with the event or state, the meaning of 'when' generally produces as reference time the duration of the event or state (approximately). Hence the 'approximate coincidence' relationship mentioned above is a direct result of using 'when' as the time-binder. If we set up an event or state as the reference time without using a time-binder, i.e. implicitly in a dialogue, then the effect is very similar to using 'when'. The time-relationship conveyed in (135) seems closer to that conveyed in (136) than either of those in (137).

(135)
A: Did you cook the meat?
B: Yes. The smell was overpowering.

(136) When I cooked the meat, the smell was overpowering.

(137)
(a) After I cooked the meat, the smell was overpowering.
(b) Before I cooked the mat, the smell was overpowering.

(This is a very weak point — intuitions vary greatly.) This would fit in quite well with the description of 'when' as a regular 'wh'-word. A clause beginning with 'wh-' ('what', 'who', etc.) can be regarded as a pattern to describe some item, where the 'wh'-word conveys the semantic class of item (time, thing, person, etc.) and the clause gives a partial description of it. Thus 'when I cooked the meat' is roughly paraphraseable as '(at) the time at which I cooked the meat'. This is just how Isard uses 'when'-clauses — they are patterns describing times. Hence, if we postulate that the meaning of 'when' merely converts the meaning of a clause into a pattern for a time then we are saying no more than that 'when' is the 'wh'-word for time.

12.4. Disembodied Time References

Under the Isard analysis, a 'when'-clause causes the value of the tense slot to change, but in some sense the 'meaning' of the 'when'-clause is not itself acted upon by a higher grammatical rule. (In computational terms the clause has side-effects but leaves no results.) Under the analysis suggested here the clause passes up a result (a time structure) for a SCR to use. Hence the analysis of partial utterances in exchanges like (138) changes. (The conversation is about 'taking' squares in a tic-tac-toe game; the squares are referred to by numbers between one and nine.)

(138)
(a) Had you taken two?
(b) Under what circumstances?
(c) When you took eight.

Isard's program tries to understand (a) and finds it has nothing in its REMOTE slot; it therefore ask for a time reference in (b). The clause (c) is interpreted and executed and the program attempts once again to interpret the initial utterance (a); the execution of the 'when'-clause should have set the REMOTE slot accordingly. Under the analysis here (c) would merely present the program with a ready-made reference point — the program would have to 'know' what to do with it (i.e. use it to fill the 'REMOTE' slot), and it could then continue from where it left off. This distinction may seem fairly minor but the new approach will allow (139) (b) to be treated similarly to (138) (c).

(139)
(a) When did you see me?
(b) When you left the building.

That is, uttering an isolated 'when'-clause is regarded as offering a time-structure to the hearer — the way that the hearer reacts to this will depend on what he is expecting. An alternative which could be adopted under the Isard analysis is to suggest that the act of setting a value into the tense slot can be regarded as answering a question (e.g. in (139)), but this seems slightly counter-intuitive.

This is not to say that the time-structures created for the 'when'-clause does not end up in one of the tense slots; the point is that the clause meaning itself (or the time-binder 'when') should not perform this task. If we allocate such decisions to rules outside the 'when'-clause, then (138) (c) and (139) (b) can be treated identically at the clause level, but any differences can be described at the conversational level, in that the time structure is being used in different ways by different conversational routines (cf. 'localised semantic description' in Section 10.9).

12.5. Tense Clash

Once a 'when'-clause has set up a reference time the main clause has to use it or oddity results:

(140) *When he walks in, I greeted him.

This is not a constraint on keeping tenses in different clauses of a sentence the same:

(141)
(a) Although she sells sea shells, she was once an admiral's daughter.
(b) Because she helped Fred, he is very grateful.
(c) Fred said that Gladys knows that Evelyn left.

If the time-binder (under Isard's analysis) or the time-adjunct rule (under this analysis) merely alters the value of the tense-slot there is no reason why the main clause should have to use this slot. There seems no neat way of accounting for this constraint but it may be that within each clause there is some notion of 'current tense slot'. That is, one of the two slots is selected, on the basis of time-adjunct and tense information in the sentence, and it becomes the reference time for that clause. The difficulty (in sentences like (140)) is then not because the two clauses have different 'current tense slots', but because the process of interpreting the time-adjunct selects the tense slot for the main clause using the reference time of the subordinate clause; the main clause itself tries to select a tense slot using its tense. If these attempted selections are different (as in (140)) a clash results. This is *ad hoc*, but it is not clear what else would fit in with the other suggestions.

12.6. A Summary of the Tense-Slot System

Let us summarise the modifications to the Isard/ Longuet-Higgins analysis. The task of the time-binder words is solely to convert a clause-meaning into a time structure. This time structure can then be used as the answer to a question, or may become the argument for a SCR which handles time adjuncts. The basic form of time adjunct is the 'when'-clause, which indicates a moment or interval of time using an event or state which has roughly that duration. Time adjuncts may occur in forms other than bound clauses (e.g. prepositional phrases) but are handled in a similar way. The time adjunct SCR rule selects the tense slot indicated by the time adjunct to be the 'current' tense slot for the main clause, and puts the time structure supplied by the tense of the time adjunct into that slot. In interpreting the main clause a selection is made of a 'current' tense slot on the basis of the clause's tense, and the interpretation proceeds using the reference time held in that slot (or perhaps by searching a stack of stored values — see above).

12.7. Time Semantic Structures and Relationships

Before discussing the details of the various semantic categories and SCRs needed to describe such structures let us examine informally the kind of information that will have to be represented.

The way in which an event can be used to convey a time structure can vary. For example, (142) seems to refer to a definite point in time, whereas (143) seems to describe an interval of time:

(142) When I opened the box . . .
(143) When I was opening the box . . .

This distinction affects the way in which a main clause is interpreted; if we append (144) to (142) the interpretation is that the leaving followed the opening, but if it is appended to (143) the interpretation is that the leaving occurred at some stage during the opening.

(144) . . . he left.

If we assume that events and states are located on a simple 'time-line' the appropriate primitives seem to be 'points' and 'intervals'. (These are left as unanalysed primitives whose mnemonic names should be intuitively useful.) One way to describe an interval of time is to mention a state which existed during that period:

(145) When I was at school . . .

The verb 'be', together with a complement, is a simple way to achieve this. As illustrated in (143), the use of a progressive verb form can also describe an interval of time. (Some generalisation might be possible about the meaning of copular 'be' and progressive 'be', regarding its use for describing states of affairs; this will not be attempted here.) If a sentence attempts to relate two intervals (in the way described above) the interpretation is often that the state of affairs described in the 'when'-clause held for a subinterval of the duration of the state described in the main clause:

(146) When I was at school, de Gaulle was still alive.

Some examples can be found where there seems to be a slight implication that the two time intervals are co-extensive —

(147) When the sun was shining, the room was quite warm.

However, it is rather difficult to find examples where the main clause describes a subinterval (proper) of the interval indicated by the 'when'-clause — the reverse use, as in (146) seems more natural. It may be that the suggestion of co-extensiveness in sentences like (147) derives from some kind of 'conversational implication'. The sentence just asserts that the state of affairs described in the main clause existed throughout the duration of the situation described in the 'when' clause, i.e. a subinterval relationship, as in (146). The feeling that the state of affairs did not hold outside the interval described by the 'when'-clause may be a deduction from the fact that there must be some point to saying (147). If we add '. . . and when the sun went down we turned on the heater to keep it that way' to (147), there is no contradiction; (147) does not assert that the state of affairs described in the main clause failed to hold outside the smaller interval.

Point reference times can be described by the non-progressive forms of certain verbs, as in (143). As observed above, relating two point reference times leads to some interpretation of 'approximate coincidence' (see (122)). Here is a case where 'world knowledge' is necessary to sort out the exact relationship between the two events — the syntax/semantics can only provide the 'approximate coincidence' relationship. This vague relationship seems to be paraphraseable as 'just before, during or just after', where there is no absolute definition of 'just after' or of 'just before'; these depend on the 'scale' of the event, in some sense:

(148)
(a) When the bell rang, I opened the door.
(b) When the Americans dropped the atomic bombs, Japan surrendered.

It may seem rather glib to keep allotting various problems to 'world knowledge' and 'higher-level inferences', but there are limits to what should be crammed into the grammar. One further non-grammatical aspect of (148) is the slight implication of causality that some people may extract from sentences like (148) (b). However, this nuance does not come directly from the use of 'when', but rather from the juxtaposition of the mentions of the events. Compare (149), which conveys a similar sense of causality (or fails to, according to your intuitions).

(149) The Americans dropped the atomic bombs. Japan surrendered.

The use of the 'when'-clause does help to draw attention to the temporal proximity of the two events, and hence may spark off some deductions in the hearer's mind, but there is no need to cram these inferences into the grammar of time clauses.

If the sentence describes a point event and an interval the relationship between the two seems to be the same no matter which occurs in the 'when'-clause:

(150)
(a) When I was quite young, Fred hit me with a shovel.
(b) When Fred hit me with a shovel, I was quite young.

(There is no suggestion that these two sentences are synonymous — merely that the time relationships expressed in them are the same.) As pointed out in (142) and (143) there are two ways of using an event to refer to a reference time — either as a point or as an interval. As in (122) (b) two points events can be related by being coincident:

(122)
(b) When they built the fifth bridge, they used the best materials.

If we wish to state that one event occurred at some stage during another event describing them as point events is awkward; it seems more natural to describe the 'surrounding' event as an interval:

(151)
(a) ??? When they built the fifth bridge, a workman drowned in the river.
(b) When they were building the fifth bridge, a workman drowned in the river.

Also, if both clauses describe events as 'points' they cannot be interpreted as locating the event described by the when-clause during the event described in the main clause:

(152) ??? When he put in salt, he cooked the meat.

Thus there are certain possible ways of relating time-points and time-intervals using 'when'-clauses:

'When'-clause	*Main clause*	*Relationship*
point x	point y	x approx. coincides with y
point x	interval i	x contained in i
interval i	point x	x contained in i
interval i	interval j	i a subinterval of j

The ways in which point and interval time structures can be conveyed by different verb forms is quite complex (or even messy). As commented already, an interval can be described by either

(153)
(a) The copular 'be'
(b) the progressive form of a verb

Certain other verbs can also serve to describe states of affairs and produce interval time structures without the use of progressive verbs. Stative verbs, like 'believe', for example:

(154) When I believed in deep structure, life was much simpler.

This does not seem too odd, since stative verbs usually do not have a progressive form and seem to contain already the sense normally associated with progressive verbs. However, there seem to be verbs which are semi-stative, in that they have a progressive form, they describe a state of affairs even in non-progressive form and they fail some of the standard syntactic tests for stative verbs. 'Live', in the sense of 'dwell' or 'reside' is one such verb. The oddity of (155) (a) suggests that this is a stative verb, but the acceptability of (b) and (c) suggest that it may not be:

(155)
(a) ??? I lived in London and he did so too.

(b) What he did was to live in London.
(c) Live outside London — the rents are lower.

The two sentences in (156) seem almost synonymous; in particular, the time relationships conveyed are the same.

(156)
(a) When he was living in London, the rents were high.
(b) When he lived in London, the rents were high.

If we try to use the 'when'-clauses of (156) to describe an interval within which some event occurred the two verb forms are not equally suitable:

(157)
(a) When he was living in London, someone bombed the GPO Tower.
(b) ??? When he lived in London, someone bombed the GPO Tower.

As pointed out ((142) and (143)) the progressive form of a verb is more suitable for describing an interval during which some point event occurred. It may be that (157) (b) sounds odd because of its similarity to the completely non-stative, non-progressive verb form (cf. (151)), whereas (157) (a) sounds better because of some similarity to the standard form. The whole issue seems very messy.

So far, the only time structure associated with totally non-stative, non-progressive verbs has been the simple point reference time. If we now look at the use of such verbs to describe habitual events, further complications arise. Roughly speaking, a habitual occurrence can be regarded as a series of events which together define an interval (namely, the interval within which they occurred). Thus a clause like:

(158) When I travelled in by tube . . .

is ambiguous between (at least) two possibilities:

(159)
(a) it refers to a single event; consider adding to (158) the

clause: '. . . I left my briefcase behind'

(b) it refers to an interval during which the event occurred several times; consider adding to (158) the clause: '. . . I was able to claim expenses'

This may be the only way in which a non-progressive, non-stative verb can describe an interval — by describing some habitual action which took place within that interval. An interesting consequence of this is the way in which the ambiguity of (158) is preserved even when a progressive marker is added:

(160) When I was travelling in by tube . . .
(a) . . . someone stole my briefcase.
(b) . . . they raised the fares.

There seems to be no grammatical way of disambiguating these — again some resort is necessary to extra-linguistic knowledge.

12.8. Perfect Aspect

As mentioned previously, the use of perfect aspect generally indicates that the event time of a clause precedes the reference time of the clause. This information can be used in two ways: if the reference time is known it locates the event time; if the event time is known it helps to define the reference time. The rules for determining whether to use a verb with perfect aspect, rather than a past tensed verb, (i.e. 'I have seen him' rather than 'I saw him') are unclear. One relevant factor may be a reluctance (or inability) on the part of the speaker to specify an exact reference time at which the event occurred. This alone would not account for all the nuances that the present perfect seems to convey, but it is outside the scope of this chapter to examine this wider problem. (McCawley (1971b) gives an inconclusive discussion of several examples.)

There has not been time to develop a full analysis of perfect aspect here, as it is probably the most difficult part of the English tense/aspect system. The MCHINE program (Chapter 13) included some *ad hoc* devices to allow it to respond to questions which used perfect aspect.

12.9. Some Rules and Structures

Let us examine in slightly more detail how the rules and structures could operate for time clauses. As pointed out above it seems plausible to regard time-binder words like 'after' and 'before' as combining with a clause-meaning to form some kind of 'time-descriptor'. That is, we could have semantic categories — 'time-binders' and 'time-descriptors' — and an SCR (say, 'Time-Bind') which performs the combination. Surface-trees like (161) would be the result:

(161)

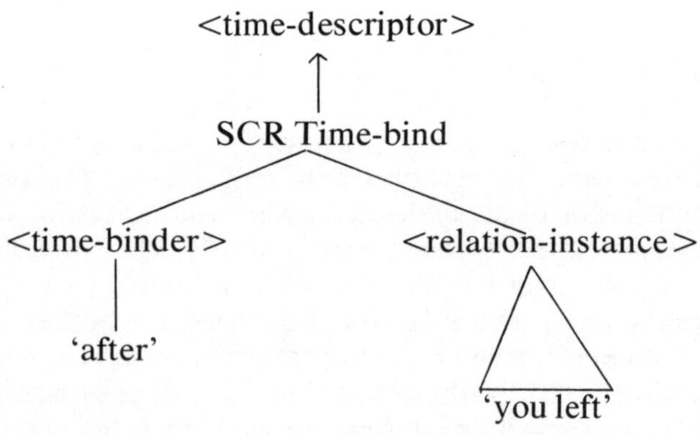

In order to relate these time-descriptors to another clause there would have to be a further SCR (say, 'Time-Adjunct') which relates adjuncts to main clauses. Trees like (162) would follow, where the semantic category of the overall result is yet to be discussed (see below).

(162)

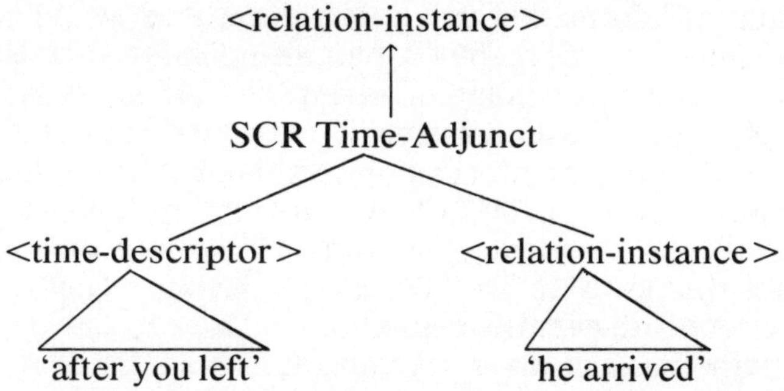

By separating these two functions into separate SCRs we allow other time-descriptors (e.g. (133) above) to combine with main clauses in the same way, and time-descriptors to be created independently, as in (163) (b).

(163)
(a) When did he arrive?
(b) After you left.

The overall structure produced by SCR Time-Adjunct is hard to characterise. It seems to express a relationship between a time and an action, or state of affairs. We can represent this (in a rather *ad hoc* fashion) with a semantic network relation 'AT-TIME'.

Let us consider what characteristics a 'time-descriptor' will require to represent the time relationships discussed above (i.e. in the table in Section 12.7). The first important point is that a time-descriptor is at the level of intensional semantics (see Chapter 7), not referential semantics. The 'points' and intervals' used in Section 12.7 above are abstract constructs which enter into the relationships sketched here; they are distinct from 'points' and 'intervals' in time. Time-descriptors *denote* segments of the traditional 'time-line', but they are at a different level of description. The duration of a particular event may define one segment of time, but it may have several different linguistic descriptions, with these different descriptions behaving in different ways (cf. (142) and (143)). It might seem that the minimum amount of information that a time-descriptor would need is the segment of time involved, plus an indication of whether it is to be treated as a 'point' or an 'interval'. If we consider the way that time-clauses are used, it turns out that this is not the appropriate kind of information. Although the point/interval indication is necessary if we are to systematise time relationships as above, the exact times involved may be totally unknown to speaker and/or hearer. Time-clauses serve to locate events or situations *relative to one another*, not with respect to some absolute time-line. A time-descriptor should therefore contain a representation of the event (or situation) involved, and an indication of how the start and end of the 'point' or 'interval' are defined by the start and end of the event. For example, in a clause like (164) the end point of the event provides the start of the interval described.

(164) After he arrived.

In all the time clauses examined so far the 'points' and 'intervals' can be described directly in terms of the start and finish of the event or situation, with the further option of being 'undefined'. Hence a time-descriptor can be represented fairly simply, containing just a description of the reference event, a point/interval marker and an indication of how the event's end-points define the end-points of the time described. The SCR Time-Bind will act on a clause (which contains an event description) and a time-binder (which will provide some of the information to construct the other markings) to produce a time-descriptor.

12.10. 'When' Clauses

One obvious way to describe 'when' clauses would be to class 'when' as a time-binder, along with 'after' and 'before'. That would not capture certain other patterns concerning 'when'. In particular, 'when' is a 'wh'-word (see Chapter 11 above), and it would be neater if clauses like (163) (a) could be processed by the general wh-clause grammar, as in Chapter 11. Also, it might be difficult to process question 'when'-clauses (e.g. (163) (a)), answer 'when'-clauses (e.g. (138) (c)) and subordinate 'when'-clauses (e.g. (142)) all in the same way if the latter are to be described as time-binder + clause combinations, since (163) (a) does not seem to produce a time-descriptor.

As discussed in Chapter 11 wh-clauses can be looked on as a pattern which identifies some item (or items) and this pattern can be used to insert a reference to that item into a sentence (via a relative clause) or to seek more information about that item (via a wh-question). 'When'-clauses fit into this description, since most subordinate 'when'-clauses can be regarded as relative clauses, with a paraphrase using 'at the time at which' instead of 'when'. Questions (e.g. (163) (a)) also fit the general 'wh'-clause system, since they indicate an item (in this case, a time) about which the speaker requires more information. As pointed out in Chapter 11 the meaning of a wh-clause is a semantic structure with one component marked as 'blank' in some way. If we are to treat 'when'-clauses similarly some suitable semantic structure of this general form will have to be devised.

This can be achieved as follows. An independent 'what'-clause like (165) is given a surface-tree like (167), with a semantic network representation as in (166).

(165) What did John bring?

(166)

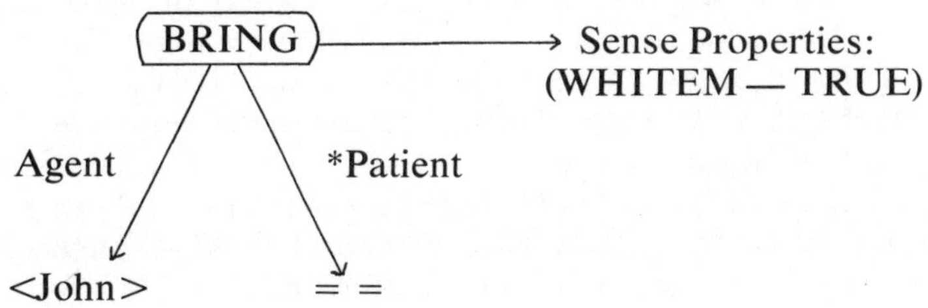

(167)

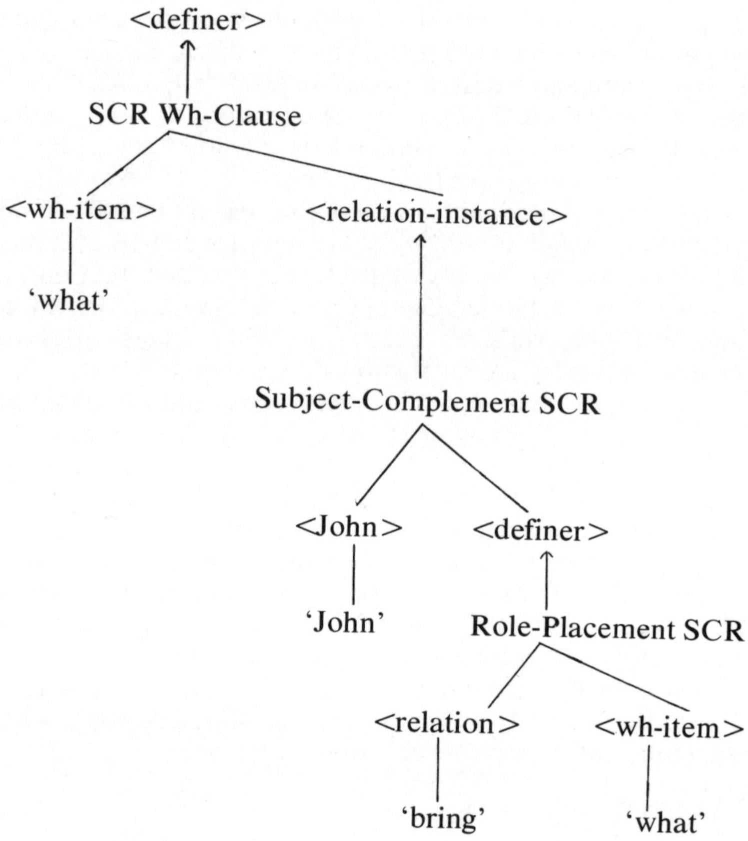

(168) When John arrived.

Similarly, a 'when'-clause (168) can be given the structure in (169) for its surface tree. That is, 'when' is regarded as a 'wh' form of time-descriptor which can thus fill the second argument of SCR Time-Adjunct in the same way that the meaning of 'what' can fill an argument in a role-placement rule. The resulting AT-TIME relation-instance will have a component marked as a 'wh'-form, and SCR Wh-Clause will work on this as usual to produce a network like (170).

(169)

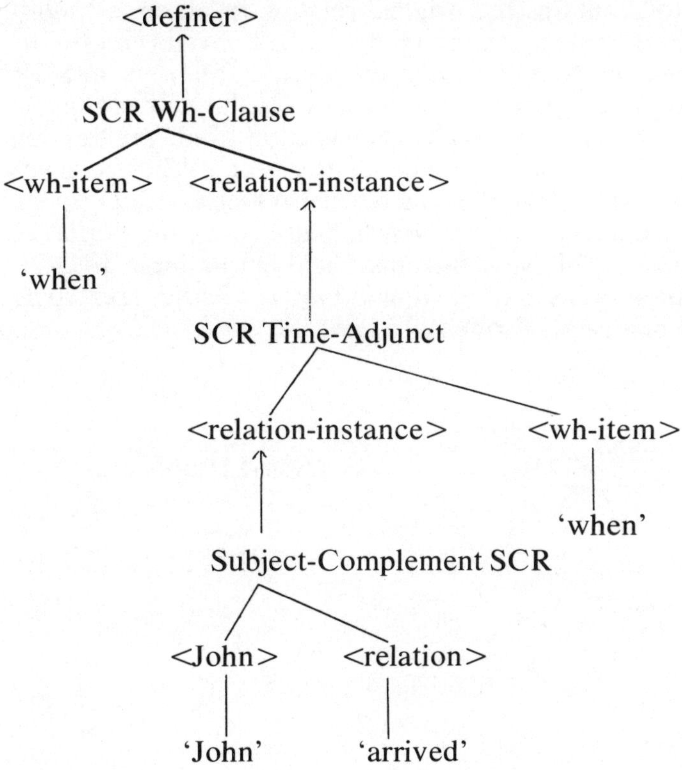

This means that a 'when'-clause will be a definer which singles out the time associated with the state or event described in the main part of the clause. Thus, this item describes a time, but is not a 'time-descriptor' as created by the Time-Bind SCR described above.

12.11. Summary of Rules

Let us summarise the representation of time-clauses. There

is an SCR Time-Bind which combines a 'time-binder' with a relation-instance to form a 'time-descriptor'. The time-descriptor contains the original relation-instance, a 'point' or 'interval' indicator and an indication of how its end-points are to be used to delimit the time period. There is an SCR Time-Adjunct which inserts the tense as the 'current' tense in the current conversational section and creates an 'AT-TIME' relation-instance as its result. 'When' clauses are treated as wh-clauses which will produce a definer (in the normal wh-clause way) which indicates the time period of some event. This structure may also act as input to SCR Time-Adjunct, as may any time-adjunct (whether created by an SCR or already formed as a lexical entry).

(170)

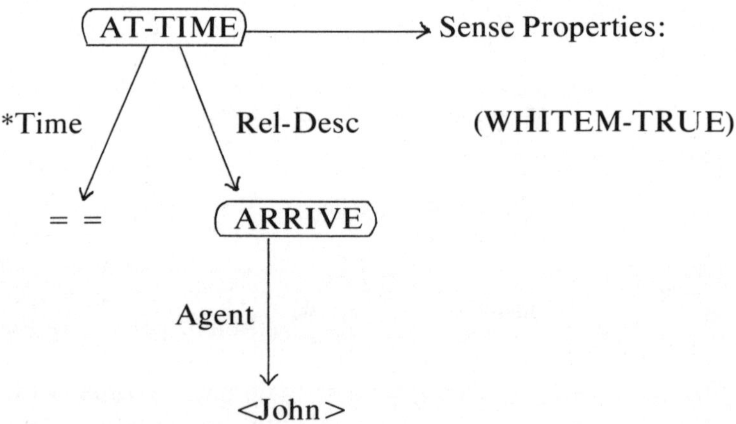

CHAPTER 13

A COMPUTER IMPLEMENTATION

13.1. The MCHINE Program

As discussed in Chapter 1 computer implementation is a principal research technique for computational grammar. Many of the ideas described in earlier chapters evolved during a project to write an English dialogue program. The details of the program are not of great theoretical interest, but a summary is included here to emphasise that computational grammar has developed from the empirical battlefield of grammar-writing and program-debugging. The program (which was given the rather confusing name of MCHINE) was useful as a test-bed for certain ideas, but unspectacular in its conversational performance.

The program could run in two modes — isolated sentence analysis or conversation. In the former mode, the user could type in a single sentence or phrase and the program would try to construct a data structure representing the semantic network associated with that sentence or phrase. This structure (which would be the word 'NIL' if the analysis had been completely unsuccessful) could then be printed out and examined by the user. In conversational mode the program could carry on a series of typed exchanges with the user, answering simple questions and responding to statements.

The program was written in POP-2 (Burstall, Popplestone and Collins (1971)) as implemented at the Department of Artificial Intelligence, University of Edinburgh, and ran on the TOPS-10 operating system on the DEC System 10 with a KA-10 processor. The compiled code occupied approximately 45K of 36-bit words, in addition to the 11K used by the POP-2 system. While running in conversational mode the program used additional storage (to 'remember' the conversation) and could perform a dialogue of about twenty exchanges in 109K (+11K) of core. The processing time used to analyse an input sentence varied from about five seconds for a short simple sentence to about one minute for a two-clause sentence. The real response time varied depending on how heavily loaded the DEC System 10 was, but under optimal conditions (typically, 3.00am with no other users on the machine) conversational replies could vary from eight seconds to two minutes (real time). That is, the program was very slow.

13.2. Overall Structure

All the components described in Chapter 10 were implemented, to varying levels of sophistication.

There was a facility for specifying ATN grammars and an ATN interpreter which used these rules to analyse sentences. Several structural combining rules were defined and there was a semantic network data-base for storing 'knowledge'. The flow of control was handled by a sequence of nine 'conversation games' (as in Chapter 9). There was a simple lexicon to give each word syntactic and semantic information and a rudimentary *ad hoc* mechanism to allow the program to type out simple answers (e.g. 'Yes', 'No') to questions.

The semantic network system was intended to be general, in the sense that it could be used to represent any relational structure. The particular toy world that was used for testing the conversational system was simpler than the SHRDLU BLOCKS world (see Section 2.10). The world comprised items called PERSONs, where a PERSON consisted of three components: a name, an associated 'state of the world' (to represent that PERSON's 'beliefs') and a 'credibility rating' (1 or 0, depending on whether or not a statement coming from that PERSON was to be believed). There were a set of relations which could hold between PERSONs — FATHER, MOTHER, etc. — and some unary relations (i.e. predicates of one argument) which could be used to attribute properties to a PERSON — MAN, WOMAN, etc. This strange 'world' was chosen, rather than, say, a table-top BLOCKS world, to allow the possibility of investigating indirect speech and past tense. Questions like 'Did Harry say that Fred likes Mary?' seemed to fit more naturally into a world populated by PERSONs (albeit a barren world of primitive PERSONs).

Dialogues proceeded in a series of conversations between the 'self' of the program (with its own 'knowledge' of the world) and different PERSONs. The conversation games were arranged so that the 'farewell' game always restarted the 'greeting' game (to prepare for a new interlocutor), and this went on until the program was terminated by the programmer. At the change-over between conversations the identity of the new interlocutor was taken from a pre-set list.

13.3. Sample Dialogues

The following conversations are based on a ludicrously simple 'world' inhabited by five 'PERSONs'. GLADYS is the MOTHER of HIRAM and of BORIS. BORIS is the FATHER of DELIA. Both GLADYS and DELIA have 'FAIR' marked on the property 'HAIR', and so can be referred to as BLONDE (using the elaborated form of this description — see Section 6.3). HIRAM has 'DOCTOR' marked on the property 'JOB' and so can be referred to as a DOCTOR, also by way of an elaborated form. GLADYS, HIRAM and DELIA are given a credibility rating of 1 (i.e. their statements are accepted), but BORIS and EGBERT have a credibility of 0 (i.e their statements are not believed).

All the dialogues are short as the program soon runs out of space and becomes inconveniently slow.

In Example 5 MCHINE becomes confused over GLADYS's SONs because of the crude matching routines in the program, which match the first example found when answering a 'wh' question, but scan all possibilities in a 'yes-no' question.

The meaning given to SURPRISE is that P SURPRISES X if X BELIEVES not-P. In Example 3 MCHINE's failure to spot that GLADYS does not believe BORIS to be clever (i.e. that STUPID (X) => NOT (CLEVER (X))) is because the relationship between the two relations is by means of their elaborated forms (see Section 6.3), and the elaboration system does not make the distinction between FALSE and UNKNOWN correctly when the proposition is embedded in a BELIEVE relation.

Example 1

:.CONVERSE;
GLADYS: HAVE YOU SPOKEN TO THE DOCTOR?
MCHINE: PARDON?
GLADYS: HAVE YOU SPOKEN TO THE DOCTOR?
MCHINE: NO
GLADYS: CHEERIO.
MCHINE: CHEERIO

*****

BORIS: GOOD AFTERNOON!
MCHINE: GOOD AFTERNOON
BORIS: HAS THE BLONDE SPOKEN TO YOU?
MCHINE: WHICH BLONDE?
BORIS: GLADYS.
MCHINE: YES
BORIS: GOODBYE.
MCHINE: GOODBYE

*****

Example 2

:.CONVERSE;
GLADYS: GOOD MORNING!
MCHINE: GOOD MORNING
GLADYS: BORIS, WHO IS STUPID, LIKES EGBERT.
MCHINE: REALLY?
GLADYS: GOODBYE!
MCHINE: GOODBYE

*****

EGBERT: HI!
MCHINE: HI

EGBERT: IS IT TRUE THAT GLADYS BELIEVES THAT BORIS IS STUPID?
MCHINE: YES
EGBERT: DOES ANYONE LIKE ME?
MCHINE: YES
EGBERT: WHO LIKES ME?
MCHINE: BORIS
EGBERT: CHEERIO.
MCHINE: CHEERIO

*****

DELIA: GOOD MORNING!
MCHINE: GOOD MORNING
DELIA: HAVE YOU SPOKEN TO EGBERT?
MCHINE: YES
DELIA: DO YOU BELIEVE THAT GLADYS BELIEVES THAT EGBERT IS LIKED BY BORIS?
MCHINE: YES

Example 3

:.CONVERSE;
GLADYS: HI!
MCHINE: HI
GLADYS: BORIS IS STUPID.
MCHINE: REALLY?
GLADYS: IS BORIS CLEVER?
MCHINE: NO
GLADYS: DO I BELIEVE BORIS TO BE CLEVER?
MCHINE: DUNNO
GLADYS: DO I BELIEVE BORIS TO BE STUPID?
MCHINE: YES

Example 4

:.CONVERSE;
GLADYS: HI!

MCHINE: HI
GLADYS: HIRAM, WHO IS CLEVER, LIKES BORIS.
MCHINE: REALLY?
GLADYS: IS HIRAM CLEVER?
MCHINE: YES
GLADYS: DO I BELIEVE THAT HIRAM IS CLEVER?
MCHINE: YES
GLADYS: DOES IT SURPRISE YOU THAT HIRAM IS CLEVER?
MCHINE: NO

Example 5

:.CONVERSE;
GLADYS: HI!
MCHINE: HI
GLADYS: HIRAM LIKES DELIA.
MCHINE: REALLY?
GLADYS: HAS IT BEEN SAID THAT HIRAM LIKES DELIA?
MCHINE: YES
GLADYS: DOES MY SON LIKE DELIA?
MCHINE: YES
GLADYS: WHO IS MY SON?
MCHINE: BORIS
GLADYS: DOES BORIS LIKE DELIA?
MCHINE: DUNNO
GLADYS: CLOT!
MCHINE: PARDON?
GLADYS: WHO IS DELIA'S FATHER?
MCHINE: BORIS

13.4. Comparison with Other Programs

Although Chapter 2 discussed the ideas of computational grammar and their relationship to other frameworks no comparison was offered of the more mundane details of actual programs. It is difficult to make fair or accurate comparisons between natural language programs in artificial intelligence since there is a dearth of real statistics about the performance of the programs. It is good that such prosaic details have not assumed undue prominence at the expense of the principles involved, but it makes it difficult to summarise what practical work is being done.

Three programs have been documented in sufficient detail to allow some comparison, so this section will provide a discussion of the relative merits and deficiencies of the MCHINE program with respect to the Thorne-Bratley-Dewar parser (referred to here as the TBD program for short), Winograd's SHRDLU and Soul's TESSA (Thorne *et al.* (1968), Winograd (1972), Soul (1975)). Unfortunately these programs are very similar in theoretical orientation and so the survey here will be somewhat narrow.

The TBD program produced a labelled bracketing of the input string, with special markings for indicating any constituents that were not in 'deep structure position', and where these constituents had been 'transformed' from. That is, it was a wholly syntactic parser, operating on single sentences. It occupied 16K of 48-bit words on the English Electric KDF9, and took between 0.5 and 2.2 seconds to analyse sentences, depending on complexity.

SHRDLU was an entire dialogue system, but it contained as a (separable) subpart a syntactic analyser. This analyser could be run autonomously on isolated sentences and could produce analyses for all the sentences in the list published for the TBD program in Thorne *et al.* (1968), but its performance on the sentences in Dewar *et al.* (1969) is not known. The SHRDLU system as a whole could deal with a narrower range of sentences but its performance was not trivial. The analyser alone occupied about 25K of 36-bit words on the PDP-10, and the whole system took about 80K (both figures include the underlying LISP system). The system responded to sentences in between five and twenty seconds.

TESSA was an improved implementation of the grammar described in Winograd (1972). (The SHRDLU program did not include all the grammatical constructions exactly as described in the written paper.) It ran on isolated sentences, performing no semantic processing, and included some elaborations of the SHRDLU grammar. The program occupied about 30K of 36-bit words on the PDP-10, plus an 11K POP-2 system. The time taken to analyse a sentence was about two to three seconds.

As stated above, the MCHINE program could run either in isolated sentence mode (when it built a semantic network for each phrase or sentence) or in conversational mode. It could therefore be compared with the performance of all three programs on isolated sentences and with the conversational ability of SHRDLU. In isolated sentence mode MCHINE's performance was spectacularly cumbersome. Not only did it occupy 56K total core space, it was by far the slowest of the programs (by a factor of about fifteen). However, it must be borne in mind that the MCHINE program constructed a semantic network as it proceeded and so was performing what many other systems would treat as two stages. The conversational ability of the MCHINE program also seemed to be inferior to that of SHRDLU, if we assume that Winograd's 'sample dialogue' is a typical sample (as opposed to a one-off performance). The only mitigating factor for MCHINE was that it was fairly robust (by the standards of such programs) in conversational mode, and several sample dialogues were produced without error.

Although this summary has been included for completeness it must be admitted that certain details are almost completely irrelevant to artificial intelligence and linguistics. The processing time consumed by a program is of little interest as it depends so directly on implementation details and the particular programming language used. For example, POP-2 subroutines can be defined as 'functions' (held in general purpose identifiers) or as 'operations' (with their own syntactic type). Since functions therefore require run-time checks that are redundant for operations, the call of an operation is about twenty-five per cent faster. Most of the routines in the MCHINE program were defined as 'functions' and hence the program could be speeded up simply by redefining them as 'operations'. Such an improvement is hardly of theoretical importance. Thorne,

Bratley and Dewar (1968) included in their data the number of ATN states visited in each analysis. This is a somewhat more interesting statistic but unfortunately similar figures are not available for the other programs.

The point made in Section 1.4 could be emphasised here. It is not the superficial performance of the program that is important but the principles embodied in it. MCHINE's pedestrian performance can perhaps be attributed to the aim of developing general mechanisms rather than of achieving a virtuoso performance.

The coverage of the programs is difficult to compare, since different workers tend to use slightly differing vocabulary and constructions. However, it is possible to produce an imaginary 'master sample set' by combining the published data from all the programs and making some reasonable assumptions about 'equivalent' examples. One can only speculate about how the programs would fare on these standardised examples, but some reasoned estimates, tempered with charity, are possible. Ritchie (1977) contains such a hypothetical standard sample set and an estimate of the performance of each program.

13.5. Summary of Grammar

It is hard to give the full grammar used by the program without including large lists of ATN states and actions. Nevertheless, it is interesting to list all of the structural combining rules, features and properties which were used, as this illustrates not only the type of categories which were found necessary but also how few rules and categories are necessary to span the subset of English involved.

Syntactic Features

DETERM: determiner
CN: common noun
NP: noun phrase
PPN: personal pronoun
STARTNP: possible initial word in noun phrase

ADJ: adjective
RA: restrictive adjective
NRA: non-restrictive adjective
VB: verb
MAJOR: major verb
AUX: auxiliary
NTAUX: negative auxiliary
COP: part of 'be'
MODAL: modal verb
ASPECT: part of 'have'
DO: part of 'do'
WH: wh-word
WHDET: can start a wh-phrase
WHFUL: can start an independent embedded wh-clause
WHREL: relative pronoun
TBIND: time-binder
THATS: introduces embedded question or statement

Syntactic Properties

AGREEMENT: three values, marked on noun phrases.
INFLECTION: eleven values, marked on verbs.
OBJECT-INFORMATION: an SCR and list of states, marked on major verbs.

Structural Combining Rules

Determiner-Head: carries sense properties from determiner to head phrase.
NP-of-NP: combines head phrase with 'of' phrase.
Possessive: combines possessive with noun phrase.
R-adjective: combines adjective and head-phrase restrictively
NR-adjective: combines adjective and noun phrase to make assertion about things referred to by the phrase.
NP-Modifier: combines a verb-phrase post-modifier with a head phrase.
Subject-Complement: inserts the subject into the slot of the predicate.
It+that+S: inserts an embedded clause in the meaning of

another.
Time-Adjunct1: relates a time adjunct to a following clause.
Time-Adjunct2: relates a time adjunct to a preceding clause.
Time-Binder: combines a time-binder and a clause to form a time-descriptor.
WH-Phrase: carries the wh-marking from a wh-determiner to a head phrase.
Relative Clause: combines a head phrase and a wh-clause to form a wh-item.
NR-Relative Clause: given a term and a wh-item, makes an assertion about the term.
Role-Placement Rules: there are ten rules for constructing meanings for verb phrases from the meaning of its verb and its objects, as follows:

Active: 1 intransitive, 2 single-object, 3 double-object
Passive: 2 intransitive, 2 single-object, no double object.

Sense Properties

(All binary-valued, except MODALMK, ILLOCMK and NUMBERPT)
DEFINITE: marked on meanings of NPs. See Section 6.2.
SPECIFIC: marked on meanings of NPs. See Section 6.2.
INDEXIC: marked on meanings of NPs. See 'deictic' in Section 6.2.
NUMBERPT: semantic number; marked on noun and NP meanings.
WHMK: indicates whether a 'wh'-item.
TENSEMK: REMOTE or PRESENT; marked on clause meanings.
POLARMK: sentence-negation; marked on clause meanings.
MODALMK: value of modal verb; marked on clause meanings.
ILLOCMK: illocutionary category; marked on clause-meanings.
NEGMK: verb-phrase negation; marked on VP meanings.
PERFMK: perfective aspect; marked on VP meanings.
PROGMK: progressive aspect; marked on VP meanings.

CHAPTER 14

CONCLUSIONS, PROBLEMS AND SPECULATIONS

14.1. Preamble

Computational grammar is an attempt to combine various artificial intelligence techniques into a practical framework for linguistic description. It is merely an early sketch for a possible model of natural language and still has many deficiencies. In this chapter we will point out some of the more interesting of the unsolved problems and outline some of the parts of the framework which need to be developed further. There is not a full grammar of English within any formal model at present, so it is not realistic to criticise computational grammar on the grounds that it has not furnished a comprehensive description of all grammatical constructions. (Notice that the description of time and tense in Chapter 12 has been superseded by a more detailed account in Ritchie (1979).) We will therefore concentrate here on aspects of the theoretical mechanisms involved, rather than on areas of English yet to be investigated. One or two references will be made to new research which is relevant, but this is not a survey of recent work.

14.2. Structural Combining Rules

The main advantage of structural combining rules, as currently defined, is that they provide an interface between what are traditionally known as syntax and semantics. The hierarchical grouping of surface constituents which has been so much part of previous linguistic theories has often been regarded as syntactic, necessitating the development of syntactically-motivated rules (e.g. phrase-structure grammars). The compromise represented by SCRs is to accept that there are tree-like patterns in surface structure, but to stipulate that the rules which express these groupings must be devised on semantic grounds, and that the operations that these rules perform should be on semantic structures.

One obvious shortcoming of the entire computational grammar framework is the lack of any means of sentence production and the one-directional rules which have resulted from this bias. A possible refinement is to see how much of the information used by the analyser is also useful in sentence production, and to try to factor out those parts into rules which are interpretable in both directions (cf. Section 1.2). It is not obvious whether this would be best tackled by writing a separate production grammar, or whether the current grammar should be modified. The first step would probably be to make SCRs bidirectional, since they will be needed in production. The experimental form of SCRs, described in Section 3.4, where the operation of the rule was subdivided into separate components, one for each argument, would be more easily reversed than the form in which all computation is done in one unanalyseable block. Much of the recognition grammar might remain one-directional, since it is aimed at a strongly directional task, but even in that area some information regarding constituent-ordering might be extracted into the dual-purpose part of the grammar. One major problem is that the recognition rules often test for some *sufficient* condition before taking some action (not always a *necessary* condition) and some rules test simply for the presence of some particular marking or structure, without testing all the details of that item. Hence these rules might not be fully reversible.

As discussed in Sections 10.6 and 10.9, SCR trees are built in a strict left-to-right fashion with any re-ordering of constituents being performed by the ATN part of the grammar before the re-ordered items are built into the tree. This approach is particularly suitable for English, where much of the linguistic information is conveyed by word-order, but it raises doubts about the generality and flexibility of computational grammar. If grammars are to be written for languages which make much less use of sequential arrangement as a communicative device (using, for example, inflections instead) new problems arise. It is far from clear what criteria would be used for such grammars for choosing an ordering for the places in SCRs. This whole issue is very complex and some of the arguments have already been raised within transformational linguistics in the discussion of 'underlying word order' and 'universal bases' (cf. McCawley (1970), Peters and Ritchie (1969)).

One of the many areas of linguistic communication which computational grammar has not touched is that of 'topic' and 'focus'. Different arrangements of semantically similar sentences can be regarded as differing in the emphasis that they put on the various items of information in the sentence, and in the way that they separate 'new' information from 'given' information (cf. Halliday (1967a, b, 1968)). This is an obvious point for further investigation, since very little work has been done in this area computationally (but see Davey (1974) and Kay (1975) for some suggestions). Within computational grammar as defined here the best way to describe such a notion would be to incorporate these aspects into the SCRs, so that, for example, 'passive' rules would have different consequences, in terms of 'topic', 'focus' and 'new/given' characteristics, from 'active' rules.

14.3. The Analysis Procedure

Most of the ATN system used in computational grammar is fairly standard. The most interesting modification is the NEWLEVEL . . . NIL construct which allows the grammar writer to specify a new processing level without having to state what will follow the constituent for which the new level is needed. However, writing the ATN rules for the experimental grammar highlighted some of the inadequacies of ATN formalism as it stood.

One disadvantage of the ATN formalism is that it has been developed mainly as a way of expressing a top-down search strategy. As discussed in Section 8.6 the decomposition of networks into subnetworks promotes a classic top-down approach and the analyser can do little with an input item that is not explicitly specified as a possible option in the current state. Many English constructions allow items to occur at any one of several points in the sentence (e.g. adverbs), and grammars should be a little more flexible in the way that they handle such constructions. There are other circumstances where it might be neater to let the input items guide the analyser, rather than having the analyser search single-mindedly for all possible options. For example, some verbs can take various configurations of objects, as in (171).

(171)
(a) We gave Veronica a teaset.
(b) We gave a teaset.
(c) He never gives to charity.
(d) We gave a teaset to Veronica.
(e) The chef is cooking.
(f) The chef is cooking something exotic.

At the moment, these are covered by having the analyser explore an exhaustive network representing all the possibilities for the given verb (see Section 3.7 and 8.6). It would be neater if the analyser could in some way process whatever objects are present and then allocate them to nodes in the surface-tree. The grammar-writing system outlined by Marcus (1978) seems better suited than the traditional ATN to such a strategy.

Also, a relative clause may, under certain circumstances, be separated from its antecedent, as in (172).

(172) A man came in who had been at the party.

The relative clause is generally understood as modifying the most recent noun phrase in the sentence (cf. Grosu (1972)), so this seems to require a procedure which searches back for an antecedent on encountering the relative clause. However, that would necessitate a grammar capable of analysing a detached relative clause, even if it was not anticipated, without assuming that it was an independent embedded wh-clause as in (173) below.

(173) We told him *who had been at the party*.

Whether these kinds of 'optional' constituent need a new formalism, or merely a more imaginative use of the ATN mechanism, remains to be seen.

One of the difficulties in trying to construct a semantically motivated processing model is the problem of relating predictions made during the analysis of a sentence (possibly in some semantic terms) to methods of processing actual words. This has been discussed elsewhere, (see Sections 2.8 and Ritchie (1978a, 1978b)), but no solution to the problem has emerged..As pointed out in Ritchie (1978a) the ATN mechanism, as currently used, is an implicit (and rather unprincipled) way of effecting the conversion from high-level semantic predictions to low-level processing procedure. The first step in tackling this awkward area is to make this conversion explicit in order to see what relationships do exist between semantic and syntactic categories. If we introduced a set of 'category conversion rules' we might at least see what was going on as a preliminary to systematising the process.

Over recent years a particular form of control structure has been used for various processing models in artificial intelligence. It is based on the concept of a 'demon' (Charniak (1973)) and has been used for English language programming by Marcus (1975) and Riesbeck (1974). (See Sections 2.8 and 2.11 for a fuller exposition.) As observed in Section 8.5 there are various formal similarities between the ATN 'arcs' and 'states' and Marcus' 'demons' and 'packets'.

The main differences between the two formalisms are in the possible ways of activating and de-activating the units. A packet is usually a smaller unit than an ATN state and several packets may be active at one time, whereas each path in an ATN analysis has only one active state. This extra flexibility in the packet method might avoid the unsuitability of the ATN states for expressing alternative groupings of arcs and the unions of states (see Ritchie (1977)).

This leaves unresolved the question of de-activating demons and packets. Since an ATN analysis path has only one currently active state the de-activation procedure is simple — once all the arcs in the state have been processed (i.e. tested against the input word, and appropriate action taken) that state is no longer active. Each arc has to supply a new state for activation on the path it creates. If a demon-and-packet analyser is maintaining a list of active demons there is not such a simple way of deciding when to remove a given demon from the list. Marcus (1978) has a system whereby whole packets are de-activated at a time by explicit commands within the body of other rules. That is, the flow of activation and de-activation is wholly under the control of the grammar-writer, with no implicit de-activation built into the system.

14.4. Semantic Representation

The semantic network system adopted for computational grammar is general and includes some useful facilities (such as the 'expanded' and 'elaborated' forms for relations), but in most respects it adds very little to the proposals of Rumelhart and Normal (1973), or Norman and Rumelhart (1975). The only novel item is the discovery of a particular kind of network structure (the 'definer') which is especially useful in specifying semantic structures which can undergo a variety of operations and which interface neatly with the syntactic constructs.

The concept of 'semantic anomaly' has been used, rather uncomfortably, for some time within language research (e.g. Katz and Fodor (1963), McCawley (1968), Winograd (1972), Wilks (1975)), but there is still no clear way of characterising the distinction between semantically well-formed and ill-formed meanings. If a sentence-analyser is to use referential semantic considerations to guide its processing (e.g. choosing between two possible analyses by selecting the one which offers the 'better' meaning) then this whole area will have to be examined much more thoroughly. The over-simplified notion of 'selectional restrictions' has been regarded as theoretically inadequate for some time, but computational models still resort to it, for want of anything else. Computational grammar includes the improvement of not treating violation of selectional restrictions as an all-or-nothing matter (as in the Wilks system — see Section 2.7), but that just scratches the surface, particularly as there are no principles developed yet concerning how semantic combinations are to be graded for ill-formedness. There are a few preliminary proposals concerning ways of 'choosing better interpretations' (e.g. Wilks (1973), Charniak (1972)) but the theoretical side has not been developed.

If we are to have structures for certain noun phrases that allows them to describe different objects in different contexts, then the question arises of which context should be used when a particular expression is evaluated. Using the analogy of Section 6.1 let us identify a 'state of the world' with an 'environment', where 'environment' is used in the programming sense (cf. Davies (1973), Stansfield (1975), Moses (1970)), meaning a set of values for variables. When a pattern is used to produce an item from the data-base (as has been suggested here for the semantics of specific, definite noun phrases) the item(s) produced will depend on the current values in the data-base — different environments will produce different 'referent sets'. The appropriate environment may be the hearer's model, the speaker's model, or some other state of affairs, possibly hypothetical or associated with some third person.

This means that the linguistic model will need some way of keeping track of which 'environment' is to be used for evaluating the various referring expressions in a sentence or dialogue. (See Ritchie (1976) for some of the problems involved here.) This device will have to operate within the sentence analyser (not just in some global conversational routine) as the relevant context may vary within a sentence.

It is perhaps worth including some speculation concerning the possible connection between this problem and the notions of 'specific' and 'generic' discussed in Section 6.2. For example, compare the two uses of 'someone' in (174) (a) and (b).

(174)
(a) Did someone attack that man?
(b) Someone attacked that man.

The 'someone' in (a) seems to be non-specific, in that it is being offered to the hearer as a pattern; in this respect (a) is similar to 'Did anyone attack that man?' where 'anyone' is non-specific. In order to respond to the question the hearer uses the pattern to search his world model for any appropriate items. The 'someone' in (b) seems to be specific, in that it represents some item that the speaker does not expect the hearer to be able to identify further. There is a certain symmetry here. In (a) the speaker has no information about the referent but assumes that the hearer has; in (b) the hearer has no information about the referent but assumes that the speaker has. Possibly notions like 'specific' could be re-defined in terms of the way that referring expressions are handled in the two contexts — speaker's and hearer's (cf. Hintikka (1973)).

14.5. Syntactic Markings

Computational grammar has tried to clarify the role that syntactic information plays in the sentence-analyser, by separating those devices that seem to be wholly non-semantic, without constructing a full 'syntactic component'. If syntactic features, properties and rules are allowed to be used in the grammar, but there is no commitment to giving a syntactic explanation to every phenomenon, the amount of syntax needed can be assessed more accurately.

If we were to disallow any device that resembles 'traditional syntax' (as Schank (1972a) and Riesbeck (1974) seem to advocate) we would bias the investigation from the outset. Conversely, trying to provide a full 'syntactic analysis' for every sentence may introduce pseudo-problems, in that there may not be an appropriate way of describing some aspects of a sentence in a syntactic structure.

The experimental grammar showed the need for twenty-two syntactic features, three syntactic properties, and about eight property-inheritance rules (see Chapter 13). This is interesting, but not spectacular. It remains to be seen how this view of the role of syntax can be refined by further grammar-writing, since it is hard to generalise from so few examples of syntactic properties and property inheritance rules.

14.6. Methodology

Chapter 1 provides the metatheoretical background to computational grammar, but the issues are discussed at greater length in Pylyshyn (1978). The position adopted in this book is not unusual within the field of artificial intelligence, as can be seen from the discussion following that article.

The guidelines used in devising linguistic descriptions are very rarely made explicit and some of the intuitive meta-rules are so widely accepted that a linguist may not realise that he is tacitly using certain methodological axioms. Section 10.9 attempted to articulate some of the more important criteria that were employed in writing the experimental grammar, since some of the reasoning used in the linguistic descriptions would seem unfounded otherwise. This setting-out of methodological axioms for grammar-writing is an important step, since lack of acknowledgement of such assumptions could lead to confusing disputes between workers following different schools of thought (cf. Householder (1965, 1966), Chomsky and Halle (1965)). Although many of the principles are very general, and might be adopted by many linguistic frameworks, some of the guidelines are specific to this particular framework. It is an advantage of computational grammar that it makes even its peripheral assumptions explicit.

Linguists place great stress on the 'elegance' or 'neatness' of a particular grammatical description, and, as commented in Chapter 1, this is one of the main means of assessing descriptions when there is more than one possible solution. In a processing grammar the elegance may be assessed at more than one stage. Firstly, there is the 'static' elegance of the grammatical rules as stated — are they obviously *ad hoc* or redundant, or are they general and simple? Secondly, there is the 'dynamic' elegance of the grammar in operation

— does the analyser thrash round exploring many dead ends, or is it efficient enough to constrain its searching? (In programming terms static elegance concerns the source code, but dynamic elegance concerns the run-structure.) Only Marcus (1974, 1975) seems to have considered the latter as a topic, but it may be an increasingly interesting area in future. There is often a trade-off between the two forms of elegance since a completely general static description of the options in a grammar may give no guidance on how these constructs are to be found. On the other hand, a more complicated description (containing more information to guide the analyser) may produce a shorter, neater processing stage. Anyone attempting to write recognition grammars should be conscious of this distinction and perhaps consider what his methodological priorities are. The MCHINE grammar (Chapter 13) slid confusingly between these two criteria, trying to gain the best of both forms of elegance, and that project might have benefited from an earlier realisation of this trade-off.

14.7. Constraints

One major metatheoretical deficiency of computational grammar is the lack of any constraints imposed on any of its devices. For example, to state that registers are used for temporary information storage during analysis is to say almost nothing, unless some further claims are made concerning the various ways that these registers can and cannot be used. The classification set out in Chapter 5 is a foundation on which an investigation of register usage can be built, but much work remains to be done.

Some of the register principles used in the experimental grammar have been developed independently by other ATN users (see Woods (1973)), and this reinforces the case in favour of these constraints. Woods (1973) uses a general work register called the HOLD list for temporary structure storage, and imposes the following general principle: 'the constituent saved on the HOLD list must be used by some virtual arc, either at the current level or at some embedded level before a POP from the level at which it was saved can be taken.' (p. 119) This is exactly the 'tidying-up principle' which was found useful in computational grammar (see Section 10.9). Woods comments:

> The presence of such a facility in the model raises a number of questions of theoretical linguistic interest: for example, should the HOLD list be constrained so that constituents can be taken off only in the reverse of the order in which they are put on . . . or can constituents be taken off in any order? Our experience in writing grammars within this model has not turned up any examples which would resolve this question. (p. 120)

The constraint that Woods postulates here would have a similar effect to the use of stack registers in the MCHINE grammar. In particular, the patterns described in Section 11.2 would be partly covered by such a principle.

This area appears to be a promising one for further exploration.

14.8. Conversational Rules

Computational grammar has included a level of conversational description in its model of sentence-processing, since the 'conversation games' of Chapter 9 provided a systematic way of structuring a dialogue in such a way that the conversational information could interact with the sentence analyser. This is yet another area where the barest skeleton has been constructed, but at least the first step has been taken.

One area for major improvement is the interaction between the conversational games and the sentence analyser. The interface implemented in the MCHINE program (Chapter 13) allows arbitrary information to pass in either direction, since the games call the analyser as a subroutine, any part of the program may call a game if required, and the analyser returns the semantic structure of the sentence as a result to the game which called it. In practice, the interactions are limited, and there are very few places where either of the two levels directs the flow of control at the other level.

In some games the illocutionary type (interrogative, imperative, etc.) of the 'result' passed up by the analyser determines which game is to be initiated next. In one or two places the semantic routines can call CGQUERY (the routine for gathering further details) if they lack information. The current conversation game always selects the initial state for the analyser to use. Beyond these brief communications the analyser and the games plod forward without consulting each other much.

It should be emphasised that the practical facility for arbitrary interaction is already present in the MCHINE program (in that both levels are programmed in the same programming language), but this is not the point. What would be interesting would be to find exactly what intractions are needed and to try to formalise these within the given framework (or modify the framework to allow it, if this proved necessary.)

14.9. Epilogue

Computational grammar, as outlined in this book, is in danger of being obsolete immediately, since computational work on English language is proceeding so fast.

In the area of semantics, simple semantic networks have been superseded by more complex systems based on 'frames' (Minsky (1975)) and investigations have been carried out into specialised programming systems for knowledge representation (e.g. Bobrow and Winograd (1977)).

Transformational grammar bears little resemblance to the 'Aspects' model referred to extensively here, following the development of 'trace' theory (Chomsky (1976)). As this newer model is more concerned with surface syntax than previous versions of transformational grammar it may prove particularly fruitful in its influence on computational approaches; Marcus (1978) has already presented a very neat recognition-grammar-writing system which uses trace-based surface structure. Marcus claims not only that his system is highly constrained but also that it captures many significant generalisations which previous systems ignored.

Speech understanding is another area where interesting processing techniques for natural language have been developed. These include enhancements of the traditional ATN (Woods *et al.* (1976)) and general multi-processing (Lowerre (1976), CMU Speech Group (1973, 1974)). The latter techniques are pertinent to the comments above on 'demons', since it is possible to describe them in terms of 'production systems' (i.e. sets of test+action rules).

The speech understanding research may give rise to suitable processing strategies for the English language, but these may not provide obvious linguistic descriptive techniques. We may be approaching an important stage in the development of formal grammars at which the complexity of the model (as demanded by the complexity of the phenomenon of language) is so great that it is unsuitable for traditional, semi-formal linguistic analysis. Large detailed computer programs may be the only feasible way to work with sophisticated processing models, and simple informal descriptions (e.g. Chapters 11 and 12 above) may be impossible. This would be unfortunate, but it is a consequence of the need to develop adequate theories of the way language operates; we cannot confine the model to some relatively simple level just so that linguistic analysis is 'easier'.

Although these innovations may supplant some of the detailed suggestions made in this text, many of the theoretical arguments remain valid and relevant. Computational grammar may thus serve as a stepping stone to a more adequate linguistic theory.

REFERENCES

AUSTIN, J. L. (1962) 'How To Do Things with Words'. Oxford University Press, Oxford.

AYER, A. J. (1936) 'Language, Truth and Logic'. Penguin Books, 1972.

BACH, E. (1968) 'Nouns and Noun Phrases'. In Bach and Harms (1968).

BACH, E. AND HARMS, R. (1968) 'Universals in Linguistic Theory'. Holt Rinehart and Winston, New York.

BAR-HILLEL, Y. (1954) 'Indexical Expressions'. Mind 63, pp. 359–79.

BOBROW, D. G. AND FRASER, J. B. (1969) 'An Augmented State Transition Network Analysis Procedure'. First International Joint Conference on Artificial Intelligence, Washington, D.C. Mitre Corporation, Bedford, Massachusetts.

BOBROW, D. G. AND WINOGRAD, T. (1977) 'An Overview of KRL, A Knowledge Representation Language'. Cognitive Science Vol. 1, No. 1

BOLINGER, D. L. (1965) 'The Atomisation of Meaning'. Language 41, No. 4, pp. 555–73.

—— (1967) 'Adjectives in English: Attribution and Predication'. Lingua 18, pp. 1–34.

BRESNAN, J. (1970) 'On Complementizers: Toward a Syntactic Theory of Complement Types'. Foundations of Language 6, pp. 297–321.

BROWN, R. (1958) 'Words and Things'. Free Press, New York.

BRUCE, B. C. (1975) 'Case Systems for Natural Language'. BBN Report 3010 (A1 Report 23), Bolt Beranek and Newman, Cambridge, Mass. (Also in Artificial Intelligence 6.)

BURSTALL, R. M., POPPLESTONE, R. J. AND COLLINS, J. S. (1971) 'Programming in POP-2'. Edinburgh University Press, Edinburgh.

BURT, M. K. (1972) 'From Deep to Surface Structure'. Harper and Row, New York.

CAREY, P. W., MEHLER, J., AND BEVER, T. G. (1970) 'When do we compute all the interpretations of an ambiguous sentence?'. In 'Advances in Psycholinguistics', ed. Flores d'Arcais and Levelt. North Holland, Amsterdam.

CHARNIAK, E. (1973) 'Toward a Model of Children's Story Comprehension'. Memo AI-TR-266, AI Lab, MIT, Cambridge, Mass.

—— (1975) 'A Brief for Case'. Working Paper No. 22, Institute for Semantic and Cognitive Studies, Castagnola.

CHOMSKY, N. (1955) 'The Logical Structure of Linguistic Theory'. Microfilm, MIT, Cambridge, Mass.

—— (1956) 'Three Models for the Description of Language'. IRE Transactions in Information Theory, pp. 113–14. (Reprinted in Luce, Bush and Galanter (1965).)

—— (1957) 'Syntactic Structures'. Mouton, The Hague.

—— (1958) 'A Transformational Approach to Syntax'. Third Texas Conference on the Problems of Linguistic Analysis in English. (Reprinted in Fodor and Katz (1964).)

—— (1959) 'On Certain Formal Properties of Grammars'. Information and Control 1, No. 2, pp. 137–67. (Reprinted in Luce, Bush and Galanter (1965).)

—— (1961) 'On the Notion 'rule of grammar' '. In Jakobson (1961). (Reprinted in Fodor and Katz (1964).)

—— (1964) 'Current Issues in Linguistic Theory'. Mouton, The Hague. (Reprinted in Fodor and Katz (1964).)

—— (1965) 'Aspects of the Theory of Syntax'. MIT Press, Cambridge, Mass.

—— (1966) 'Topics in the Theory of Generative Grammar'. Mouton, The Hague.

—— (1971) 'Deep Structure, Surface Structure and Semantic Interpretation'. In Steinberg and Jakobovitz (1971).

—— (1972) 'Some Empirical Issues in the Theory of Transformational Grammar'. In Peters (1972).

—— (1976) 'Reflections on Language'. Fontana, London.

CHOMSKY, N. AND HALLE, M. (1965) 'Some Controversial Questions in Phonological Theory'. Journal of Linguistics 1, No. 2, pp. 97–138.

—— (1968) 'The Sound Pattern of English'. Harper and Row, New York.

CMU Computer Science Speech Group (1973). 'Working Papers in Speech Recognition II'. Department of Computer Science, Carnegie-Mellon University, Pittsburgh.

CMU Computer Science Speech Group (1974). 'Working Papers

in Speech Recognition III'. Department of Computer Science, Carnegie-Mellon University, Pittsburgh.

CONWAY, M. E. (1963) 'Design of a Separable Transition-Diagram Compiler'. CACM Vol. 6, No. 7. July 1963, pp. 396–408.

DAVEY, A. C. (1974) 'The Formalisation of Discourse Production'. PhD. Thesis, School of Artificial Intelligence, University of Edinburgh, Edinburgh.

DAVIES, D. J. M. (1973) 'Popler 1.5 Reference Manual'. TPU Report No. 1, School of Artificial Intelligence, University of Edinburgh, Edinburgh.

DEWAR, H., BRATLEY, P. AND THORNE, J. P. (1969) 'A program for the Syntactic Analysis of English Sentences'. CACM Vol. 12, No. 8, pp. 476–9.

DOUGHERTY, R. C. (1969) 'An Interpretive Theory of Pronominal Reference'. Foundations of Language 5, pp. 488–519.

FILLMORE, C. J. (1968) 'The Case for Case'. In Bach and Harms (1968).

—— (1972) 'On Generativity'. In Peters (1972).

FILLMORE, C. J. AND LANGENDOEN, D. T. (1971) 'Studies in Linguistic Semantics'. Holt Rinehart and Winston, New York.

FODOR, J. A. AND GARRETT, M. F. (1967) 'Some syntactic determinants of sentential complexity'. Perception and Psychophysics 2, pp. 289–96.

FODOR, J. A., GARRETT, M. F. AND BEVER, T. G. (1968) 'Some syntactic determinants of sentential complexity, II: Verb Structure'. Perception and Psychophysics 3, pp. 453–61.

FODOR, J. A. AND KATZ, J. J. (1964) 'The Structure of Language'. Prentice-Hall, Englewood Cliffs, New Jersey.

FOSTER, J. M. (1970) 'Automatic Syntactic Analysis'. McDonald/Elsevier, London.

FOWLER, H. W. AND FOWLER, F. G. (1906) 'The King's English'. Oxford University Press, Oxford, 1973.

FREGE, G. (1892) 'On Sense and Reference'. In 'Translations from the Philosophical Writings of Gottlob Frege', Geach and Black. Blackwell, Oxford, 1960.

GARRETT, M. F. (1970) 'Does ambiguity complicate the perception of sentences?'. In 'advances in Psycholinguistics', ed. Flores d'Arcais and Levelt. North Holland, Amsterdam.

GOLDMAN, N. (1973) 'Sentence Paraphrasing from a Conceptual Base'. International Conference on Computational

Linguistics, Pisa, September 1973.

GRINDER, J. AND POSTAL, P. M. (1971) 'Missing Antecedents'. Linguistic Inquiry 2, No. 3, pp. 269–312.

GROSS, M. (1972) 'Mathematical Models in Linguistics'. Prentice-Hall, Englewood Cliffs, New Jersey.

GROSU, A. (1972) 'The Strategic Content of Island Constraints'. Working Papers in Linguistics No. 13, Department of Linguistics, Ohio State University.

HALLE, M. (1962) 'Phonology in Generative Grammar'. Word 18, pp. 54–72. (Reprinted in Fodor and Katz (1964).)

HALLIDAY, M. A. K. (1967a) 'Notes on Transitivity and Theme Part I'. Journal of Linguistics 3, No. 1, pp. 37–81.

—— (1967b) 'Notes on Transitivity and Theme Part II'. Journal of Linguistics 3, No. 2, pp. 199–244.

—— (1968) 'Notes on Transitivity and Theme Part III'. Journal of Linguistics 4, No. 2, pp. 179–215.

HARRIS, Z. (1946) 'Morpheme to Utterance'. Language 22.

HEMPEL, C. G. (1966) 'Philosophy of Natural Science'. Prentice-Hall, Englewood Cliffs, New Jersey.

HINTIKKA, J. (1973) 'Language-Games for Quantifiers'. In 'Logic Language-Games and Information', Hintikka, 1973. Oxford University Press, Oxford.

HOPCROFT, J. E. AND ULLMAN, J. D. (1969) 'Formal Languages and their Relation to Automata'. Addison-Wesley, Reading, Mass.

HOUSEHOLDER, F. W. (1965) 'On Some Recent Claims in Phonological Theory'. Journal of Linguistics 1.

—— (1966) 'Phonological Theory: A Brief Comment'. Journal of Linguistics 2.

HUDSON, R. A. (1971) 'English Complex Sentences'. North Holland, Amsterdam.

ISARD, S. D. (1974) 'What would you have done if . . .'. Theoretical Linguistics 1, No. 3.

ISARD, S. D. AND LONGUET-HIGGINS, H. C. (1973) 'Modal Tic-tac-toe'. In 'Logic, Language and Probability', ed. Bogdan and Niiniluoto. Reidel Publishing Co, Dordrecht.

JACKENDOFF, R. S. (1968) 'An Interpretive Theory of Pronouns and Reflexives'. Indiana University Linguistics Club, Bloomington, Indiana.

—— (1973) 'Semantic Interpretation in Generative Grammar'. MIT Press, Cambridge, Mass.

JAKOBSON, R. (1961) Proc. 12th Symposium in Applied Mathematics. American Mathematical Society, Providence,

Rhode Island.

KAPLAN, R. M. (1971) 'Augmented Transition Networks as Psychological Models of Sentence Comprehension'. Second International Joint Conference on Artificial Intelligence, London. British Computer Society, London.

KATZ, J. J. (1967) 'Recent Issues in Semantic Theory'. Foundations of Language 3, pp. 124–94.

—— (1970) 'Interpretive Semantics vs. Generative Semantics'. Foundations of Language 6, pp. 220–59.

—— (1971) 'Generative Semantics is Interpretive Semantics'. Linguistic Inquiry 2, No. 3, pp. 313–32.

—— (1972) 'Semantic Theory'. Harper and Row, New York.

KATZ, J. J. AND FODOR, J. A. (1963) 'The Structure of a Semantic Theory'. Language 39, No. 2, pp. 170–210.

KATZ, J. J. AND POSTAL, P. M. (1964) 'An Integrated Theory of Linguistic Descriptions'. MIT Press, Cambridge, Mass.

KAY, M. (1975) 'Syntactic Processing and Functional Sentence Perspective'. In Schank and Nash-Webber (1975).

KEENAN, E. L. (1975) 'Formal Semantics of Natural Language'. Cambridge University Press, Cambridge.

KIMBALL, J. (1974) 'Six or Seven Principles of Surface Structure Parsing'. Indiana University Linguistics Club, Bloomington, Indiana. (Also in Cognition 2.)

KUHN, T. S. (1970) 'The Structure of Scientific Revolutions'. Chicago University Press, Chicago.

KURODA, S-Y. (1966) 'English Relativization and Certain Related Problems'. In 'Modern Studies in English', ed. Reibel and Schane, Prentice-Hall, Englewood Cliffs, New Jersey.

LAKOFF, G. (1970) 'Repartee'. Foundations of Language 6, pp. 389–422.

—— (1971) 'On Generative Semantics'. In Steinberg and Jakobovitz (1971).

LAKOFF, G. AND ROSS, J. R. (1967) 'Is Deep Structure Necessary?'. Indiana University Linguistics Club, Bloomington, Indiana.

LEVIN, J. A. AND MOORE, J. A. (1976) 'Dialogue Games: A Process Model of Natural Language Interaction'. Proc. AISB Conference, July 1976. Department of Artificial Intelligence, Edinburgh.

LONGUET-HIGGINS, H. C. AND ISARD, S. D. (1970) 'The Monkey's Paw'. New Scientist, Vol. 47, No. 717, Sept. 1970.

LOWERRE, B. T. (1976) 'The HARPY Speech Recognition System'. PhD Thesis, Computer Science Department,

Carnegie-Mellon University, Pittsburgh.
LUCE, R. D., BUSH, R. AND GALANTER, E. (1965) 'Readings in Mathematical Psychology'. Wiley, New York.
LYONS, J. (1968) 'Introduction to Theoretical Linguistics'. Cambridge University Press, Cambridge.
McCAWLEY, J. D. (1968) 'The Role of Semantics in a Grammar'. In Bach and Harms (1968).
—— (1970) 'English as a VSO Language'. Language 46, No. 2, pp. 286–99.
—— (1971a) 'Pre-lexical Syntax'. Report of the 22nd Annual Round Table Meeting on Linguistics and Language Studies. (Georgetown Monographs 22).
—— (1971b) 'Tense and Time Reference in English'. In Fillmore and Langendoen (1971).
McDERMOTT, D. V. (1973) 'Assimilation of New Information by a Natural Language-Understanding System'. MSc Thesis, Department of Electrical Engineering, MIT, Cambridge, Mass.
MCDERMOTT, D. V. AND SUSSMAN, G. J. (1972) 'CONNIVER Reference Manual'. AI Memo No 259a, AI Lab, MIT, Cambridge, Mass.
MARCUS, M. (1974) 'Wait-and-See Strategies for Parsing Natural Language'. Working Paper 75, AI Lab, MIT, Cambridge, Mass.
—— (1975) 'Diagnosis as a Notion of Grammar'. In Schank and Nash-Webber (1975).
—— (1978) 'A Theory of Syntactic Recognition for Natural Language'. PhD Thesis, MIT, Cambridge, Mass.
MILLER, G. A. AND ISARD, S. D. (1964) 'Free Recall of self-embedded English Sentences'. Information and Control 7, No. 3, pp. 292–303.
MINSKY, M. (1975) 'A Framework for Representing Knowledge'. In P. Winston (ed.), 'The Psychology of Computer Vision'. McGraw-Hill, New York.
MONTAGUE, R. (1968) 'Pragmatics'. In 'Contemporary Philosophy: A Survey', ed. Klibansky. La Nuova Editrice, Florence.
—— (1970a) 'Universal Grammar'. Theoria 36, pp. 373–98.
—— (1970b) 'English as a Formal Language I'. In 'Linguaggi nella societa e nella tecnica', ed. Visentini *et al*. Edizioni di Comunita, Milan.
—— (1972) 'Pragmatics and Intensional Logic'. In 'Semantics of Natural Language', ed. Harman and Davidson. Reidel Publishing Co., Dordrecht.

MOSES, J. (1970) 'The function of function in LISP'. AI-199, MAC–M–428, Project MAC, MIT, Cambridge, Mass.

NORMAN, D.A. AND RUMELHART, D.E. (1975) 'Explorations in Cognition'. McGraw-Hill, New York.

PARTEE, B. H. (1970) 'Negation, Conjunction and Quantifiers: syntax vs. semantics'. Foundations of Language 6, pp. 153–65.

—— (1971) 'On the requirement that transformations preserve meaning'. In Fillmore and Langendoen (1971).

PETERS, P. S. (1972) 'Goals of Linguistic Theory'. Prentice-Hall, Englewood Cliffs, New Jersey.

PETERS, P. S. AND RITCHIE, R. W. (1969) 'A note on the universal base hypothesis'. Journal of Linguistics 5, No. 1, pp. 150–52.

—— (1971) 'On Restricting the Base Component of Transformational Grammars'. Information and Control 18, No. 5, pp. 483–501.

—— (1973) 'On the Generative Power of Transformational Grammars'. Information Sciences 6, No. 1.

PETRICK, S. (1973) 'Semantic Interpretation in the REQUEST System'. International Conference on Computational Linguistics, Pisa, September 1973.

PLATH, W. (1973) 'Transformational Grammar and Transformational Parsing in the REQUEST System'. International Conference on Computational Linguistics, Pisa, September 1973.

POSTAL, P. M. (1964) 'Constituent Structure'. Indiana University Press, Bloomington, Indiana.

—— (1972) 'The Best Theory'. In Peters (1972).

POWER, R. J. (1974) 'A Computer Model of Conversation'. PhD Thesis, School of Artificial Intelligence, University of Edinburgh, Edinburgh.

PYLYSHYN, Z. (1978) 'Computational Models and Empirical Constraints'. The Behavioural and Brain Sciences 1, pp. 93–127.

QUILLIAN, M. R. (1969) 'The Teachable Language Comprehender: a simulation program and theory of language'. CACM Vol. 12, No. 8, August 1969.

REICHENBACH, H. (1966) 'The Elements of Symbolic Logic'. Free Press, New York.

RIEGER, C. (1974) 'Conceptual Memory'. PhD Thesis, Computer Science Department, Stanford University, Stanford, California.

RIESBECK, C. (1973). 'Expectation as a Basic Mechanism of

Language Comprehension'. International Conference on Computational Linguistics, Pisa, September 1973.

—— (1974) 'Computational Understanding: Analysis of Sentences and Context'. PhD Thesis, Computer Science Department, Stanford University.

—— (1975) 'Computational Understanding'. In Schank and Nash-Webber (1975).

RITCHIE, G. D. (1976) 'Problems in Local Semantic Processing'. Proc. AISB Conference, Edinburgh, July 1976. Department of Artificial Intelligence, Edinburgh.

—— (1977) 'Computer Modelling of English Grammar'. PhD Thesis CST–1–77, Department of Computer Science, University of Edinburgh.

—— (1978a) 'Augmented Transition Network Grammars and Semantic Processing'. Internal Report CSR–20–78, Department of Computer Science, University of Edinburgh.

—— (1978b) 'Predictions and Procedures in Semantically-Based Grammar'. Proc. AISB/GI Conference, Hamburg, July 1978. Department of Artificial Intelligence, University of Edinburgh.

—— (1979) 'Temporal Clauses in English'. Theoretical Linguistics, Vol. 6, No. 1

ROBINSON, J. (1970) 'Dependency Structures and Transformational Rules'. Language 46, No. 2, pp. 259–85.

ROSS, J. R. (1967) 'Constraints on Variables in Syntax'. PhD Thesis, Department of Linguistics, MIT, Cambridge, Mass. (Also Indiana University Linguistics Club, Bloomington, Indiana.)

RUMELHART, D. E. AND NORMAN, D. A. (1973) 'Active Semantic Networks as a Model of Human Memory'. Proc. Third International Joint Conference on Artificial Intelligence, Stanford University, Stanford, California. Stanford Research Institute, Menlo Park, California.

RUSSELL, B. (1905) 'On Denoting'. Mind 14, pp. 479–93.

RUSTIN, R. (1973) 'Natural Language Processing'. Algorithmics Press, New York.

SCHANK, R. C. (1969) 'Linguistics From A Conceptual Viewpoint (Aspects of Aspects of the Theory of Syntax)'. Memo AI–88, AI Project, Stanford University.

—— (1970) ' ''Semantics' in Conceptual Analysis''. Memo AIM–122, AI Project, Stanford University.

—— (1972a) 'Conceptual Dependency: A Theory of Natural Language Understanding'. Cognitive Psychology Vol. 3, No. 4, pp. 552–630.

—— (1972b) 'Adverbs and Belief'. Memo AIM–171, Stanford University.

—— (1975) 'Using Knowledge to Understand' In Schank and Nash-Webber (1975).

SCHANK, R. C. AND COLBY, K. M. (1973) 'Computer Models of Thought and Language'. Freeman, San Francisco.

SCHANK, R. C. AND NASH-WEBBER, B. L. (1975) Proceedings of the Workshop on Theoretical Issues in Natural Language Processing, MIT, June 1975. Cambridge, Mass.

SCHANK, R. C. AND TESLER, L. (1969) 'A Conceptual Parser for Natural Language'. Proc. First International Conference on Artificial Intelligence, Washington, D.C. Mitre Corporation, Bedford, Mass.

SCHOENFIELD, J. (1967) 'Mathematical Logic'. Addison-Wesley, Reading, Mass.

SIMMONS, R. F. (1965) 'Answering English Questions by a Computer: A Survey'. CACM Vol. 8, No. 1. pp. 53–70.

—— (1973) 'Semantic Networks: Their Computation and Use for Understanding English Sentences'. In Schank and Colby (1973).

—— (1975) 'The CLOWNS Microworld'. In Schank and Nash-Webber (1975).

SMITH, C. S. (1964) 'Determiners and Relative Clauses in a Generative Grammar of English'. Language 40, No. 1, pp. 37–52.

SOUL, M. J. (1975) 'Parsing and Reference Determination'. PhD Thesis, Computing Centre, University of Essex, Colchester, Essex.

STANSFIELD, J. L. (1975)'Programming a Dialogue Teaching Program'. PhD Thesis, Department of Artificial Intelligence, University of Edinburgh.

STEINBERG, D. AND JAKOBOVITZ, L. (1971) 'Semantics: an Interdisciplinary reader in philosophy, linguistics and psychology'. Cambridge University Press, Cambridge.

STOCKWELL, R. P., SCHACHTER, P. AND PARTEE, B. H. (1973) 'The Major Syntactic Structures of English'. Holt Rinehart and Winston, New York.

SUSSMAN, G. J., WINOGRAD, T. AND CHARNIAK, E. (1972) Micro-Planner Reference Manual. AI Memo No. 203a, AI Lab, MIT, Cambridge, Mass.

THOMPSON, S. A. (1971) 'The Deep Structure of Relative Clauses'. In Fillmore and Langendoen (1971).

THORNE, J. P., BRATLEY, P. AND DEWAR, H. (1968) 'The

Syntactic Analysis of English by Machine'. In 'Machine Intelligence 3', ed. Michie. Edinburgh University Press, Edinburgh.

WEINREICH, U. (1966) 'Explorations in Semantic Theory'. In 'Current Trends in Linguistics, Vol. III', ed. Sebeok. Mouton, The Hague.

WEIZENBAUM, J. (1966) 'ELIZA — A Computer Program for the Study of Natural Language Communication Between Man and Machine'. CACM Vol. 9, No. 1. pp. 36–45.

WELLS, R. (1947) 'Immediate Constituents'. Language 23.

WILKS, Y. (1972) 'Grammar, Meaning and the Machine Analysis of Language'. Routledge Kegan Paul, London.

—— (1973) 'The Stanford Machine Translation Project'. In Rustin (1973).

—— (1975) 'Preference Semantics'. In 'Formal Semantics of Natural Language', ed. E. L. Keenan. Cambridge University Press, Cambridge.

—— (1976) 'Processing Case'. American Journal of Computational Linguistics 56.

WINOGRAD, T. (1972) 'Understanding Natural Language'. Edinburgh University Press, Edinburgh.

WOODS, W. A. (1968) 'Procedural Semantics for a Question Answering System'. Proc. AFIPS Fall Joint Computer Conference, Vol. 33, Pt. 1.

—— (1970) 'Transition Network Grammars for Natural Language Analysis'. CACM Vol. 13, No. 10, Oct. 1970, pp. 591–606.

—— (1973) 'An Experimental Parsing System for Transition Network Grammars'. In Rustin (1973).

WOODS, W. A. *et al*. (1969) 'Augmented Transition Networks for Natural Language Analysis'. Report CS–1 to the NSF, Computation Laboratory, Harvard University.

WOODS, W. A., NASH-WEBBER, B. L. AND KAPLAN, R. M. (1972) 'The Lunar Sciences Natural Language System: Final Report'. BBN Report No. 2265, Bolt, Beranek and Newman, Cambridge, Mass.

WOODS, W. A. *et al*. (1976) 'Speech Understanding Systems — Final Report; Vol. IV'. BBN Report No. 3438, Bolt Beranek and Newman Inc., Cambridge, Mass.

YNGVE, V. (1960) 'A Model and An Hypothesis for Language Structure'. Proc. American Philosophical Society 104, No. 5, pp. 444–66. Philadelphia.

—— (1961) 'The Depth Hypothesis'. In Jakobson (1961).

SUBJECT INDEX

(References are to chapters and sections)

abstract syntax 6.6, 7.3
acceptable 1.3
active 3.7
adjectives 3.5, 3.6, 6.5
agent 3.7, 6.4
agreement 3.3, 11.1
ambiguity, ambiguous 1.2, 1.4, 2.2, 2.7, 8.5, 10.6, 11.2
anomalous, anomaly 1.3, 8.1, 10.9
antonym sets 2.3, 6.6
approximate coincidence 12.1, 12.3, 12.7
arc 2.9, 4.1, 4.2, 8.3, 8.4, 8.5, 8.6, 10.3, 10.6, 14.3
arc-action 2.9, 4.1, 8.7, 10.3, 10.5, 10.6
arc-head 4.1, 10.3, 10.5, 10.6
arc-test 2.9, 8.5, 8.6, 10.6
associated arc-set 8.5, 10.5, 10.6
associated state 8.5, 10.5, 6.1
ATN, augmented transition network 1.4, 2.9, 2.10, 2.12, Ch.4, Ch.5, 8.2, 8.4, 8.5, 10.3, 10.6, 11.1, 14.3, 14.9
auxiliary verb 1.2, 3.3, 10.9

backtracking 1.1, 8.2, 10.9
bi-directional rules 1.2, 14.2
BLOCKS world 2.10, 6.1, 13.2
bottom-up 1.1, 8.4, 8.5
breadth-first 1.1, 1.6, 8.2, 8.3, 8.4, 11.2

case frame 2.3, 2.11, 2.12, 3.4, 3.7, 6.3, 6.4, 6.5
centre-embedding 1.2, 4.3, 4.5, 4.6
classifier 3.6
competence 1.6
complexity of grammar 1.1, 10.9, 14.6
of model 1.1, 1.4, 14.9
of sentence 1.2, 1.6, 4.3, 4.5, 4.6
complex noun phrase constraint 11.2
computer program 1.4, 1.5, 1.6, 4.6, 6.1, Ch.13, 14.9
concrete syntax 7.3
conceptual dependency 2.1, 2.8, 6.3
context 1.2, 1.3, 2.6, 6.1, 6.2, Ch.9, 10.6, 12.1, 12.2, 14.4
constraints 1.2, 2.11, 4.5, 11.2, 14.7
continuation 4.1, 4.2, 4.4, 4.5, 4.6, 5.2, 10.6, 10.7
conversation 1.2, 1.4, 2.6, Ch.9, 10.8, 12.1, 12.2, 12.3, 12.4, 12.7, 13.1, 13.2, 13.3, 14.8
conversation game 9.2, 9.3, 10.8, 14.8
conversational implication 12.7
cooccurrence relations 6.4, 10.9
coreference table 2.4
counter-example 1.1

debugging 1.4
deep structure 1.2, 2.2, 2.3, 2.4, 2.5, 6.4, 7.3, 13.4
definer 6.5, 6.6, 10.4, 11.3, 12.10, 14.4
definite 6.2, 6.5

Index

deictic 6.2
demon 1.1, 2.8, 2.11, 8.4, 14.3
demon words 2.10, 8.5
denote 6.1
dependency grammar 2.3
depth 4.3, 4.4, 4.6
depth-first 1.1, 1.6, 8.2, 8.3, 8.4
derivation 2.2, 2.4, 2.5, 8.2
determiner 3.5, 7.1
deterministic processing 2.11, 8.2, 8.6
differential diagnostic 2.11
distributed knowledge 1.1
dummy nodes 3.2, 10.6

elaborated form 6.3, 10.4, 13.3, 14.4
elegance 1.1, 2.5, 8.2, 10.9, 14.6
ELIZA 1.4
embedding Ch.4
empirical 1.6
environment 1.1, 6.1, 14.4
evaluation of SCR 10.6
event time 12.1, 12.2, 12.3, 12.8
expanded form 6.3, 10.4, 14.4
expectation 2.8, 8.4

feature, syntactic 2.10, 2.11, 3.1, 3.2, 3.3, 7.2, 7.3, 8.5, 10.5, 10.6, 13.5, 14.5
flags 5.2, 10.9
flow of control in analyser 2.10, 2.11
  in conversation games 9.2, 10.8
focus 3.7, 14.2
formula 2.7
frame 14.9
framework 1.1, 2.1
future 12.1

garden-path sentence 8.2
generative semantics 2.5
generic 6.2, 14.4
given-new 14.2
global derivational constraints 2.5
goal-directed 9.2
grammaticality 1.2, 1.3, 1.6, 2.4
grammatical judgments 1.2, 1.3, 1.6, 2.4
grammatical register 5.2, 10.6, 10.7, 10.9, 11.1, 11.2

habitual events 12.7

idiom 9.1, 11.2
ill-formed 1.3, 2.2, 14.4
illocutionary force 9.1, 9.2, 14.8
inappropriate 1.3
indefinite 6.2
indexical expression 2.6, 6.1
inference 1.2
inflections 3.3
input specification 10.2
intensional semantics 6.1, 7.3
interacting goals 1.1
interpretive semantics 1.2, 2.1, 2.3, 2.4
interpreter, ATN 2.9, 4.1, 4.2, 4.4, 5.2, 8.5, 8.6, 10.6, 10.9
interpreter register 5.2, 10.6, 10.7
interval of time 12.7, 12.9, 12.11

left-branching, left-embedding 3.5, 4.3, 4.4
left-right order 3.7, 10.6, 10.9, 14.2, 14.3
levels of processing 2.9, 2.10, 2.11, Ch.4, 5.2, 10.6, 11.1
lexical entry 2.10, 3.3, 3.6, 3.7, 8.5, 10.6, 10.9
linguistic theory 1.1
localised semantic description 10.9, 12.4
local variables 5.2, 11.2
look-ahead 2.11, 8.4, 8.6, 10.9
LSNLIS 2.9, 2.10, 3.4, 8.2, 11.1

machine translation 2.7, 2.8
MCHINE 2.6, 3.5, 8.5, 8.7, 9.3, Ch.13, 14.6, 14.8
methodology Ch.1, 2.10, 8.1, 10.9, 14.6
middle-out 1.1
modifier 3.6
module 2.11, 8.4

Index

named register 5.2, 8.6
nesting, syntactic 2.8, 2.9, 2.10, 2.11, Ch.4, 8.5, 8.7, 10.6, 11.2
 of conversation games 9.2, 9.3, 10.8, 12.2
 of tense 12.2
NEWLEVEL 4.1, 4.2, 4.5, 4.6, 8.5, 8.7, 10.3, 10.6, 14.3
node of syntax tree 2.2, 2.3, 2.4, 2.5, 2.6, 2.10, Ch.3, 4.4, 4.5, 6.4, 10.5, 10.6, 10.7
non-restrictive adjective 3.5
non-restrictive relative clause 11.4
noun 3.6
noun phrase 1.3, 2.8, 2.9, 3.5, 3.6, 4.3, 4.4, 4.5, 6.1, 6.2, 6.5, 7.2
number 3.3

object 3.7, 4.6, 6.4, 8.5, 11.1
oddity 1.3, 1.6, 8.1, 8.2, 10.9
opaque context 2.4
output specification 10.2

packet 2.11, 14.3
paradigm 1.1
paradigmatic 3.1, 3.3, 3.5, 3.6, 7.1, 7.2
paradigmatic ordering rule 2.12
paraplates 2.7
parser – see 'sentence analyser'
passive 3.7, 6.4, 10.9, 14.2
past tense 12.1 (see also 'remote tense')
pattern invocation 1.1, 2.8, 10.9
perfect aspect 12.1, 12.8
performance 1.6
phonological component 2.2
phrase structure 2.2, 2.6, 14.2
plan formation 1.1
point in time 12.7, 12.9, 12.11
pointer-holding register 5.2, 10.7
POP, POPUP 2.9, 2.10, 4.1, 4.2, 4.5, 10.6, 11.1
possessives 3.5, 4.3, 4.4, 7.1
predicate logic 1.2, 2.5, 2.6, 2.9, 2.12
predictions 2.8, 2.11, 4.1, 4.2, 8.6, 8.7, 14.3
preference 2.7, 8.3
preference semantics 2.7, 8.3
present tense 12.1
primitive semantic representation 2.1, 2.7, 2.8, 6.3
procedural embedding 1.1, 6.3
processing time 2.11, 13.4
PROGRAMMAR 2.8, 2.10, 4.1, 4.5, 8.5, 10.3
programming language 1.4, 2.8, 2.10, 6.1
projection rule 2.3, 2.6, 3.2, 10.2
pronouns 1.4, 6.2, 9.1
pronominalisation 3.6
properties, sense 6.5, 6.6, 7.3, 10.2, 10.4, 13.5
 syntactic 3.3, 7.3, 8.5, 10.2, 10.5, 10.6, 13.5, 14.5
property inheritance rule 3.3, 10.2, 10.5, 10.6, 14.5
PUSH 2.8, 2.9, 2.10, 4.1, 4.2, 4.5, 8.4, 8.5, 8.6, 8.7
psychological evidence 1.6

question-answering 2.8, 2.9

recognition rules 1.2, 1.3, 1.6, 2.2, 2.6, 2.8, 2.9, 2.11, 3.1, 3.3, Ch.8, 10.3, 10.6, 10.9
recursion 4.4
redundancy rules 2.3
reference evaluation 6.1, 6.2, 8.3, 9.3
reference time 12.1, 12.2, 12.3, 12.4, 12.6, 12.7, 12.8
referent 6.1, 6.2, 14.4
referent recognition 6.1
referential classes 6.6, 7.3, 10.2
referential semantics 2.4, 2.6, 6.5, 6.6, 7.3, 14.4
registers Ch.5, 8.6, 8.7, 10.6, 10.7, 10.9, 14.7
relation 2.12, 3.7, 6.3, 6.4, 10.4
relation-instance 6.3, 6.4, 6.5, 10.4, 11.3
relative clause 4.6, Ch.11, 14.3
relevance 6.2

remote tense 12.1, 12.8
restart 8.5, 10.6
restrictive adjective 3.5
right-branching, right-embedding 3.5, 4.3, 4.5
role 3.7, 6.3, 6.4, 6.5, 8.5, 10.4, 10.9
role-placement 3.4, 3.7, 6.4, 6.5, 8.5
role-restrictions 3.4, 10.4, 11.3
rule-body 10.2
rule-component 3.4

SCR – see 'structural combining rule'
self-referential 1.4
selectional restrictions 14.4
semantic anomaly 1.3, 2.3, 2.7, 6.6, 14.4
  component 2.2, 2.3, 2.4, 2.6, 2.9
  interpretation 1.2, 2.2, 2.3, 2.4, 2.9, 2.10, Ch.3, Ch.6
  marker 2.3, 2.4, 2.7
  network 2.12, 6.3, 6.4, 6.5, 6.6, 10.4, 13.2, 14.4
  representation 2.3, 2.4, 2.9, 2.10, Ch.6, 14.4
  similarity 1.2, 1.6, 6.3, 6.4
  specialist 2.10, 3.1, 3.2, 7.1, 10.2
  structure 1.2, 2.3, 2.4, 2.5, 2.7, 2.8, 2.10, 2.12, 3.2, Ch.6, 10.6, 10.9, 14.4
semi-stative 12.7
sense and reference 2.6, 6.1, 7.3
sense classes 6.6, 7.3, 10.2
sentence analyser 1.6, 2.4, 2.7, 2.8, 2.9, 2.10, 2.11, 3.1, 3.2, 3.3, 3.4, 3.7, Ch.4, Ch.5, Ch.8, 9.2, 9.3, 10.6, 10.8, 13.1, 13.2, 13.4, 14.3
sentence production 1.2, 1.6, 2.2, 2.6, 4.3, 14.2
SHRDLU 2.10, 3.4, 6.1, 9.1, 11.1, 13.4
simplicity 1.1, 2.3, 2.5, 8.2, 10.9, 14.6
speech act 9.1
speech understanding systems 14.9
specific 6.2, 6.5, 14.4
stacks 5.2, 10.6, 10.7, 11.2, 14.3, 14.7
state 2.9, 4.1, 4.2, 8.4, 8.5, 8.6, 10.3, 10.5, 10.6
state-specification 10.3, 10.6
stative verbs 12.7
structural combining rule 2.12, Ch.3, 5.2, 6.3, 7.3, 8.5, 10.2, 10.6, 10.9, 13.5, 14.2
structure-holding register 5.2, 8.6, 10.6, 10.7, 10.9, 11.1
subject 3.7, 4.6, 6.4, 11.1
subject-complement rules 6.2, 6.4, 6.5, 7.3
subnetwork 10.3
subroutine 1.1, 2.9, 4.6, 13.4
surface structure 2.4, 2.9, 2.10, 2.12, Ch.3, 7.1, 8.3, 8.6, 8.7, 10.6, 10.9, 14.2
syntactic component 2.2, 2.3, 2.4, 2.5, 2.6, 2.9, 14.5
syntagmatic 3.1, 3.5, 7.1, 7.2, 10.9
systems network 2.10

template 2.7
temporary storage 2.11, 3.4, 3.5, Ch.4, Ch.5, 8.2, 8.6, 10.6, 10.7
tense 12.1, 12.2, 12.3, 12.4, 12.5, 12.6, 12.11
tense clash 12.5
tension 8.3
TESSA 8.6, 13.4
thematic hierarchy 2.4
theory of language 1.1, 1.4, 1.5, 1.6
tidying-up 10.6, 10.7, 10.9, 11.1
time Ch.12
time-adjunct 11.1, 12.3, 12.5, 12.6, 12.9, 12.10, 12.11
time-binder 12.1, 12.3, 12.5, 12.6, 12.8, 12.9, 12.10, 12.11
time descriptor 12.8, 12.9, 12.10, 12.11
time structure 12.3, 12.4, 12.6,

12.7, 12.9
top-down 1.1, 4.2, 8.4, 8.5, 14.3
topic 3.7, 14.2
trace theory 14.9
transformational grammar 1.1, 1.2, 1.6, 2.2, 2.3, 2.4, 2.5, 3.1, 8.2, 10.9, 11.1, 14.9
tree structure 2.2, 2.5, 2.6, 2.10, Ch.3, 4.1, 4.2, 4.3, 4.4, 4.5, 8.7, 10.2, 10.6, 10.9, 14.2
truth-value 2.6, 10.4
Turing machine 1.1, 2.9

verbs 2.12, 3.3, 3.4, 3.7, 6.3, 6.4, 6.5, 8.5
verb categorisation 2.2, 3.4, 3.7, 6.3, 6.4, 8.5

weighting 8.3, 10.6
well-formed 1.2, 1.4, 2.2, 2.4, 14.4
wh-clause 4.6, Ch.11, 12.10, 12.11, 14.3
wh-phrase 11.1, 11.2, 11.3
wh-word 11.1, 11.4, 12.3, 12.10
when-clause 12.1, 12.3, 12.4, 12.6, 12.7, 12.10, 12.11
work register 5.2, 10.9
world model 2.6, 2.10. 3.5, 6.1, 6.2, 6.3, 9.2, 10.6, 10.8, 13.2, 13.3

AUTHOR INDEX

(References are to chapters and sections)

Austin 9.1

Bach 2.5, 6.5
Bar-Hillel 2.6, 6.1
Bobrow 2.9, 10.9, 14.9
Bolinger 3.6, 6.6
Bratley 8.2, 8.5, 13.4
Bresnan 2.4
Brown 3.3, 6.1
Bruce 6.4
Burstall 13.1
Burt 10.9, 11.1

Carey 1.6
Charniak 2.8, 6.3, 6.4, 8.4, 14.3, 14.4
Chomsky 1.2, 1.3, 1.6, 2.2, 2.3, 2.5, 2.6, 2.10, 3.1, 3.3, 4.3, 6.4, 7.3, 10.6, 10.9, 11.1, 14.6, 14.9
Collins 13.1
Conway 2.9

Davey 6.2, 14.2
Davies 6.1, 14.4
Dewar 8.2, 8.5, 13.4
Dougherty 2.4

Fillmore 1.1, 1.3, 2.3, 3.7, 6.4
Fodor 2.3, 2.6, 2.7, 3.2, 6.6, 10.2, 14.4
Foster 4.4
Fowler 3.5
Frege 2.6, 6.1
Fraser 2.9, 10.9

Garrett 1.6
Giuliano 1.4
Goldman 2.8
Gross 1.1
Grosu 14.3

Halle 2.2, 2.3, 14.6
Halliday 2.10, 14.2
Harris 3.1
Hempel 1.1
Hintikka 14.4
Hopcroft 1.1
Householder 14.6
Hudson 3.1, 3.3

Isard 1.4, 4.3, 4.6, 10.9, 12.1, 12.2, 12.3, 12.4, 12.5, 12.6

Jackendoff 2.4, 3.2

Katz 2.1, 2.2, 2.3, 2.5, 2.6, 2.7, 3.2, 3.3, 6.1, 6.6, 10.2, 14.4
Kay 1.2, 14.2
Kimball 10.9
Kuhn 1.1
Kuroda 11.1

Lakoff 2.5, 6.4, 10.9
Langendoen 1.3
Longuet-Higgins 1.4, 12.1, 12.2, 12.6
Lowerre 14.9
Lyons 3.5

McCawley 1.3, 2.5, 6.2, 10.9, 12.1, 12.2, 12.8, 14.2, 14.4

McDermott 6.1

Marcus 2.7, 2.8, 2.11, 7.2, 8.1, 8.2, 8.3, 8.4, 14.3, 14.6, 14.9
Miller 4.3, 4.6
Minsky 14.9
Montague 2.3, 2.6, 3.1, 3.2, 3.6, 6.1, 10.2
Moses 14.4

Nash-Webber 6.3
Norman 2.12, 6.2, 6.3, 14.4

Partee 2.5
Peters 1.1, 14.2
Petrick 8.2
Plath 8.2
Popplestone 13.1
Postal 2.2, 2.3, 2.5, 3.1
Power 9.2, 10.8
Pylyshyn 14.6

Quillian 2.12, 3.6

Reichenbach 12.1
Rieger 2.8, 3.4
Riesbeck 2.8, 3.4, 8.4, 14.3, 14.5
Ritchie, G.D. 1.4, 1.5, 2.8, 2.10, 2.12, 5.2, 6.1, 6.3, 8.5, 8.6, 10.1, 10.2, 10.6, 13.4, 14.1, 14.3, 14.4
Ritchie, R.W. 1.1, 14.2
Robinson 2.3
Ross 2.5, 6.4, 10.9, 11.1, 11.2, 11.4
Rumelhart 2.12, 6.2, 6.3, 14.4
Russell 6.1

Schank 1.4, 2.1, 2.8, 6.3, 9.2, 14.5
Schoenfield 1.2, 2.12
Simmons 1.4, 2.12
Smith 11.4
Soul 8.6, 13.4
Stansfield 6.1, 14.4
Sussman 6.1, 9.2

Thompson 11.4
Thorne 8.2, 8.5, 13.4

Ullman 1.1

Weinreich 6.6
Weizenbaum 1.4
Wells 3.1
Wilks 2.6, 2.7, 6.3, 6.4, 8.3, 14.4
Winograd 1.4, 2.7, 2.10, 3.1, 3.2, 3.4, 3.6, 4.4, 6.1, 6.2, 6.4, 7.1, 7.2, 8.3, 8.5, 9.1, 9.3, 10.2, 13.4, 14.4, 14.9
Woods 2.7, 2.8, 2.9, 2.10, 5.1, 8.3, 8.6, 14.7, 14.9

Yngve 4.3, 4.4